4e

THE UNIVERSITY OF LIVERPOOL

EDUCATION LIBRARY

This book is due for return on or before the last date shown above. The loan may be renewed on application to the Librarian if the book is not required by another reader.

Attention is drawn to the penalties for failure to observe Library regulations laid down in Rules 4 and 5.

INDIVIDUAL DIFFERENCES IN COGNITION
Volume 2

Individual Differences in Cognition

VOLUME 2

Edited by

Ronna F. Dillon

*Department of Educational Psychology
and Department of Psychology
Southern Illinois University
Carbondale, Illinois*

1985

ACADEMIC PRESS, INC.

(Harcourt Brace Jovanovich, Publishers)

Orlando   San Diego   New York   London
Toronto   Montreal   Sydney   Tokyo

ACADEMIC PRESS, INC.
Orlando, Florida 32887

United Kingdom Edition published by
ACADEMIC PRESS INC. (LONDON) LTD.
24–28 Oval Road, London NW1 7DX

Library of Congress Cataloging in Publication Data

Main entry under title:

Individual differences in cognition.

Includes bibliographies and indexes.
1. Cognition--Research--Methodology. 2. Difference
(Psychology)--Research--Methodology. 3. Human informa-
tion processing--Research--Methodology. I. Dillon,
Ronna F. II. Schmeck, Ronald F.
BF311.15 1985 153 82-22788
ISBN 0-12-216402-4 (v. 2 : alk. paper)

PRINTED IN THE UNITED STATES OF AMERICA

85 86 87 88   9 8 7 6 5 4 3 2 1

Contents

7. Assaying, Isolating, and Accommodating Individual Differences in Learning a Complex Skill
Dennis E. Egan and Louis M. Gomez

8. The Role of Individual Differences in Learning Strategies Research
Larry W. Brooks, Zita M. Simutis, and Harold F. O'Neil, Jr.

Contributors

Numbers in parentheses indicate the pages on which the authors' contributions begin.

Phillip L. Ackerman[1] (35), Department of Psychology, University of Illinois at Urbana-Champaign, Champaign, Illinois 61820

Larry W. Brooks (219), U.S. Army Research Institute, Instructional Technology System, PERI-IC, Alexandria, Virginia 22333

Lynn A. Cooper (67), Department of Psychology, Learning Research and Development Center, University of Pittsburgh, Pittsburgh, Pennsylvania 15260

Dennis E. Egan (173), AT&T Bell Laboratories, Murray Hill, New Jersey 07974

Drew H. Gitomer[2] (1), Department of Psychology, University of Pittsburgh, Pittsburgh, Pennsylvania 15260

Louis M. Gomez[3] (173), Bell Laboratories, Murray Hill, New Jersey 07974

Daisy L. Hung (119), Department of Psychology, University of California, Riverside, California 92521; and The Salk Institute, San Diego, California 92101

Joel R. Levin (145), Department of Educational Psychology, University of Wisconsin, Madison, Wisconsin 53706

Dennis L. Molfese (95), Department of Psychology, Southern Illinois University at Carbondale, Carbondale, Illinois 62901

[1] Present address: Department of Psychology, University of Minnesota, Minneapolis, Minnesota 55455.

[2] Present address: Educational Testing Service, Princeton, New Jersey 08541.

[3] Present address: Bell Communications Research, Inc., Morris Research and Engineering Center, Morristown, New Jersey 07960.

Victoria J. Molfese (95), Department of Psychology, Southern Illinois University at Carbondale, Carbondale, Illinois 62901

Randall J. Mumaw (67), Learning Research and Development Center, University of Pittsburgh, Pittsburgh, Pennsylvania 15260

Harold F. O'Neil, Jr. (219), U.S. Army Research Institute, PERI-IZA, Alexandria, Virginia 22333

James W. Pellegrino (1), Department of Education, University of California, Santa Barbara, California 93106

Michael Pressley (145), Department of Psychology, University of Western Ontario, London, Ontario N6A 5C2, Canada

Walter Schneider (35), Department of Psychology, University of Illinois at Urbana-Champaign, Champaign, Illinois 61820

Zita M. Simutis (219), U.S. Army Research Institute, Instructional Technology Systems, PERI-IC, Alexandria, Virginia 22333

Ovid J. L. Tzeng (119), Department of Psychology, University of California, Riverside, California 92521; and The Salk Institute, San Diego, California 92101

Preface

Volume 1 of *Individual Differences in Cognition* appeared in 1983. It was compiled to bring together current work on individual differences in cognitive mechanisms underlying task performance in a range of subject areas. The goal of the current volume is to add to our understanding of individual differences underlying performance in several domains. In this regard, Volume 2 complements and extends Volume 1 in presenting various individual-difference dimensions and approaches. For example, the current volume adds to Volume 1's coverage of verbal processes by including detailed treatment of individual-difference approaches to computer-based text editing and to mnemonic systems of instruction across a range of skills including vocabulary acquisition and text processing. This volume discusses other individual-difference dimensions of very recent interest: specifically, work in individual differences in long-term memory retrieval and in automatic and controlled information processing accounting for performance-ability relationships. Coverage of individual-difference approaches of equally recent attention, such as the use of electrophysiological data to elucidate relevant individual differences, is also included. Finally, work centering on spatial aptitude complements coverage in Volume 1 by presenting individual differences at a different level of analysis.

Work in some of these areas is just beginning. As with Volume 1, a choice was made to include new areas of inquiry, with contributors assuming a forward-looking perspective. We hope that future work might be enhanced by our suggestions and implications. The chapters are written at a level appropriate for advanced students and researchers.

Preparation of this volume was supported, in part, by a Spencer Fellowship awarded by the National Academy of Education. The continued assistance of the staff of Academic Press is gratefully acknowledged.

1

Developmental and Individual Differences in Long-Term Memory Retrieval

Drew H. Gitomer and James W. Pellegrino

INTRODUCTION

It is both true and trite to state that there are developmental and individual differences in the retrieval of information from long-term memory. The purpose of the present chapter is to review research that has been conducted on the specifics of such differences within the context of theories and paradigms that focus on details of these retrieval differences. Our emphasis will be on the efficiency of accessing and processing information of an abstract or semantic nature in long-term memory. A general theoretical consensus has emerged that there are various types of information stored in long-term or permanent memory. One such distinction is between declarative and procedural knowledge. *Declarative knowledge* is conceived of as static, basic conceptual knowledge, that is, "knowing what" or "knowing that." Examples include *knowing what* a dog is and *knowing that* a fish can swim. *Procedural knowledge* is generally defined as "knowing how." Examples of this type of knowledge include *knowing how* to do addition, solve a problem, tie one's shoe, and so on.

Our focus is on the retrieval of declarative information. It is important to note that one can also distinguish two types of declarative knowledge, generally referred to as semantic and episodic in nature. Declarative knowledge in long-term memory includes information about the meanings of concepts, as well as information about specific personal experiences with concepts and objects in the real world. A typical assumption is that *semantic information* is context-independent and part of the knowledge store of most people in a culture. This type of knowledge makes communication between individuals possible because of a shared knowledge base. In contrast, *episodic information* is tied to an individual's experiences, is contextually bound in time and space, and is not shared among individuals. A further difference between semantic and episodic information is that retrieval of the former is presumed to be relatively automatic and effortless, whereas retrieval of the latter is more effortful, error-prone, and context-dependent (Tulving, 1972).

In the first section of this chapter, we review a range of studies that focus on developmental and individual differences in the retrieval of semantic-memory information. The studies focus on differences in the speed of fact retrieval, the organization of information in semantic memory, and the mechanisms that govern the activation and processing of such information. In the next section, we provide an overview of basic assumptions about how information is represented and organized in semantic memory and how it is accessed and processed for the purpose of simple question answering or fact verification. Basic paradigms for pursuing these issues are also discussed in this section. The third section is a review of research exploring these issues from a developmental perspective. The fourth section is a similar review, but from the perspective of individual differences within age groups. The final section is an overview of basic conclusions and directions for future research.

MEMORY STRUCTURE AND PROCESSING

Semantic memory is conceptualized as a network structure in which concepts are represented as nodes. Related concepts are linked together in a semantically organized fashion, the links representing specific types of relationships. The more associated two concepts are, the greater the degree of linkage between them. Linkage may be thought of as the number of semantic features common to both concepts or as a measure of the strength of the direct association between them. For example, *baseball* and *football* may have a high degree of linkage because they share many features, such as sport, ball, stadium, team members. On the other hand, *baseball* and *hot dog* may also be highly linked, but not because of a large number of common features. Rather, the playing of baseball and the eating of hot dogs often occur together and are thus highly associated. Regardless of the nature of the linkage, the basic premise is that the more associated two concepts are, the closer their respective nodes will be in the semantic memory network.

Much of the theorizing about the structure and content of semantic memory has focused on two types of information about concepts: categorical relations and specific properties. It is generally assumed that concepts are organized in a network structure reflecting superordinate–subordinate relations among individual concepts. Thus, *dog, cat, cow,* and *horse* are linked to the more general concept *animal,* although they may vary among themselves in the strength of this linkage. Tests of the retrieval of information from semantic memory and the organization of its contents have been based upon speeded fact–verification tasks. The essence of these tasks is to present a simple statement (explicitly or implicitly) and ask an individual to verify that it is true. The dependent measure is the speed of fact verification. By comparing the latencies for verifying different types of facts, we draw inferences about the structure and organization of information in semantic memory. For instance, the time to verify category statements varies as a function of the level of the superordinate. Verifying that a robin is a bird is faster than verifying that it is an animal (Collins & Quillian, 1969), suggesting a semantic structure that has *robin* linked to *animal* via the intermediary concept *bird.* There are also differences among instances of a given category in the speed of verifying their category membership. It is faster to verify that a *robin* is a *bird* than to verify that a *penguin* is a *bird* (Rips, Shoben, & Smith, 1973). This is generally referred to as the *prototypicality effect* and is presumed to result from differences between concepts in their feature overlap or strength of the associative linkage. Much of the research that we consider subsequently is based upon paradigms and tasks examining semantic verification speed. The basic question asked in such studies is, Are there age- or ability-related differences in the speed of retrieving different types of information from semantic memory?

In addition to studying the structure of semantic memory, much theoretical and empirical work has attended to the processes that operate on the semantic structures. Several theories have been advanced that conceive of long-term memory as the product of two distinct processes (Collins & Loftus, 1975; Posner & Snyder, 1975; Schneider & Shiffrin, 1977; Schvanaveldt & Meyer, 1974). Basically, one process is automatic and not under conscious control, while the other involves conscious attention and is dependent upon the use of strategies. The effect of prior context on the processing of ensuing information has been interpreted via these two-process models. The processing of one concept results in faster decisions about a second concept if that concept is semantically related to the first. This facilitation is known as a *priming effect*. For instance, decisions about the word *nurse* are faster when it follows *doctor* than when it follows *bread* (Meyer & Schvanaveldt, 1976).

Automatic processing is generally associated with the idea of spreading activation along network pathways in semantic memory (Collins & Loftus, 1975). Activation results in quicker access of the related concept than if no activation spread has taken place. In addition, when a concept is stimulated or processed, activation spreads from that concept to related nodes, activating them to some degree. Activation spread decreases as the strengths of the relationships between the stimulated concept and other nodes in the network decrease; therefore, the most related nodes will receive the greatest amount of activation when a particular concept is stimulated. The origin of this stimulation may be internal or external to the individual.

Automatic processes are thought to occur without intention, without giving rise to any conscious awareness, and without interfering with other ongoing mental activities. They are fast acting but also are characterized by a rapid decrease in activation over time and/or intervening activity. It is important to note that the activation of related nodes does not occur at the expense of unrelated nodes. That is, although related nodes may be accessed more quickly, unrelated concepts are not accessed any more slowly than if no prior stimulus had been given.

The second component process of memory retrieval can be considered strategic, conscious, and employing a limited-capacity attentional system. Given a concept, an individual can make a conscious effort to attend to certain related concepts in memory. In contrast to automatic processing, conscious attention to a small subset of memorial concepts results in inhibition in the processing of other nonattended concepts. This strategic process is also thought to be slower acting than the automatic activation component (Posner & Snyder, 1975).

A good deal of research has been concerned with the interpretation of priming effects in terms of the two-process theory of memory retrieval. The basic logic involves the presentation of a stimulus (e.g., a picture or a word) that serves to activate or prime a portion of the semantic network. Following the prime, a target is presented and the subject must make some decision about the target. Targets highly related to the prime should be activated by the prime and are processed more quickly than if no prime has preceded them. Thus, Rosch (1975) finds that, for adults, category names serve to facilitate the speed with which category decisions are made about typical exemplars of the category. Conversely, decisions about atypical exemplars are actually slowed, relative to no prime conditions, a function of attentional resources being directed towards typical concepts in memory (Neeley, 1977). Analysis of priming effects in children can offer insights into the organization of semantic memory by looking at the sorts of concepts that serve to facilitate and inhibit processing of other concepts. Facilitatory effects can be due to automatic activation and/or conscious processing, whereas inhibition is a product of conscious processing only.

Tweedy, Lapinski, and Schvanaveldt (1977) support the idea that attentional processing is used when individuals perceive an advantage in consciously attending to associates. By varying the percentage of associated pairs within a lexical decision task, they found differences in the magnitude of both the facilitatory and inhibitory effects. Similarly, Rosch (1975) found that when the prime was misleading one-third of the time, both facilitatory and inhibitory effects were markedly reduced. Because of the unreliability of the prime, subjects chose to ignore the prime and thus, did not exercise attentional processing.

In the sections that follow, we discuss results from studies employing four major paradigms for assessing retrieval and processing in long-term memory. The first such paradigm is referred to as the *attribute comparison task* and was developed by Posner and Mitchell (1967). In this task, pairs of letters, words, or pictures are presented simultaneously or sequentially. The subject's task is to decide if the items are the same given a particular decision criterion, which can be either physical, name, or semantic category identity. Much of the work done with this paradigm has focused on the contrast between name identity (NI) and physical identity (PI) decision times. Generally, it is faster to make a physical identity decision than a name identity decision. This NI–PI difference is taken as an index of the amount of additional time to retrieve a more abstract name code in long-term memory before attribute comparison can occur. It has also been shown that it takes longer to make category identity decisions (CI) than name identity decisions. This time difference is attributed to the additional time to retrieve semantic category information. In essence, physical, name, and category information can be viewed as different levels of abstraction, with higher levels having longer retrieval times. A question of interest is whether there are systematic developmental and individual differences in the time to retrieve information at these different levels. The results from these studies typically focus on the NI–PI difference and the CI–NI difference when category information is also tested.

The second major area of research focuses on semantic-verification and simple-fact–verification tasks. As discussed earlier, the basic task is to verify a simple assertion and typically involves category or property verification for a single concept. These studies are interested in developmental and individual differences in the speed of semantic verification, as well as differences in the latency patterns observed across item types. For instance, some studies are concerned with the issue of whether the prototypicality effect in category verification is demonstrated by children of different ages. These studies focus on developmental and individual differences in the contents and organization of semantic memory.

The third major paradigm deals with priming effects in decision tasks. Studies of this type examine developmental and individual differences in the mechanisms for semantic memory activation and processing. The primary concerns are whether automatic processes based upon activation spread are evidenced for different age and ability groups and for different types of materials and whether the employment of conscious processing increases over development. We also consider some research that uses semantic search tasks to explore related issues of speed of access for different types of semantic attributes. This research is concerned with the efficiency of retrieving and processing different attributes of concepts.

DEVELOPMENTAL DIFFERENCES

The efficiency with which individuals perform information-processing tasks typically increases developmentally. For example, improvements in short-term memory span and operating efficiency have been given various interpretations, including the increased use of rehearsal and organizational strategies (e.g., Belmont & Butterfield, 1977; Ornstein & Naus, 1978), increased processing speed (Case, Kurland, & Goldberg, 1982), and a better developed knowledge base (Chi, 1978). The development of long-term memory access can also be considered in terms of these issues.

The speed of performance on tasks that require the retrieval of information stored in long-term memory typically exhibits a developmental increase. A present goal is to survey this area of research in terms of theoretical positions that might explain this developmental phenomenon. Our plan is not to contrast these positions in hopes of defending a single, most favored position but instead to provide a comprehensive picture of the several factors that play important roles in memory retrieval access.

One class of explanation is concerned with possible developmental change in the general processing efficiency of the individual. In this view, the increased speed with which concepts are accessed is a function of a general, system-wide efficiency factor. This factor is often related to physiological correlates, so that the speed with which certain responses are executed is often associated with patterns of cortical activity (e.g., Courchesne, 1978; Surwillo, 1977).

Although such maturation may be an integral part of development, our contention is that it is not sufficient to explain the relevant data. If development were simply a function of maturational variables, the expectation could be that identical developmental trends will be observed regardless of the material to be processed. Maturational changes have been shown to be inadequate in explaining short-term memory development (Chi & Gallagher, 1982), and we argue that they are also incomplete in accounting for the findings of research examining long-term memory retrieval. Developmental change in retrieval is not simply a consequence of maturation but is dependent on knowledge and stimulus factors as well.

A second class of explanation involves knowledge: its representation, acquisition, and organization. For instance, if the representational form of knowledge changes through development (e.g., Bruner, 1964), then retrieval of different information could exhibit different developmental patterns. An important issue is whether increases in retrieval speed are due to an increased tendency to organize semantic information or whether organization is present at all stages while the basis of that organization undergoes change. For instance, the fact that younger children may categorize items on the basis of perceptual rather than taxonomic features (e.g., Saltz, Soller & Sigel, 1972) implies that even young children organize, though the guiding principles of that organization may change.

A third possible contribution to a developmental increase in retrieval efficiency may be attributable to processes engaged in during retrieval. A person can become more skilled in the use and efficient execution of speeded retrieval process strategies with development. The importance of conscious strategy usage in development has been extensively documented. For speeded processes, which do not require such conscious awareness, the pattern of development is not as clear. Development may entail the acquisition of new processes or the reorganization of existing ones.

The contribution of these three factors to developmental increases in retrieval efficiency are examined in the context of tasks that demand retrieval from semantic memory. Other possible influences, such as metacognitive awareness, are not overviewed for several reasons. First, the methodologies exploring metacognitive variables typically do not assess speeded memory retrieval, and second, a clear understanding of metacognition has not yet been attained (Cavanaugh & Perlmutter, 1982).

ATTRIBUTE COMPARISON

The NI–PI paradigm has been studied developmentally to assess whether children differ from adults in the relative speed with which they access name information compared with physical information from a stimulus. If it is correct that development is characterized by a decreasing dependence on physical information, it is expected that the NI–PI difference will decrease over age. If, by school age, individuals are predominantly dependent upon conceptual information, one expects little change in additional name retrieval latency.

Modifications of the Posner task have been made so as to make the tasks amenable to experimentation with children. In several studies, the stimuli were pictures, rather than letters, while in others, multiple judgments were involved per trial so as to reduce the extreme response variability of young children in reaction-time studies. Nevertheless, the logic of all studies is similar, involving the comparison of conditions in which decisions can be based solely on physical information with other conditions in which the names of the to-be-compared stimuli must be retrieved.

Although the experiments reviewed here have all found significant NI–PI differences across the age range tested, the evidence concerning developmental changes in the magnitude of the effect is mixed. Henderson (1974) had second, fourth, and sixth graders search through lists containing 40 sets of five letters, with the first letter and one of the four remaining letters having the same name. In physically identical lists, the letters were in the same case (e.g., E–BEHF), whereas in the name-match lists the target case differed from the remaining letters (e.g., E–behf). Subjects were asked to search through the lists and draw a line through the letter with the same name as the target for each letter set, with the number of letters canceled in a given time period the dependent measure. Henderson found that all subjects were able to search the physically identical lists faster than name identical lists and that this difference did not interact with grade at all.

In a study by Keating and Bobbitt (1978), developmental differences were found in name-retrieval time for letters. Third, seventh, and eleventh graders were asked to sort a deck of cards based on either physical (e.g., A–A) or name identity (e.g., A–a). Name identity sorts took longer at each grade level, and the NI–PI difference decreased with grade. Thus, in the Keating and Bobbitt study, the ability to access name codes from memory was found to be related to age.

Two studies used pictures as stimuli, in which physically identical pictures served as PI stimuli, and different perspectives of the same concept were used as NI stimuli. Results with these stimuli are also equivocal regarding developmental trends. Bisanz, Danner, and Resnick (1979) presented pairs of black line drawings of common objects to third, fifth, and seventh graders and college students. Physically different–name identical stimuli were created by varying the state of the stimulus, depicting it in either an open or closed position (stimuli were *umbrella, banana, jack-in-the-box,* and *book*). The additional time to make name judgments as opposed to physical judgments was significant for all groups. However, the difference generally decreased with age, although the finding that the difference for third graders was less than for fifth graders is puzzling.

Hoving, Morin, and Konick (1974) presented successive line drawings of animals to subjects in kindergarten, third grade, and college. In one condition, the onsets of the stimuli were separated by 700 msec, and name matches took longer than visual matches by approximately the same amount of time for all subjects. However, when stimulus onset asynchrony (SOA) was 3000 msec, the two older groups made both matches equally fast. Although the kindergarteners still took longer on the name matches in the first study, two subsequent replications with kindergarteners and first graders showed that name and visual matches took the same time in the 3000 msec SOA condition. Attributing the kindergarteners' results from the first experiment to sampling error, the authors conclude that all subjects were able to use visual information more efficiently than name information only for relatively short periods. The data suggest that, after a short period, even for kindergarten children, name information from pictures is automatically accessed.

The application of the Posner task to developmental research has led to some general conclusions, as well as to some questions that await resolution. First, there is consistent evidence that with simultaneous presentations or with successive presentations close together, judgments based on physical information are made faster than those based on name information. This effect is quite robust, being observed across a wide range of ages and stimuli. Another developmental invariant is that this effect disappears when successive presentations are sufficiently separated.

Why the pattern of developmental change across studies is inconsistent is unclear. One way to resolve this ambiguity is to understand better the tasks themselves by precisely defining the processes employed in task performance. For example, Henderson (1974) found that, over trials, name retrieval speed increased while physical judgment latencies remained stable. Thus, it is suggested that subjects may learn to generate a physical representation of the target (e.g., generate e for E) and then engage in a physical comparison with the other stimuli. In later trials, the NI–PI difference may not represent name retrieval for each item, but rather the time to transform the target letter to its opposite case.

Bisanz et al. (1979) broke down their task into several component processes. Three classes of stimuli were created—physical different–name different (PDND), physical different–name same (PDNS), and physical same–name same (PSNS)—and were all presented in the name-match and physical-match conditions. By employing a subtractive logic, they were able to isolate five component processes of the task: a base encoding-and-response parameter a, the additional time to make a different response r, the additional time to make name as opposed to physical judgments n, the additional time to make a name match in the presence of conflicting physical information ϕ, and the additional time to make a physical match in the presence of conflicting name information v. For example, in the physical-match task, in the PDNS condition, the subject must respond negatively in the presence of conflicting name information, whereas in the PDND condition, the name information is consonant with the physical information. Thus, in the former example, the latency should be equal to $a + r + v$, and in the latter, the latency should equal $a + r$, the difference between the conditions yielding an estimate for v. Similarly, in the name-match task in the PDNS condition, the latency should include, in addition to base encoding and response, the time to make a name judgment plus the additional time to make the name judgment in the face of conflicting physical information $(a + n + \phi)$. By analyzing the task in such a manner, Bisanz et al. found different developmental trends for different processes. The effect of conflicting physical information was significant only for the youngest subjects, while the effect of conflicting name information was significant only for the two older groups.

Bisanz et al. also found that r was significant at all ages. Why different decisions are more difficult than same decisions is still an unresolved question (Nickerson, 1978), but decision asymmetry is found throughout development (e.g., Blake & Beilin, 1975). Gitomer, Pellegrino, and Bisanz (1983) found that the asymmetry is greater across ages when an active decision *and* response are required, rather than when a simple decision, but no response, is made. Whatever the nature of the decision process, it does not appear to be characterized by major developmental changes, though this does not suggest that decision criteria are not subject to developmental change (Blake & Beilin, 1975).

Thus, the Posner task research indicates that 5-year-olds, as well as adults, are able to utilize physical information more quickly than name information. However, any developmental change in the magnitude of this difference is still unclear because of the many processes that may be involved in the task. The NI–PI difference may represent not only semantic retrieval time, but also stimulus transformation time, interference effects, and decision processes. Until a clearer specification of the processes employed in these tasks is determined, it is equivocal, based on this class of evidence, whether adults retrieve semantic information any faster than children.

SEMANTIC VERIFICATION

Speeded retrieval of semantic information has also been examined in order to assess the development of category and property knowledge of concepts. Studies of unspeeded recall and other production tasks have typically found large developmental increases in the degree to which taxonomic knowledge is utilized to facilitate performance. While young children's deficits have been attributed to differences in strategic organizational processes (e.g., Lange, 1978), an alternative view is that the organization of knowledge in memory affects the degree of structure imposed on information (Chi, in press). Speeded retrieval of semantic information allows for an examination of the knowledge structure that is less dependent upon sophisticated organizational strategies. Thus, by using semantic-verification tasks, the relative saliency of facts stored in memory, as well as the developmental course of any changes that may occur, can be assessed. Studies of priming effects, which are discussed later, also permit insights into the structure of semantic memory.

One well-studied semantic verification task requires the subject to verify that some concept is a member of a superordinate class (e.g., "a bear is an animal"). Rosch (1973) found that 9–11-year-old boys were slower than adults by about 1300 msec in verifying that good exemplars were members of a category, while the difference for poorer exemplars was more than 1600 msec. For both groups of subjects, good exemplars were verified significantly faster. Rosch's latency differences included encoding and response components in addition to semantic retrieval time. To help partial out these processes, Landis and Herrmann (1980) presented two tasks to third and twelfth graders. In the first task, subjects were simply asked to name aloud category exemplars and nonexemplars. In the second task, they were asked to verify whether an exemplar was a member of a previously presented category. Landis and Herrmann propose that the latency difference between the two tasks is a better estimate of semantic categorization time, although it should be noted that the nature of the response was quite different in the two tasks (exemplar name vs. "yes–no"), thereby confounding the experiment somewhat. Nevertheless, the authors found latency differences on the verification task similar in magnitude to Rosch, but they also found large differences in the naming task. Thus, their estimates for categorization time was close to 600 msec for the younger subjects and 100 msec for the older group (based on true sentences). Landis and Herrmann therefore conclude that the developmental difference Rosch found was due, only in part, to semantic-retrieval time.

The Rosch finding that, for both children and adults, good exemplars were verified faster than poorer ones, is consistent with a network theory of representation in which both children and adult memories are organized along similar dimensions. Other researchers have explored this issue; and all lend support to the idea that the basic organization of memory does not change, although basic retrieval speed invariably increases over age. Ford and Keating (1981) had fourth and eighth graders and adults perform a semantic verification task. To account for encoding and response times, their dependent measure was the slope of the reaction time as a function of associative ratings taken from a large sample. For each subject, a slope was calculated based on average latencies for items with high, medium, or low association to a category; and the slope was deemed to be an index of retrieval efficiency. Large developmental differences were found, with slopes displaying a marked decrease over grades. Additionally, slopes were negatively correlated with verbal ability for fourth and eighth graders but not for adults, indicating that retrieval efficiency may be an integral aspect of cognitive development. Large developmental differences in efficiency were found, despite the lack of group differences in other tasks that required subjects to produce and rate category exemplars. The lack of differences in these latter tasks is probably due to the fact that the youngest subjects were in the fourth grade, an age by which general memorial strategy usage is evident. Nevertheless, retrieval efficiency continued to improve across this group of mature strategy users.

The studies reviewed to this point suggest that, although the speed with which category information is retrieved increases with age, the basic organization of memory does not, with better exemplars accessed faster at all ages. However, Sperber, Davies, Merrill, and McCauley (1982) demonstrate that the development of efficient retrieval is not identical across all categories. Verification times were measured for responses to basic and superordinate descriptions of pictures (e.g., "this is a dog" vs. "this is an animal", respectively). The latency difference between the two types of decisions was deemed to be a measure of category decision time. Superordinate categories were divided into two classes, those in which the exemplars were perceptually similar (e.g., *insects*) and those in which they were not (e.g., *toys*). Perceptual similarity was based on ratings of an independent sample, and subjects were second, fifth and eleventh graders. Sperber et al. found that for perceptual categories, category decision time decreased across all three groups, whereas, for nonperceptual categories, only the eleventh graders differed from the other children. Thus, developmental change in category decision speed occurs sooner for categories in which exemplars are more visually similar.

Two other studies in which researchers examined the organization of knowledge employed different methodologies, yet it was concluded in both that developmental differences were minimal across the age range tested. McFarland and Kellas (1975) had fourth, sixth, and eighth graders decide whether a probe word was a member of either of a pair of categories, which were either intuitively similar (e.g., *fruit-vegetable*) or dissimilar (e.g., *tool-vegetable*). Although overall times decreased with age, at each grade level, reaction times for similar categories were faster, with positive and negative trials differing only on dissimilar categories. The results are interpreted as supporting a parallel, exhaustive search through similar categories, causing no difference in positive and negative latencies. For dissimilar categories, a serial, self-terminating search is proposed, resulting in longer negative trials because the search is always exhaustive, while for positive trials, a positive decision after processing the first category will terminate processing. For all grades, the similarity of categories allowed a consolidation, thereby permitting a simultaneous activation of both categories and a parallel search within the consolidated category. Thus, all subjects utilized the semantic overlap that characterized the similar categories.

Mansfield (1977) presented kindergarteners, first, third, and fifth graders, and college students with simple sentences followed by a recognition probe word, for which the subject had to verify that it had appeared in the sentence. False items were either related or unrelated to the target word in the sentence and, if related, were created in one of four ways: superordinate (e.g., *flower-rose*), subordinate (e.g., *rose-flower*), part-whole (e.g., *leaf-tree*) and whole-part (e.g., *tree-leaf*). Semantic organization was inferred by examining the effect of the false items on correct rejection times, with the hypothesis being that the more closely related the concepts in memory, the slower rejection should be. All subjects took significantly longer to reject superordinate distractors than unrelated words. The other three classes of distractors significantly interfered for the three youngest groups, whereas for the fifth graders, only part-whole items interfered, and for college students, no other relations slowed reaction time. However, for all age groups, the superordinate-subordinate relations were more effective than the part-whole relations in producing interference, indicating that memory is organized along taxonomic dimensions rather than simple feature overlap.

Taken together, the category verification tasks indicate that little change in the nature of semantic organization occurs after children enter school. While basic speed increases, all individuals seem to organize their memories on the basis of taxonomic structures with good exemplars being most closely related to their superordinate and with search across categories relatively invariant. Estimates of semantic organization are certainly greater than those derived from tasks that have assessed more active strategy usage, such as free-recall clustering. One possibility is that, despite the relatively early establishment of semantic categories in memory, the efficiency of accessing that information continues to increase (e.g., Sperber et al., 1982). As efficiency increases, more attentional capacity is available for complex strategy execution (Case, et al., 1982), resulting in the apparent use of more sophisticated organizational strategies and the production of more semantically organized output.

A second general class of semantic verification tasks has subjects verify properties of concepts such as *x has y* and *x can y*. These studies examine developmental changes in the relative accessibility of different dimensions, such as whether the properties are typical, salient, or dynamic. The evidence indicates that, in addition to general developmental increases in speed, certain property dimensions stabilize developmentally sooner than others, although the basic structural organization seems relatively invariant.

Keller (1982) had second and fourth graders and adults verify sentences of the form *x has y* or *x can y*. Sentences varied on two dimensions: the typicality of *x* within its superordinate category and the feature dominance of *y* relative to *x*. Thus, *a robin has wings* is typical and high dominant, while *a penguin has eyes* is atypical and low dominant. All subjects responded to high dominant properties faster than low dominant, but only the adults exhibited a significant typicality by dominance interaction, such that dominance effects occurred only for typical items. Thus, it is concluded that though all subjects represent exemplars in terms of dominant properties, only the older subjects have developed superordinate prototypes. The major developmental difference is a reweighting of superordinate features.

Nelson and Kosslyn (1975) presented 8-, 11-, and 13-year-olds and adults with sentences pairing animal names and properties. Properties varied in their saliency and specificity to the particular animal concepts. Thus, *a leopard has spots* is high in saliency and specificity, while *a mink has a nose* is low on both dimensions. At all ages, properties low in specificity and high in saliency were verified fastest. While the saliency effect is as expected, the specificity results are intriguing. On the basis of Collins and Quillian's (1969) model of semantic memory, it is expected that low specificity properties will be verified more slowly because retrieval has to be conducted via a mediating superordinate (e.g., *mammal*). Why the opposite occurred is unclear, although for the present discussion, the important finding is the lack of any developmental change in organization from the age of eight.

Prawat and Cancelli (1977) designed a study to examine whether the developmental invariance noted by Nelson and Kosslyn extended to even younger children. Kindergarteners and third graders were orally presented sentences about animals and asked to verify them. Saliency and property type were varied, with three levels of property type: static, dynamic, and relational. Static properties are permanent qualities (e.g., *a horse has legs*), dynamic properties refer to animal functions independent of human interaction (e.g., *a horse can run*), and relational properties refer to functions that entail human interaction (e.g., *a horse can buck*). For low saliency items, the third graders were faster at all property levels, with no age-by-property interaction. For highly salient items, third graders were faster for relational and static properties but not for dynamic properties. This suggests that highly salient, functional properties are acquired earliest, a view consonant with theories of conceptual development (Nelson, 1974). Despite this difference, both groups verified salient properties fastest, supporting the view that even kindergarteners have a fairly well-structured semantic memory.

Mansfield (1977), in an experiment with the same basic design as the previously mentioned study, examined the effects of synonyms and antonyms, which were either weak or strong associates of the target. For all subjects, related concepts caused more interference than unrelated concepts, with no effect of associative strength. There was no effect of antonymy–synonymy for the older groups, although kindergarteners and first graders were slowed more by synonyms. Thus, a semantic organization that represents the sharing of common dimensions develops later for antonyms than for synonyms.

The data obtained from property-verification tasks indicate that little change occurs in the organization of property knowledge. Whatever change there is generally occurs by the second grade. Even for kindergarteners, there is strong evidence that well-structured organization exists, certainly more than has been inferred from tasks that require active strategy usage. The studies discussed here have not controlled for encoding and response times, so that comparisons of property retrieval time per se cannot be made, despite the consistent finding of increases in speed with age.

PRIMING STUDIES

Priming studies have been employed to study automatic and conscious processes in memory, as well as the organization of memory itself. Duncan and Kellas (1978) orally presented a category prime followed by two pictures to second, fourth, and sixth graders, as well as adults. Subjects were required to decide whether both pictures represented instances of the same category. Category exemplars were either typical or atypical instances, and unprimed trials were preceded by a neutral statement of "ready." When picture pairs were physically identical, the three older groups exhibited significant priming facilitation for typical instances and significant inhibition for atypical exemplars. Second graders showed significant inhibition for atypical exemplars but no facilitation for the typical instances. Duncan and Kellas conclude that priming effects are caused by the category concept eliciting the prototypical features of the category. Second graders have not yet developed complete prototypical structures, resulting in decreased priming effects for identical stimuli. However, the fact that category primes serve to facilitate both atypical and typical exemplars in the same category–different item and different category conditions indicates that some degree of category organization is present at all ages tested. The lack of a typicality interaction for nonidentical stimuli is a common, yet poorly understood, finding.

Two other studies have also noted a developmental change in priming effects as a function of the type of information to be processed. McCauley, Weil, and Sperber (1976) had kindergarteners and second graders name successively presented pictures one at a time. Picture pairs were of four types and varied according to associative relatedness (high–low) and categorical relatedness (high–low); for example, *cat–dog* is high in associative and categorical relatedness, *dog–bone* is high associative but low categorical, *lion–dog* are low associative, high categorical, and *airplane–dog* is low on both dimensions. There was a main effect of associative relatedness, which did not interact with grade at all, with high associates of the first member of the word pair being named faster. However, the target pictures in the high categorical pairs were named faster than in low categorical pairs for the second graders only. Thus, it was concluded that the kindergartener memory system is characterized by associative relationships, whereas categorical relations are well established by second grade.

Sperber, Davies, Merrill, and McCauley (1982) demonstrate, however, that not all category concepts exhibit the same pattern of development. As in their verification study, categories were manipulated in terms of the perceptual similarity of their exemplars. Subjects from the second, fifth and eleventh grades were asked to name line drawings after hearing either a superordinate prime or a neutral preparatory signal. For perceptual categories, all but the second graders exhibited significant priming effects. For the nonperceptual categories, only the eleventh graders named the pictures faster in the presence of the superordinate prime. Thus, just as for the verification task, Sperber et al. find a faster developmental progression for categories in which members are perceptually similar.

An important issue is whether the same processes are responsible for the priming effects observed across the range of ages tested in the preceding studies. In work with adults (e.g., Neeley, 1977), priming effects are attributed to two processes discussed earlier: automatic activation and conscious attention. It is asserted that those processes that are automatic do not undergo much developmental change, while processes that require conscious strategy usage exhibit the most development (e.g., Hasher & Zacks, 1979). From this perspective, Simpson and Lorsbach (1983) examined whether the priming effects observed in children are attributable to both processing components or are simply a function of automatic processes.

In one Simpson and Lorbach (1983) study, second, fourth and sixth graders, and college students, were asked to judge whether two simultaneously presented letters were the same. Preceding the letter pair was one of three stimuli, a neutral plus sign, a related prime letter, which was the same as the letters that appeared in the subsequent pair, or an unrelated prime, which was a different letter from the target pair. For all age groups, significant facilitation by the related prime was observed. However, only the three older groups exhibited significant inhibition by the unrelated prime. Since inhibition is a product of conscious attention (Posner & Snyder, 1975), it was concluded that the effects exhibited by the second graders were due to automatic processing components only and that the older groups were affected by both classes of processes.

In a second study, Simpson and Lorsbach (1983) varied the predictiveness of the prime, so that in one condition a word prime preceded an associate of the word 75% of the time, while in another condition, a word pair was predictive of an associate only on 25% of the trials. Any differential effects of the prime in the two conditions would be due to conscious processing, since they would indicate a sensitivity to probability and appropriate allocation of attentional resources. Subjects were the same ones who had participated in the first study. Predictiveness of the prime affected the sixth graders and adults, with inhibition observed only in the .75 condition. For the younger groups, facilitation only was observed in both conditions.

The Simpson and Lorsbach (1983) studies suggest that automatic processing is operative by the second grade but that conscious processing does not play a major role until later. These studies also illustrate some of the problems inherent in using sophisticated reaction-time methodologies across a wide range of ages. First, it is difficult to interpret the relative magnitude of effects because of the different baseline latencies for each group. Simpson and Lorsbach claim that the facilitatory effect decreases with age from 89 msec in the second graders to 44 msec in the adults, a common finding. However, if the data are considered in terms of percent of facilitation relative to a neutral baseline, the amount of facilitation remains fairly stable across the age range tested (between 10 and 13% across the four age groups). Second, the reaction-time variance is typically quite large when testing children, decreasing with age. This has two effects. First, power is low, increasing the possibility of a Type II error, especially for the younger groups. In Simpson and Lorsbach's first study, inhibition scores for the second graders were in the right direction but did not achieve significance. In fact, Duncan and Kellas (1978) did find significant inhibition for second graders. Second, large heterogeneity of variance forces separate group analyses, eliminating strong tests of any hypotheses involving age interactions. Therefore, with this type of methodology, the need for many trials and also experimental replications is imperative. Of course, it is no easy task to have a second grader sit through a large number of trials, making replication all the more important.

Taken together, the priming research leads to several conclusions. First, even children as young as kindergarteners exhibit facilitation by semantically related primes, suggesting that, at all ages examined, knowledge is organized along semantic lines and activation spreads to related concepts upon the processing of an initial concept. Second, the effectiveness of certain primes changes as the child matures. The evidence indicates that children proceed from an organization based more on perceptual and associative features to one less dominated by such features. The effectiveness of superordinate primes, at least to some degree, by the second grade indicates a semantic-memory organization that has superordinate relations as an integral part. Third, automatic processes are evident in the young child, whereas conscious processing effects probably do not become well established until somewhat later.

Overall, the verification and priming experiments can be similarly interpreted. First, there is unequivocal evidence of well-developed organization of semantic memory at all ages studied. The organization appears to be based on similarity of concepts in terms of properties, including taxonomic ones. However, the relative weighting of different features in memory changes with development. Various features are relatively more salient at different stages of development, and this saliency has been reflected in various methodologies. The evidence suggests little change in the structural mechanisms of semantic memory, although it points to significant alterations in the contents of what is stored.

Verification and priming tasks have been employed in the study of children to assess the organization of memory, while minimizing the influence of encoding and retrieval strategies. The results of these endeavors is a conceptualization of the young child as possessing a memory that is much more organized semantically than has been assumed on the basis of production tasks. Retrieval from semantic memory that does not require a great deal of conscious processing is relatively invariant across development. Differences that emerge do so because of changes in the salient features of concepts represented in memory.

SEMANTIC SEARCH TASKS

The methodologies discussed to this point have contributed significantly to our understanding of semantic-memory processing, although several questions are left unanswered. Among these are, What is the relative speed of access of different semantic information independent of response processes? and, What are the developmental trends? Also, What is the development of the organization and execution of subprocesses involved in the semantic decision? Aside from the McFarland and Kellas (1975) study, little attention has been paid to this issue in long-term memory research, although it has been explored in the short-term memory literature (e.g., Ashcraft, Kellas, & Keller, 1976; Hoving, Morin, & Konick, 1972; Naus & Ornstein, 1977). To answer these questions, Gitomer, Pellegrino, and Bisanz (1983) conducted two experiments with third and fifth graders, as well as adults. A search task was used in which subjects had to scan through a list of items, selecting targets based on prespecified criteria. In the first experiment, subjects searched through lists of six items, searching either for a member of a prespecified category among five nonmembers or for a nonmember of a prespecified category among five members. Examples of each list are presented in Figure 1.1. Slopes and intercepts were calculated for member and nonmember conditions on the basis of latencies and positions of the targets within each list. Slopes represented semantic decision time, independent of motor response and vocalization time, and were found to decrease with age. Also, intercepts for nonmembers were substantially longer than for members, corroborating other evidence that decision processes that require a negative response are more difficult (e.g., Clark & Chase, 1972). Thus, the use of the search methodology permits assessments of semantic decision time independent of response time, and leads to conclusions consistent with those derived from other methodologies.

The purpose of the second experiment was twofold. First, it was necessary to establish that the developmental differences found in the first experiment were not simply encoding differences but also represented changes in the efficiency of semantic retrieval. While it is difficult to partial out encoding latency, it is possible to compare latencies that require the

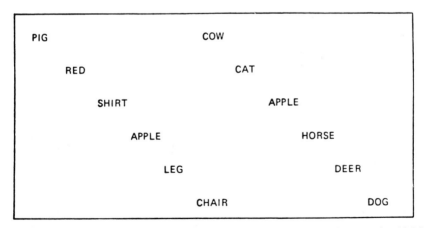

FIGURE 1.1   Example of stimulus arrays used in the member (left) and nonmember (right) conditions: Experiment 1.

retrieval of different types of semantic information. If developmental differences are not equivalent when different information must be accessed for the same concept, then it is apparent that a simple encoding hypothesis is insufficient.

Subjects read through lists composed of the following item types: large animals, small animals, large objects and small objects (e.g., *bear, cat, bed, doll,* respectively). In the category condition, subjects were asked to name aloud all animals, while in the size condition, all items that were large were to be vocalized. The number of items of each type was varied orthogonally across lists so that regression modeling of the data could be performed. For each grade, estimates of category and size decision latencies were obtained for each item type. It was found that the time to make category and size decisions were similar for the third graders but that the two older groups made category decisions significantly faster. Additionally, when the nonvocalized items were analyzed, so as not to be confounded with naming latency, a significant age effect was found for category decisions, while the increase in size decision latencies was only marginal. Therefore, although semantic-retrieval speed increased with age, the increase for category information was much greater than for size information. Developmental differences were not simply attributable to encoding but were also dependent upon the relative saliency of a concept's properties. Nonetheless, there did appear to be some general increase in retrieval speed with age.

One possible explanation for increased processing speed is that, with development, individuals become more efficient in the organization and execution of subprocesses. Two pertinent distinctions are those between parallel and serial and between exhaustive and self-terminating processes. In a *parallel* system, multiple pieces of information are processed simultaneously, while in a *serial* system, information is processed sequentially. *Self-terminating processing* ceases when information sufficient to make a correct decision has been analyzed, whereas *exhaustive processing* continues until completion, regardless of intermediate consequences.

A third experimental condition, in addition to size and category trials, was designed to examine these distinctions. Subjects were presented with the same lists but had to vocalize only large animals, having to make decisions based on size and category within the same list. Parameter estimates for each of the item types in the double-attribute condition were again calculated by a multiple regression technique. Parallel models predict that the acceptance of a large animal takes as long as the longer of the two single-attribute decisions, since both attributes are processed simultaneously. Serial models predict that positive responses in the double-attribute condition take much longer than in the single-attribute conditions, since time reflects category decision time plus size decision time plus vocalization time. Self-terminating models predict that rejections are faster, on the average, than predicted by exhaustive models, since processing terminates once a single negative attribute is processed. However, the predicted effects of self-terminating versus exhaustive processing interact with whether serial or parallel processing is executed. For a complete discussion of these issues, see Gitomer et al. (1983).

The estimates for the 12 data points (4 item types × 3 conditions) were formally fit to models that varied on the above dimensions. At all ages, parallel, self-terminating models accounted best for all the data. The parameter estimates for the best fitting model are given in Table 1.1. The only developmental difference was the relative latency for category and size decisions. For third graders, the estimates were virtually identical, while for fifth graders and adults, size estimates were 17 and 22% larger than category decisions, respectively. Across the age range tested, size-latency estimates decreased from 561 to 418 msec, while estimates of category decision decreased from 565 to 343 msec.

SUMMARY

We began this section by suggesting three possible sources of developmental differences in retrieval efficiency from long-term memory. It would have been desirable to conclude this section by stating emphatically that retrieval differences are due to maturational growth, or to development of knowledge structures, or to the development of efficient processing, and cleanly reject two of the competing hypotheses. Unfortunately, as is usually the case, simplistic explanations are just that: simplistic. It is clear from the reviewed research that any unitary explanation is insufficient to handle the data.

A simple maturational explanation implies that developmental changes in retrieval efficiency are equivalent for all types of information. This is obviously not the case. For example, there is converging evidence from multiple paradigms that retrieval of certain information undergoes more rapid development than the retrieval of other types of information. Therefore, developmental increases in retrieval efficiency cannot be attributed to maturation of the organism alone.

There is strong evidence that much of the developmental increase in retrieval speed reflects changes in the knowledge base. While there do not appear to be gross modifications in the structure of semantic memory, there seem to be reweightings of different conceptual features during development. These developmental patterns are consistent with theories of concept development derived from research that has employed other methodologies.

TABLE 1.1
Best-Fitting Models for Three Age Groups[a]

Grade	Model	R^2	RMSD (msec)	Parameters (msec)		
				c	s	v
Third	Parallel, self-terminating	.887	63	559	549	359
Fifth	Parallel, self-terminating	.754	60	431	503	190
College	Parallel, self-terminating	.918	24	339	419	123

[a] R^2 refers to the proportion of variance accounted for by each model; *RMSD* refers to root mean square deviation; c to time to make a category decision; s to time to make a size decision; v to time for vocalization. Data from Gitomer, Pellegrino, & Bisanz, 1983.

Changes in knowledge organization, though, are not sufficient to explain satisfactorily all of the findings. The work of Simpson and Lorsbach (1983) suggests that processing differences emerge under certain conditions, affecting retrieval efficiency. Second, although age differences are often attenuated for certain types of information, some developmental differences are still observed in many cases. For instance, even though Gitomer et al. (1983) found that size retrieval did not differ developmentally as much as category retrieval efficiency, marginally significant size-retrieval differences were observed. Other studies also find varying amounts of increased efficiency with age. However, most of these measures of retrieval are confounded with encoding, decisions and response processes.

The organization and execution of retrieval processes has not been studied extensively, but the available evidence indicates that processing explanations are insufficient to explain much of the data. McFarland and Kellas (1975) found no developmental change in the execution of search processes through semantic categories. Likewise, Gitomer et al. (1983) found that multiple attributes of a given concept were processed similarly across the age range tested. Finally, the priming studies have observed automatic activation effects for children as young as 5 years old. The developmental invariance of these processes preclude processing differences as the sole explanation of a developmental increase in retrieval efficiency.

Though the precise nature of retrieval efficiency development is undetermined, this area of research offers a great deal of insight into some important developmental issues. We suggest that development is not characterized by any major changes in memory structure. Organization along conceptual dimensions is present in the youngest school-age children. The degree of organization is such that it aids the processing of related information. This view of the young child's organization is not obtained with traditional production measures used to assess organization.

The execution of automatic processes is also relatively invariant across development. Young children exhibit the same patterns of automatic activation that adults exhibit. They also employ efficient searches through information stored in memory. The typical developmental finding that retrieval efficiency increases is probably not due to these more automatic processes, but rather to processes that necessitate active control by the individual. Thus, when organization is measured by methods not requiring active processing by the child, a more competent view of the child emerges.

Thus, the research on developmental differences in semantic-retrieval efficiency depicts development as a much more subtle progression than one usually finds in the developmental literature. The similarities across age groups are at least as impressive as the differences noted. However, the relation of seemingly small developmental increases to other aspects of cognitive development must be defined. Speed differences on the order of milliseconds may have important implications for the use of attentional resources; they may affect the execution of more sophisticated strategies, which certainly do exhibit large developmental differences.

INDIVIDUAL DIFFERENCES

Studies of individual differences in long-term memory retrieval attempt to relate basic information-processing skills to external reference tests, such as general intelligence or verbal aptitude measures. We know that there are substantial and readily measurable differences among individuals in their general intellectual ability and in their verbal ability. We also know that individual differences exist in the speed of semantic-memory retrieval. The question of interest is whether these two sets of individual differences are at all related. While age is a relevant individual difference variable that is related to semantic-memory retrieval, our concern in this section is with individual differences within a given age group.

Studies of individual differences in semantic-memory retrieval have employed one of three different designs. The first of these is a contrastive analysis approach in which normal individuals of high and low ability are compared in their performance on attribute comparison or semantic verification tasks. The definition of high and low ability is based upon an external reference test, such as the verbal part of the Scholastic Aptitude Test (SAT), a general intelligence test, or a measure of scholastic achievement. The second type of design that has been used is a correlational approach. Rather than selecting and contrasting high and low ability groups, a random sampling of ability in a normal population is conducted and then measures of verbal ability or intelligence in this sample are correlated with measures derived from semantic-memory retrieval tasks. The correlational design allows one to assess the magnitude of the relationship between measured ability and measures of semantic-memory retrieval. This is preferable to the contrastive design in which statistical tests typically indicate that there is a significant difference between ability groups in some component of processing. The contrastive and correlational designs are complementary and results tend to be highly consistent.

The third type of design used to examine individual differences is an extreme-groups contrastive approach. In research of this type, normal individuals are compared to special populations such as educable mentally retarded (EMR) adults and adolescents. A number of studies involving a normal versus EMR contrast have been conducted by Sperber, McCauley, and their associates.

ATTRIBUTE COMPARISON

Several studies have been conducted with the Posner task examining the magnitude of the NI–PI difference for different ability groups. Hunt (1978) reports the results of several contrastive and correlational studies using letter stimuli for the decision task. The studies varied in the procedure employed to obtain the NI–PI measure, with both card-sorting and individual pair reaction tasks being employed. All produced comparable results: high verbal individuals show a smaller NI–PI difference than those with low verbal ability. Table 1.2 contains results obtained in studies conducted by Hunt, Lunneborg, and Lewis (1975) with college students varying in verbal ability as measured by a college entrance test. Two things are obvious in the data. First, high verbal subjects are only slightly faster at physical-match decisions than low verbal subjects. Second, differences between ability groups are larger for the name-match trials. The NI–PI difference is 64 msec for high verbals and 89 msec for low verbals. Although the time difference seems very small, it is nonetheless significantly different for the two ability groups. Correlational studies have corroborated this basic contrastive finding with correlations of − .36 between NI–PI values and verbal ability measures for college students (Lansman, 1977) and − .28 for a restricted high ability sample of high school students (Poltrock, 1977).

Keating and Bobbitt (1978) conducted an extensive study of individual differences in information-processing parameters for children of ages 9, 13, and 17. One of their tasks provided a measure of the NI–PI difference for letters. At each age level, they found a larger NI–PI difference for children of average versus high intellectual ability. Ability was assessed by performance on the Raven's Progressive Matrices Test. Contrastive analyses of average versus high ability individuals within each grade, as well as correlational analyses within grade, supported a relationship between the NI–PI difference and intellectual ability.

TABLE 1.2
Reaction Time (msec) for Attribute Comparisons

Stimuli	Low verbal	High verbal	Ability difference
Letter[a]			
Physical identity (a–a)	543	524	19
Name identity (a–A)	632	588	44
NI–PI difference	89	64	—
Word[b]			
Physical identity	869	733	136
Name identity	1169	806	363
Category identity	1267	907	360
NI–PI difference	300	73	—
CI–NI difference	98	101	—

[a]Data from Hunt, Lunneborg, and Lewis (1975).
[b]Data from Goldberg, Schwartz, and Stewart (1977).

Table 1.2 also contains data obtained in a study by Goldberg, Schwartz, and Stewart (1977) that used the attribute-comparison task with word pairs. The study was conducted with college students differing in verbal aptitude. Differences between high and low verbal individuals appeared for all three types of comparison, but the differences were larger for the name and category identity judgments. Both subject groups showed the typical results, wherein category judgments took longer than name judgments, which, in turn, took longer than physical-identity judgments. The CI–NI difference did not appear to be related to verbal ability.

A general conclusion from studies using the attribute-comparison task is that verbal and intellectual ability is related to the time it takes to retrieve and compare more abstract name and semantic category codes from long-term memory. Both contrastive and correlational studies with college, high school, and elementary school students show within-age individual differences that are related to the NI–PI difference. Hunt (1978) presents a summarization of data from several studies examining the magnitude of the NI–PI difference in different samples of individuals. Table 1.3 reflects his summarization and indicates that the magnitude of the NI–PI difference increases as one moves from high verbal college students to normal children to mildly retarded children.

SEMANTIC VERIFICATION

Adult individual differences in semantic-decision tasks were studied extensively by Hunt, Davidson, and Lansman (1981). They tested 75 college students on several semantic-decision tasks, all of which were designed to

TABLE 1.3
Representative Times (msec) for Name Identity versus
Physical Identity Attribute Comparisons

Sample population	NI–PI difference
High verbal college students	64
Normal college students	75–80
Low verbal college students	89
Young adults not in a university	110
Severe epileptic adults	140
Adults over 60	170
10-year-old children	190
Mildly mentally retarded children	310

assess the speed of making category decisions. The subjects varied in verbal ability as measured by the Nelson–Denny Reading Test. One of the semantic-decision tasks involved the presentation of a category label and then a sequence of individual words or pictures that had to be judged relative to correspondence with the category label. This task was an exact replication of one used by Hogaboam and Pellegrino (1978) in a study that failed to find any significant relationship between category decision times and verbal SAT scores. A second semantic decision task used by Hunt et al. involved the presentation of two words that had to be judged relative to category identity (e.g., *dog–cat*). Their third semantic-decision task involved the presentation of a category label and a potential instance. The task was to decide if the instance was a member of the specified category (e.g., *animal–dog* vs. *animal–car*).

The testing procedures used by Hunt et al. (1981) provide highly reliable mean latencies for all three semantic-decision tasks, and performance on all three tasks is highly correlated over subjects. In addition, measures derived from all three tasks show significant correlations with scores from the Nelson–Denny test. The correlations are all in the range of − .25 to − .30 for the Nelson–Denny composite measure. Another interesting finding is that the semantic-decision speed measures do not correlate significantly with the reading-speed measure from the Nelson–Denny test. Instead, significant correlations are concentrated in the composite, vocabulary, and reading comprehension measures of the ability test.

Individual differences in semantic verification have also been explored within younger age groups in the study by Ford and Keating (1981) described in the section on developmental differences. They studied semantic-verification speed in samples of fourth and eighth graders and college students. The task was a simple category-verification procedure in which the instances varied in prototypicality. They derive a slope measure from the verification task that reflects retrieval times as a function of item typicality. These slope measures are shown to be highly correlated with verbal ability measures. The correlations are $-.59$ and $-.50$ for the fourth and eighth graders, respectively. Significant correlations are also obtained between the slope measures and scores on the Raven's Progressive Matrices Test (r's of $-.39$ and $-.35$). The college sample failed to show any significant correlation between the slope measure and a verbal ability measure. This failure may be attributable to a small sample size and restricted range of scores for both the slope measure and the verbal ability measure.

The general conclusion from studies of individual differences in semantic verification latencies is that adults and children with higher levels of verbal ability are faster at retrieving basic category information from long-term memory. Two caveats should be noted, however. First, measures of semantic-verification latency are composites of several processes such as encoding, decision, and response processes. Thus, effects observed in these studies cannot be unequivocally attributed to retrieval time alone. Second, the effects observed with college students are generally small in absolute magnitude and require large samples with highly reliable reaction-time data to obtain significant correlations. Failures to find relationships (e.g., Hogaboam & Pellegrino, 1978), can probably be attributed to such problems. When significant correlations are obtained, they are typically at the .30 level. This is also true for correlations obtained for the NI–PI difference. Thus, individual differences in attribute-comparison and semantic-verification tasks account for only a small percentage of the variance in verbal ability. It appears, however, that when a broader spectrum of ability is examined, particularly within younger age groups, there are substantial differences in semantic-retrieval times that are related to standardized measures of verbal ability.

Semantic-verification tasks have also been used to explore issues associated with the organization and retrieval of semantic information in normal and retarded populations. McCauley, Sperber, and Roaden (1978) examined differences between normal and EMR adolescents in a property verification task. Sentences that represented high and low salient action and static properties of concepts were presented orally. Examples are *bees can sting, people can sneeze, camels have humps,* and *ants have legs.* They found an overall difference between normal and EMR subjects in verification time. More importantly, they observed a substantial increase in verification time for static properties relative to action properties only for the EMR group. Their data suggest a differential organization and accessibility of semantic knowledge in EMR individuals, reflecting a differential weighting of semantic features.

Roaden, McCauley, and Sperber (1980) conducted a study similar to Mc-Cauley et al. (1978), examining intelligence-related differences in the verification of different object–property relationships. Normal and EMR subjects were compared in the speed of verifying action and static properties of animate and inanimate objects. They again found a large difference for action and static properties in the EMR sample. For EMR individuals, the static properties of animate objects and the intrinsic action properties of inanimate objects were relatively less accessible than they were for normal individuals of the same chronological or mental age.

PRIMING EFFECTS

Studies focusing on priming effects and individual differences have been limited to contrasts between normal and retarded populations. McCauley, Sperber and their associates have conducted a large number of studies using priming paradigms. Their results indicate no intelligence-related differences in priming effects, as both EMR and normal subjects show similar priming effects that are related to automatic activation processes (Davies, Sperber, & McCauley, 1981; McCauley, Parmelee, Sperber, & Carr, 1980; Sperber, McCauley, Ragain, & Weil, 1979; Sperber, Ragain & McCauley, 1976). An example is a study conducted by Weil, McCauley, and Sperber (1978). Normal and EMR subjects were tested on the time needed to name pictures of common objects. Pictures were presented in pairs that were either categorically related or unrelated. Naming times for the target items (the second item in each pair) showed a priming effect: Targets in related pairs were named faster than those in unrelated pairs. Of major interest is the finding that naming times varied as a function of both prime and target typicality. These effects were shown for both subject groups. Weil et al. interpret these results as indicating that the semantic categories of EMR individuals have an internal structure or organization similar to that of normal individuals and that even relatively atypical exemplars are functional category members for EMR individuals. A similar set of results was obtained in a study conducted by Sperber et al. (1982). A priming task was used that involved naming target pictures that were preceded either by a category or by a neutral prime. Both normal and EMR subjects showed a facilitative priming effect and this effect was only apparent for perceptual categories.

From results such as those described above, Sperber and McCauley (1984) have argued that knowledge about common superordinate–subordinate relationships and the automatic activation of such knowledge does not vary appreciably with intelligence. The failure to find any differences between EMR and normal population, other than overall latency differences, in the patterns of effects is not attributed to an insensitivity of the priming paradigm, since the primary paradigm is sensitive to other population differences, such as age. The lack of intelligence-related differences in the magnitude of the priming effect is indicative of commonalities over individuals in the automatic component of semantic processing.

Differences between normal and EMR groups appear when controlled semantic-processing effects are tested. Sperber et al. (1982) examined verification times for pictures preceded by a superordinate or basic level description. Latencies were faster for judgments about basic-level descriptions (e.g., "this is a dog"), than for category descriptions (e.g., "this is an animal"). In addition, these effects were larger for nonperceptual categories. In this task, however, larger differences between category and basic-level decision times were observed for the EMR subjects when compared to their chronological-age counterparts. Similar results were obtained in another study conducted by Davies et al. (1981) using this same paradigm.

Sperber and McCauley arrive at the following conclusions:

> Thus, the indication is that both the necessary and sufficient condition for observing intelligence-related differences in categorization processes is the requirement that subjects actively process category information. Active processing seems necessary in that we consistently fail to obtain group differences on tasks tapping only the automatic activation of categorically related concepts, and it seems sufficient in that group differences in categorization processes (specifically processing efficiency) are observed even on tasks in which the roles of strategic behavior and complex decision processes are minimized. (Sperber & McCauley, 1984, pp. 148-149)

SUMMARY

The research on individual differences in retrieval efficiency has focused on two basic concerns: The first is with the relationship between speed of access and other measures of cognitive ability in normal populations; the second is with differences in retrieval efficiency between retarded and normal groups. The questions asked in the second more closely parallel those encountered in the developmental literature.

Within normal populations, there is a highly reliable, yet typically weak, correlation between speed of semantic access and measures of intelligence, verbal ability, and so forth. This finding is consistent across both semantic-attribute and semantic-verification tasks. The pattern of results is provocative, yet the implications are unclear. We say provocative because it is intriguing that a simple task, such as retrieving the name of a letter, is reliably related to overall measures of aptitude. Since even average college students have experienced these stimuli millions of times during their lives, it is difficult to attribute retrieval differences to knowledge or experience.

Nevertheless, very good college students are faster in retrieving letter names than are average students. However, because of the weakness of the relationship, it would not be desirable to use measures of retrieval efficiency as predictors of other performance. It is also not clear how increasing retrieval speed by some method of intervention would necessarily improve general cognitive functioning.

The results from experiments that contrast normal and retarded individuals are quite similar to the developmental studies discussed in the previous section. Retarded individuals display evidence of semantic organization, although they differ from normal individuals in the relative saliency of certain features. Automatic processes appear to operate in identical fashion in both populations. Just as in the developmental research, differences emerge when more active processing of information is required.

CONCLUSION

The research presented in this chapter offers a fresh perspective on individual and developmental differences in long-term memory retrieval. The large performance differences usually associated with these contrasts are probably not attributable to structural differences in semantic memory. Instead, differences are more likely due to differences in content, to changes in the relative saliency of certain concepts and features, and to the use of active processing. Even immature groups of performers give evidence of highly organized memories and efficient automatic processing of the semantic structure.

The present methodologies allow for precise examination of the organization and contents of semantic memory, uncontaminated by sophisticated strategy usage. These techniques are sensitive to the changes in semantic memory that have been documented in the psychological literature via other experimental paradigms. Thus, there is great potential to study the development of concepts in other areas besides taxonomic knowledge. For instance, Ashcraft and Stazyk (1981) have interpreted verification latencies in order to examine the organization of processes involved in addition. As more complex conceptual domains are explored, large developmental and individual differences may be more apparent than has been demonstrated with the relatively simple concepts studied to date.

Research must also be directed toward the issue of why semantic retrieval efficiency is important. Although it is established that retrieval efficiency of very elementary concepts is related to other measures of cognitive ability, there are few specifications of why such a relationship is psychologically meaningful. However, recent theoretical work in the area of reading demonstrates how retrieval efficiency can be related to more complex processing. For example, Perfetti and Lesgold (1978) argue that word decoding is a slower process in the poor reader. Word code access is automatic for the good reader, but attentional capacity must be allocated to the decoding process for the poor reader. The use of attentional capacity for decoding leaves less capacity for other processes, such as comprehension.

Complex theories, such as that by Perfetti and Lesgold (1978), specify how the speeded retrieval of information from memory may be related to other abilities. Theories of aptitude will have to include hypotheses about how retrieval efficiency is related to ability-test performance if we are to progress beyond correlational observation.

REFERENCES

Ashcraft, M. H., Kellas, G., & Keller, D. Retrieval processes in fifth graders and adults. *Journal of Experimental Child Psychology,* 1976, *21,* 264–276.

Ashcraft, M. H., & Stazyk, E. H. Mental addition: A test of three verification models. *Memory and Cognition,* 1981, *9,* 185–196.

Belmont, J. M., & Butterfield, E. C. The instructional approach to developmental cognitive research. In R. V. Kail & J. W. Hagen (Eds.), *Perspectives on the development of memory and cognition,* Hillsdale, NJ: Erlbaum, 1977.

Bisanz, J., Danner, F., & Resnick, L. B. Changes with age in measures of processing efficiency, *Child Development,* 1979, *50,* 132–141.

Blake, J., & Beilin, H. The development of same and different judgments. *Journal of Experimental Child Psychology,* 1975, *19,* 177–194.

Bruner, J. S. The course of cognitive growth. *American Psychologist,* 1964, *19,* 1–15.

Case, R., Kurland, D. M., & Goldberg, J. Operational efficiency and growth of short-term memory span. *Journal of Experimental Child Psychology,* 1982, *33,* 386–404.

Cavanaugh, J. C., & Perlmutter, M. Metamemory: A critical evaluation, *Child Development,* 1982, *53,* 11–28.

Chi, M. T. H. Knowledge structures and memory development. In R. S. Siegler (Ed.), *Children's thinking: What develops?* Hillsdale, NJ: Erlbaum, 1978.

Chi, M. T. H. Interactive roles of knowledge and strategies in the development of organized sorting and recall. In S. Chipman, J. Segal, & R. Glaser (Eds.), *Thinking and learning skills: Current research and open questions* (Vol. 2). Hillsdale, NJ: Erlbaum, in press.

Chi, M. T. H., & Gallagher, J. D. Speed of processing: A developmental source of limitation. *Topics in Learning and Learning Disabilities,* 1982, *2,* 23–32.

Clark, H. H., & Chase, W. G. On the process of comparing sentences against pictures. *Cognitive Psychology,* 1972, *3,* 472–517.

Collins, A. M., & Loftus, E. F. A spreading-activation theory of semantic processing. *Psychological Review,* 1975, *82,* 407–428.

Collins, A. M., & Quillian, M. R. Retrieval time from semantic memory. *Journal of Verbal Learning and Verbal Behavior,* 1969, *8,* 240–248.

Courchesne, E. Neurophysiological correlates of cognitive development: Changes in long-latency event-related potentials from childhood to adulthood. *Electroencephalography and Clinical Neurophysiology,* 1978, *45,* 468–482.

Davies, D., Sperber, R. D., & McCauley, C. Intelligence-related differences in semantic processing speed. *Journal of Experimental Child Psychology*, 1981, *31*, 387–402.

Duncan, E. M., & Kellas, G. Developmental changes in the internal structure of semantic categories. *Journal of Experimental Child Psychology*, 1978, *26*, 328–340.

Ford, M. E., & Keating, D. P. Developmental and individual differences in long-term memory retrieval: Process and organization. *Child Development*, 1981, *52*, 234–241.

Gitomer, D. H., Pellegrino, J. W., & Bisanz, J. Developmental change and invariance in semantic processing. *Journal of Experimental Child Psychology*, 1983, *35*, 56–80.

Goldberg, R. S., Schwartz, S., & Stewart, M. Individual differences in cognitive processes. *Journal of Educational Psychology*, 1977, *69*, 9–14.

Hasher, L., & Zacks, R. T. Automatic and effortful processes in memory. *Journal of Experimental Psychology: General*, 1979, *108*, 356–388.

Henderson, S. E. Speed of letter cancellation on the basis of visual and name identity in young children. *Journal of Experimental Child Psychology*, 1974, *17*, 347–352.

Hogaboam, T. W., & Pellegrino, J. W. Hunting for individual differences in cognitive processes: Verbal ability and semantic processing of pictures and words. *Memory & Cognition*, 1978, *6*, 189–193.

Hoving, K. L., Morin, R. E., & Konick, D. S. Recognition reaction time and size of the memory set: A developmental study. *Psychonomic Science*, 1972, *21*, 247–248.

Hoving, K. L., Morin, R. E., & Konick, D. S. Age related changes in the effectiveness of name and visual codes in recognition memory. *Journal of Experimental Child Psychology*, 1974, *18*, 349–361.

Hunt, E. Mechanics of verbal ability. *Psychological Review*, 1978, *85*, 109–130.

Hunt, E., Davidson, J., & Lansman, M. Individual differences in long-term memory access. *Memory & Cognition*, 1981, *9*, 599–608.

Hunt, E., Lunneborg, C., & Lewis, J. What does it mean to be high verbal? *Cognitive Psychology*, 1975, *7*, 194–227.

Keating, D. P., & Bobbitt, B. L. Individual and developmental differences in cognitive-processing components of mental activity. *Child Development*, 1978, *49*, 155–167.

Keller, D. Developmental effects of typicality and superordinate property dominance on sentence verification. *Journal of Experimental Child Psychology*, 1982, *33*, 288–297.

Landis, T. Y., & Hermann, D. J. Differences in encoding and categorizing between children and adults. *Child Development*, 1980, *51*, 896–898.

Lange, G. Organization-related processes in children's recall. In P. A. Ornstein (Ed.), *Memory development in children*. Hillsdale, NJ: Erlbaum, 1978.

Lansman, M. *Paper and pencil measures of cognitive processes* (Tech. Note). Seattle: University of Washington, Department of Psychology, 1977.

Mansfield, A. F. Semantic organization in the young child: Evidence for the development of semantic feature systems. *Journal of Experimental Child Psychology*, 1977, *23*, 57–77.

McCauley, C., Parmelee, C. M., Sperber, R. D., & Carr, T. H. Early extraction of meaning from pictures and its relation to conscious identification. *Journal of Experimental Psychology: Human Perception and Performance*, 1980, *6*, 265–276.

McCauley, C., Sperber, R. D., & Roaden, S. K. Verification of property statements by retarded and non-retarded adolescents. *American Journal of Mental Deficiency*, 1978, *83*, 276–282.

McCauley, C., Weil, C. M., & Sperber, R. D. The development of memory structures as reflected by semantic priming effects. *Journal of Experimental Child Psychology*, 1976, *22*, 511–518.

McFarland, C. E., & Kellas, G. Category similarity effects in children's semantic memory retrieval. *Journal of Experimental Child Psychology*, 1975, *20*, 369–376.

Meyer, D. E., & Schanaveldt, R. W. Meaning, memory structure and mental processes. In C. N. Cofer (Ed.), *Structure of human memory*. San Francisco: W. H. Freeman, 1976.

Naus, M. J., & Ornstein, P. A. Developmental differences in the memory search of categorized lists. *Developmental Psychology,* 1977, *13,* 60–68.

Neeley, J. H. Semantic priming and retrieval from lexical memory: Roles of inhibitionless spreading activation and limited-capacity attention. *Journal of Experimental Psychology: General,* 1977, *106,* 226–254.

Nelson, K. Concept, word and sentence: Interrelations in acquisition and development. *Psychological Review,* 1974, *81,* 267–285.

Nelson, K. E., & Kosslyn, S. M. Semantic retrieval in children and adults. *Developmental Psychology,* 1975, *11,* 807–813.

Nickerson, R. S. On the time it takes to tell things apart. In J. Requin (Ed.), *Attention and performance* (Vol. 7). Hillsdale, NJ: Erlbaum, 1978.

Ornstein, P. A., & Naus, M. J. Rehearsal processes in children's memory. In P. A. Ornstein (Ed.), *Memory development in children.* Hillsdale, NJ: Erlbaum, 1978.

Perfetti, C. A., & Lesgold, A. M. Discourse comprehension and sources of individual differences. In M. Just & P. Carpenter (Eds.), *Cognitive processes in comprehension.* Hillsdale, NJ: Erlbaum, 1978.

Poltrock, S. *Individual differences in verbal ability: The role of attentional processes* (Tech. Note). Seattle: University of Washington, Department of Psychology, 1977.

Posner, M. I., & Mitchell, R. F. Chronometric analysis of classification. *Psychological Review,* 1967, *74,* 392–409.

Posner, M. I., & Snyder, C. R. R. Attention and cognitive control. In R. L. Solso (Ed.), *Information processing and cognition: The Loyola symposium.* Hillsdale, New Jersey: Erlbaum, 1975.

Prawat, R. S., & Cancelli, A. A. Semantic retrieval in young children as a function of type of meaning. *Developmental Psychology,* 1977, *13,* 354–358.

Rips, L. J., Shoben, E. J., & Smith, E. E. Semantic distance and the verification of semantic relations. *Journal of Verbal Learning and Verbal Behavior,* 1973, *12,* 1–20.

Roaden, S. K., McCauley, C., & Sperber, R. D. Intelligence-related differences in the relative salience of object-property relationships. *American Journal of Mental Deficiency,* 1980, *84,* 518–525.

Rosch, E. On the internal structure of perceptual and semantic categories. In T. E. Moore (Ed.), *Cognitive development and the acquisition of language.* New York: Academic Press, 1973.

Rosch, E. Cognitive representations of semantic categories. *Journal of Experimental Psychology: General,* 1975, *104,* 192–233.

Saltz, E., Soller, E., & Sigel, I. E. The development of natural language concepts. *Child Development,* 1972, *43,* 1191–1202.

Schneider, W., & Shiffrin, R. M. Controlled and automatic human information processing: I. Detection, search and attention. *Psychological Review,* 1977, *84,* 1–66.

Schvanaveldt, R. W., & Meyer, D. E. Retrieval and comparison processes in semantic memory. In S. Kornblum (Ed.), *Attention and performance IV.* New York: Academic Press, 1974.

Simpson, G. B., & Lorsbach, T. C. The development of automatic and conscious components of contextual facilitation. *Child Development,* 1983, *54,* 760–772.

Sperber, R. D., Davies, D., Merrill, E. C., & McCauley, C. Cross-category differences in the processing of subordinate–superordinate relationships. *Child Development,* 1982, *53,* 1249–1253.

Sperber, R. D., & McCauley, C. Semantic processing efficiency in the mentally retarded. In P. H. Brooks, R. Sperber, & C. McCauley (Eds.), *Learning and cognition in the mentally retarded.* Hillsdale, NJ: Erlbaum, 1984.

Sperber, R. D., McCauley, C. Ragain, R., & Weil, C. Semantic priming effects on picture and word processing. *Memory & Cognition,* 1979, *7,* 339–345.

Sperber, R. D., Ragain, R., & McCauley, C. Reassessment of category knowledge in retarded individuals. *American Journal of Mental Deficiency*, 1976, *81*, 227–234.

Surwillo, W. W. Developmental changes in the speed of information processing. *Journal of Psychology*, 1977, *96*, 97–102.

Tulving, E. Episodic and semantic memory. In E. Tulving & W. Donaldson (Eds.), *Organization of memory*. New York: Academic Press, 1972.

Tweedy, J. R., Lapinski, R. H., & Schvanaveldt, R. W. Semantic-context effects on word recognition: Influence of varying the proportion of items in an appropriate context. *Memory and Cognition*, 1977, *5*, 84–88.

Weil, C. M., McCauley, C., & Sperber, R. D. Category structure and semantic priming in retarded adolescents. *American Journal of Mental Deficiency*, 1978, *83*, 110–115.

2

Individual Differences in Automatic and Controlled Information Processing

Phillip L. Ackerman and Walter Schneider

INTRODUCTION

One major use of psychometric assessment procedures is to predict the performance of individuals after they experience a long training program. For example, college entrance exams are used to predict which applicants will succeed in completing a 4-year college educational program. Similarly, military candidates are tested to predict who will be the best airplane pilots after 2 years of training. Currently used test measures, though, provide only

INDIVIDUAL DIFFERENCES IN COGNITION
VOLUME 2

modest predictions of training-program success. For example, the correlation between a composite of college entrance exams and final semester college grades is $r = .21$ (Humphreys, 1968). Note that these predictors account for less than 20% of the variance in final task performance. This low level of variance-accounted-for poses serious practical problems for test-based selection.

The small proportion of variance-accounted-for also poses theoretical problems for relating intellectual abilities to training success. A basic premise of intelligence theory has been that intelligence is highly related to learning (see Simrall, 1946). However, measures of many intellectual abilities are only modest predictors of training-program success. It is theoretically discouraging to have measures of intelligence account for only 4–20% of the criterion performance variance in a training program.

In order to improve our predictions of training-program success, we need a better understanding of the relations between individual differences in abilities, underlying task characteristics, task performance, and practice effects. This requires (1) identification of changes in the characteristics of processing with practice, (2) determination of information-processing requirements for tasks, and (3) integration of theory and data concerning normative task performance and practice effects with theory and data concerning individual differences in abilities.

In this chapter we briefly review how performance and information processing change with practice. We then discuss the problems that practice effects pose for the assessment and prediction of individual differences in task performance. Next, we describe the automatic/controlled information-processing theory and discuss how it allows us to interpret the nature of practice and skilled performance. The automatic/controlled processing framework is elaborated to relate it to ability test measures and theories of individual differences in abilities. We also present the results of an experiment that illustrate the relations between abilities and performance during practice. Finally, we discuss future research on the issues relating practice and individual differences.

THE PROBLEM OF PRACTICE

BASIC PHENOMENA

The nature of human performance changes so substantially with practice that current ability measures are often poor predictors of practiced performance. As illustrated above, the correlations of most task performance measures and ability measures with practiced performance are typically small (.22–.43 for discrimination reaction time, see Fleishman & Hempel, 1955; .15–.21 for academic grades, see Humphreys, 1968). In addition, as the time on task increases, the correlation of initial performance and practiced performance decreases (e.g., $r = .05$ between Trials 1 and 16 on a micrometer adjustment task, see Jones, 1970).

Extended practice at performing a task can greatly change the performance level on normative tests. Pellegrino (1983) provided subjects about 8 hours of training on basic spatial abilities tasks of mental object rotations. Subjects that tested at the 39th percentile or below before practice, tested in the 91st percentile or above after training. This improvement in performance remained even when subjects were retested 15 weeks after training. These results demonstrate that for a group that showed poor initial performance, a "basic human ability" test score (Primary Mental Abilities—Spatial Relations) can be shifted 1.75 standard deviations in only 8 hours of practice. With such potential instability in a basic ability measure, we should not expect the assessed ability in a novel situation to predict performance following hundreds of hours of practice in a year-long training program.

Practice effects produce qualitative changes in performance of consistent tasks. In a review of the visual search literature, Rabbitt (1982, p. 58) states: "There is no single factor so neglected in experimental psychology as practice effects. In visual search we know that everything changes with practice. . . . So far as we know, no single experimental result in the visual search literature is stable with practice."

Consistent Practice

Categorical search results (Figure 2.1) illustrate the kind of changes that occur with consistent practice. In the category-search task, subjects were presented a memory set ranging from one to four taxonomic categories. Then they were presented a display of two probe words. Subjects made a positive response if one of the probe words was a member of one of the memory-set categories. There were two types of search in the experiment. For the *varied mapping* (VM) conditions, the mapping between the presented category exemplars and the subject's response varied over trials (e.g., on trials where the subject was searching for "animals," the subject made a positive response to the word *bear;* on other trials when not searching for "animals," the subject made a negative response to the word *bear*). The varied mapping condition is representative of the processing requirements of novice performance in both varied and consistent search tasks. The second type of search involved a *consistent mapping* (CM) of categories. In this condition, the subject always responded the same way to a given category ex-

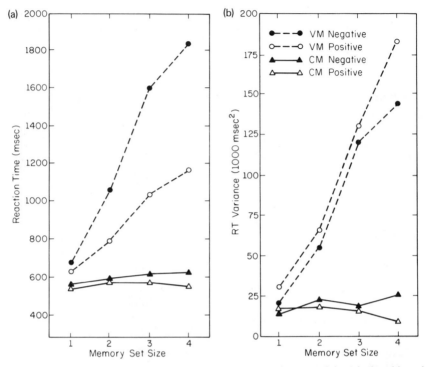

FIGURE 2.1   Reaction time means (a) and variances (b) for determining whether either of two words are members of one to four semantic categories. VM, varied mapping (unpracticed); CM, consistent mapping (practiced) search. Pos, positive—target-present responses; Neg, negative—nontarget trials. (Data from Fisk & Schneider, 1983.)

emplar (e.g., if the subject was consistently responding to "vehicles," whenever the word *jet* appeared, the subject made a positive response).

CONSISTENT VERSUS VARIED PRACTICE

Distinctions between the varied and consistent mapping conditions can be used to illustrate the gross changes that can occur with practice. For varied or novel search tasks, reaction time (RT) increases linearly with the number of items searched for (*memory-set size*); the positive (*target present*) RTs increase with number of memory items at half the rate of the negative (*no target present*) RTs; and the positive condition within-subject RT variance increase substantially faster than the negative variance. These data indicate that the varied mapping search process is a relatively slow (200 msec per comparison), serial, and self-terminating comparison process. After 13 hours of consistent practice (CM condition), neither the mean search RT levels nor the RT variance shows increases with the number of item comparisons. The search process appears to be relatively fast (only 2 msec per comparison), and access of the items in memory is parallel. A comparison of the two conditions shows that consistent practice can substantially speed the search performance (by a factor of 100) and shift the process from a serial item comparison to a parallel item comparison. In general, consistent practice at a task speeds performance, enables parallel processing, reduces cognitive effort, enables new strategies to develop, utilizes new abilities to achieve performance, makes the task less consciously demanding, and reduces subjects' control of the task processes (see Fisk & Schneider, 1983).

ABILITIES AND PRACTICE

Initial performance on complex tasks is generally a poor predictor of final performance. For example, Kennedy, Jones, and Harbeson (1980) found that the correlation between Day 1 and Day 15 performance on a grammatical reasoning task was only $r = .31$ (accounting for 9% of the variance). The subjects showed different initial performance levels, acquisition rates, and final asymptotes. Initial performance on simple tasks is also a poor predictor of practiced performance. Results from Adams (1953) show that the correlations of initial performance to final performance drop to $r = .56$ over about a half-hour of practice on a discrimination reaction time task. Similarly, Fleishman and Hempel (1955) report a correlation between initial and practiced performance of $r = .54$ for one hour of practice on a rotary pursuit task.

There are two major reasons for initial performance to be a poor predictor of final performance. First, during early performance (i.e., the first 15 minutes), many subjects perform activities that become unnecessary as skill develops. For example, they may still be interpreting the instructions, planning new strategies, evaluating performance.

The second reason for poor final task performance predictions based on initial performance is that practice effects result in radical performance changes early in training. For many skills, processing time is a power function of the number of trials. The pattern of performance is such that the log of the time to complete a response is a linear function of the number of executions of that particular response. Newell and Rosenbloom (1981) show that the power law function holds for a wide range of tasks (e.g., adding digits, editing text, detecting letters, and performing geometry proofs). The power law type of improvement function presents four problems for predicting final performance from initial performance: (1) Rapid early improvement produces large within-subject variance. (2) Differential experience with related tasks can produce a high initial performance level that is unrepresentative of final performance. (3) Subjects vary in their rate of acquisition, and acquisition rates are very difficult to estimate (see below). (4) Since practice can improve performance over large numbers of trials (e.g., 3 million trials for cigar rolling, Crossman, 1959), the person who is motivated sufficiently to keep practicing may eventually outperform either the fast learner or the fast starter.

The presence of substantial processing and performance changes during practice suggests that measures of individual differences in acquisition rate are critical for predicting final task performance. It should be noted that learning rates are rarely directly assessed during selection assessment procedures. Instead, most ability tests provide only a brief assessment of current individual differences in performance on fairly novel tasks and tests. For example, typical spatial rotations tests assess spatial ability during the first 2–30 minutes of exposure to a novel task (e.g., Educational Testing Service Kit, Ekstrom, French, Harmon, & Dermen, 1976; Differential Aptitude Test, Bennett, Seashore, & Wesman, 1977). From an information-processing viewpoint, the assessed ability levels are determined partly by the amount of previous exposure to related tasks, partly by a subject's ability to comprehend the instructions, and to a lesser, but undetermined, degree by extant learning rate and basic perceptual and motor abilities (e.g., visual acuity). On the other hand, final task performance after an extended training program is probably determined jointly by learning rate, willingness to expend the effort to learn, and abilities. The fact that individual differences on ability measures change with test practice has been well documented, especially with respect to spatial and perceptual–motor tests (e.g., see Anastasi, 1936; Woodrow, 1946). Thus, many current testing procedures provide only a limited, and certainly confounded, measure of the determinants of practiced performance.

A serious problem in the research concerned with assessment of individual differences is in the lack of appropriate data relating intellectual abilities to practice effects. In order to definitively relate these constructs, experimental studies must satisfy two criteria. First, subjects must receive substantial practice for stable performance and learning rates to be determined. For learning a relatively simple, but cognitively involving, task, as many as 10 hours of training might be required. Second, in order to obtain reliable correlations between performance and ability measures, substantial subject samples must be used (e.g., 30 subjects from a heterogeneous population). Note that when the range of abilities is restricted (as in college students), the resulting attenuation of association requires a substantially larger sample size to adequately determine ability factors. In Carroll's (1980) review of the cognitive individual difference literature, none of the reviewed studies satisfy the liberal criteria of more than 5 hours of training with more than 30 subjects from a relatively broad population. The current literature indicates that practice greatly changes performance, but we cannot, at present, relate these changes to intellectual abilities.

AUTOMATIC AND CONTROLLED PROCESSING

A THEORY OF PRACTICE

The striking changes that occur with practice have led many researchers to propose that extended practice brings about qualitative changes in mental processing (e.g., James, 1890; LaBerge, 1975; Posner & Snyder, 1975; Shiffrin & Schneider, 1977). The automatic/controlled processing framework suggests that human performance is the result of two qualitatively different forms of processing (see Schneider, Dumais, & Shiffrin, 1984; Schneider & Fisk, 1983; Shiffrin & Schneider, 1977). *Automatic processing* is a fast, parallel, fairly effortless process that is not limited by short-term memory capacity, is not under direct subject control, and is used in performing well-developed skilled behaviors. Automatic processing typically develops when subjects deal with the stimulus in a consistent manner over many trials. The rapid, effortless dialing of a well-known phone number is an example of an automatic process. The consistently mapped category search data depicted in Figure 2.1 illustrate the fast, parallel nature of this type of processing. *Controlled processing* is a slow, effortful, capacity-limited, subject-controlled processing mode that is used to deal with novel, inconsistent, or poorly learned information. Controlled processing is expected when a subject's response to a stimulus varies from trial to trial. The error-prone dialing of a novel phone number is an example of controlled processing. The varied mapping search data depicted in Figure 2.1 illustrate the slow, serial nature of controlled processing. (For a quantitative representation of automatic/controlled processing, see Schneider 1983a).

Automatic and controlled types of processing serve different information-processing roles (see Schneider et al., 1984). Automatic processing is assumed to perform consistent component processing, to interrupt ongoing controlled processing in order to reallocate attention, and to bias and prime memory. Controlled processing is assumed to be instrumental in development of new automatic processes, to deal with novel tasks that cannot be carried out by automatic processing, to maintain the activity of nodes in memory, activate nodes to enable automatic processes, and to block or modify automatic processing.

There is rarely any task for which processing is purely automatic or controlled. The two processes generally share the same memory structure and interact continuously. Automatic processing may initiate controlled processing by causing an orienting response. Controlled processing may activate an automatic process. For example, in playing tennis an expert player may adopt, via controlled processing, a strategy to place the ball in the far right corner. Automatic processes are used in executing this strategy, while controlled processing maintains the strategy.

EMPIRICAL RESULTS

The automatic/controlled processing framework has been used to organize and predict major phenomena of visual search, attention, and skill acquisition (see Schneider & Fisk, 1983; Schneider & Shiffrin, 1977; Shiffrin & Schneider, 1977). *Consistent* practice is predicted to produce substantial improvements in performance as automatic processing develops (e.g., reducing visual search comparison rates 98%, Fisk & Schneider, 1983). In contrast, *varied* (or inconsistent) practice exercises only controlled processing and produces little improvement in performance during practice (e.g., no change in letter search performance during 4 months of training, Shiffrin & Schneider, 1977).

Consistent practice greatly reduces the amount of effort necessary to perform a task, allowing controlled processing to be allocated to another task. For example, one experiment has shown that when subjects have already developed automatic processes to perform one task, they can learn to time-share another task with little or no deficit. After about 20 hours of consistent practice in both tasks, subjects were able to perform two search tasks simultaneously nearly as well as they could perform each separately (Fisk & Schneider, 1983; Schneider & Fisk, 1982a, 1982b, 1984). Once automatic processes have developed, subjects have difficulty blocking them from being implemented (e.g., Stroop, 1935; see also Shiffrin & Schneider, 1977, Experiment 4d; and other examples of negative transfer of training, Woodworth, 1938).

The acquisition of skill with practice is assumed to result from the development of automatic processes that are used to perform consistent task components. Automatic processes consist of previously learned or learned-during-practice automatic component productions (see Schneider & Fisk, 1983). These productions are condition–action rules that consistently produce a given action when their conditions are met (Anderson, 1983). The rate of development of new productions is determined by the availability of similar productions (transfer-of-training) and/or the availability of controlled processing for modifying memory (Fisk & Schneider, 1984). When a subject encounters a novel task, each stimulus must be consciously attended to and each decision consciously derived. The ability to maintain information in memory is critical during this initial phase of practice. However, as the production components become well developed, there is no longer a need for maintaining the critical information in short-term memory. As in a category-search task, when a probe word is presented, the activation part of a production is satisfied and an appropriate response is generated without a slow, sequential search. This produces the fast RT functions associated with consistently mapped search performance (Figure 2.1). For the expert, automatic processes perform consistent transformations of input stimuli and internal memory states into new memory states or responses. The expert requires controlled processing only for dealing with inconsistent aspects or time varying aspects of the task (see Schneider & Fisk, 1983).

A CONSIDERATION OF ABILITIES

We seek to develop a comprehensive theoretical framework that will relate individual differences in cognitive and intellectual abilities to individual differences in task performance before, during, and after extended task practice. The automatic/controlled processing framework provides an interpretation of when and how practice alters the nature and level of task performance. Of primary importance to this procedure is the mapping of ability-theory constructs to characteristics of automatic and controlled processing.

ABILITY THEORIES AND PRACTICE

There are three facets of ability theories that relate to predicting practice effects. These pertain to (1) aspects of hierarchical theories of intelligence, (2) aspects of the broad ability and personality theory by Horn and Cattell (1966), and (3) the concept of emergent abilities and skills. These three portions of ability theories can be extended to interpret individual differences in task practice effects.

Common to several hierarchical ability theories (e.g., Burt, 1949; Humphreys, 1962, 1979; Vernon, 1961) is the construct of a general intellectual ability factor (or g). These theories state that g represents the highest-order node in a hierarchy of ability factors. The g factor is implied by the nearly universal positive intercorrelations among cognitive–intellectual measures (Humphreys, 1979). Estimates of the influence of the general factor range between 20 and 40% of the total variance of the population of ability tests

(Vernon, 1961). In general, the hierarchical theories represent g not as a single ability, or thing-in-the-head (as in Spearman, 1904), but as a construct that represents the communality (or positive manifold) that exists at all levels of intellectual tasks (Humphreys, 1979).

The organization of these hierarchies is based on the generality or specificity of the abilities at each order of nodes. With g, or the most general ability at the highest order, less general ability factors break out at lower nodes. For example, in Vernon's (1961) representation, the second order contains broad major group factors termed *verbal:educational* and *practical:mechanical*. At the third order we find more specific abilities (or minor group factors) such as Verbal and Number below the *verbal:educational* node. As we move down the hierarchy, we would find the component abilities for the group factors (such as Vocabulary, Reading Comprehension, and Associational Fluency under the Verbal factor). Although even lower orders are rarely discussed in the literature, it is important to note that we can conceivably move far enough down such a hierarchy to discover, say, the component processes involved in the storage and retrieval of vocabulary items.

The second facet of ability theory relates to Horn and Cattell's (1966) identification of two major sources of individual differences. One source represents physiologically-based aspects of mental functioning, or *fluid* abilities. The other source, denoted *crystallized* abilities, is associated with "education or experiential influences" (Horn, 1965). Horn states that subjects use fluid abilities for tasks requiring rapid "learning and unlearning" of information and on tasks that involve the eduction of relations or use of logical reasoning. Individual differences on crystallized abilities are assumed to be related to individual differences in the familiarity of tasks, in amount of transfer of training advantage (from similar tasks), and in performance on tasks that require retrieval of information from long-term store. While we and others (e.g., Humphreys, 1982) do not endorse the particular demarcation of fluid and crystallized abilities postulated by Horn and Cattell, we do concur that abilities have specialized roles in the learning process. More detail is provided below.

The third facet of ability theories derives from the concept of *emergent abilities* (Ferguson, 1956; Guilford, 1967; Horn, 1965). The notion is that initial (*novel*) performance on a task is heavily dependent on general (*broad*) abilities that are involved in the subjects' understanding of instructions, selection of processing strategies, short-term memory limitations, reasoning skills, and so on. However, once subjects have the opportunity to practice a task, strategies are established and subjects internalize the instructions. Thus, as practice continues, the individual differences on the broad and general abilities become less influential determinants of task performance.

Finally, after extended practice, specific abilities emerge as the limiting determinants of performance (see, e.g., list of perceptual and motor abilities in Fleishman, 1966). For example, initial performance in a video game may be determined by the ability to comprehend the rules and objectives of the game. However, late in practice, perceptual–motor coordination or finger dexterity may emerge to limit performance.

PERFORMANCE AND ATTENTIONAL RESOURCES

To relate the ability and information-processing areas, we must discuss the attentional requirements of controlled and automatic processing. Norman and Bobrow (1975) propose that performance is determined by resource or data limitations. They define these limits as follows:

> Whenever an increase in the amount of processing resources can result in improved performance, we say that the task (or performance on that task) is resource-limited.
>
> [When] increasing allocations of processing resources can have no further effect on performance [i.e., performance is independent of the amount of processing resources] . . . we say that the task is data-limited. (p. 46)

In laboratory tasks we have examined resource limitations in consistent and inconsistent tasks. In one experiment, subjects performed in a dual-task search procedure. The first task was a consistent category search (e.g., "respond whenever an *animal* word occurs"); the second task was a varied mapping digit search ("respond if you see the digits *3* or *1*"). Four digits and one word were presented every 800 msec. Subjects were encouraged to maximize their digit-search performance. Subjects also performed single-task versions of category search and digit search in which they ignored the stimuli for the other task. The results are shown in Figure 2.2. The single-task digit performance shows little improvement with practice, which illustrates the fact that the resource load for varied search does not change with practice; in other words, the task remains resource-limited. The single-task consistent search is at ceiling, and hence, no practice effect can be observed (but see Fisk & Schneider, 1983, for examples of such practice effects). The dual-task conditions show marked practice effects. The category-search task accuracy improves from 55 to 99%. This improvement illustrates the fact that consistent practice can enable nearly perfect category detection while controlled processing resources are allocated to the digit-search task. This suggests that the resources needed for the varied digit-search task are no longer necessary for performing the category search. The dual-task digit search also shows an improvement with practice: Initially, the dual-task digit search accuracy was 63%, and after practice it reached 83%. This practice effect reflects the

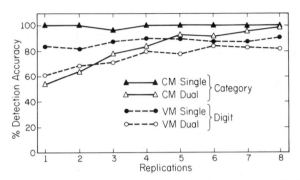

FIGURE 2.2   Detection accuracy as a function of 1-hour sessions. Filled symbols are single-task conditions, open symbols are dual-task. Solid lines are the VM (varied mapping) digit search; dashed lines are CM (consistent mapping) category search. (Data from Schneider & Fisk, 1984.)

benefit of allocating resources used initially in category search to the digit-search task.

We emphasize that the transition from resource-limited to data-limited performance practice effects shown in Figure 2.2 occurs only when *consistent* task components are involved. When subjects performed dual-task varied digit and varied category search, the resource-limited category search showed no improvement with practice over some 5,000 word searches.

Novel and inconsistent tasks require limited controlled-processing resources and hence exhibit resource limitations. Individual differences in controlled-processing resources are interpreted as differences in the *amount* or *efficiency* of attentional resources. As automatic processing develops, the availability of controlled-processing resources no longer limits performance. When this occurs, performance becomes data-limited. As automatic processing develops, individual differences in controlled processing become less important. Rather, the nature of performance differences must be described at the level of automatic processing component speed, efficiency, or level of development. Below, we identify these as individual differences in highly specific abilities.

The architecture of attentional resources provides for the mapping of controlled-processing resources to individual differences in ability. While this field of investigation is still at an early stage, two findings have been relatively well established. That is, evidence has been presented that indicates the presence of general or undifferentiated sources of attentional resources (Kahneman, 1973), as well as broad domains of differentiated attentional resources (e.g., *verbal* and *spatial* resources posited by Wickens, 1980). We propose that individual differences in controlled-processing resource availability or efficiency relate to the individual differences identified in broad and general cognitive–intellectual abilities. Individual differences in automatic-processing components, on the other hand, are mapped directly to individual differences in extremely low order, highly specific abilities.

A THEORY OF PRACTICE
AND PERFORMANCE–ABILITY RELATIONS

BASIC STATEMENT OF THE THEORY

Figure 2.3 depicts a theory in which we consider an initial domain of tasks that are novel and resource-limited at the beginning of practice and that allow all subjects to achieve a greater-than-chance (or greater-than-zero) performance level. Three main principles provide for the major effects in the theory. These are as follows:

Principle 1: Broad and general ability individual differences are equated with individual differences in amount or efficiency of attentional resources.

Principle 2: The transition from controlled to automatic processing is equated with the transition from resource-limited to data-limited performance characteristics.

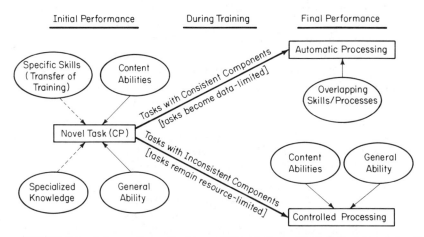

FIGURE 2.3 A theory for performance–ability relations. (If specialized knowledge is necessary, the relation between abilities and performance may be nonlinear, or even a discontinued function. Initial correlation between performance and general ability will be higher when instructions are complex, when familiarization with equipment, and so on are involved. Since these influences drop out over time, later performance will correlate less with general ability.)

Principle 3: The ability determinants of performance are associated with
the extent and type of resources required by the task.

Based on these principles, the figure illustrates what types of abilities will
be associated with naïve and practiced task performance for either consistent
or inconsistent information-processing characteristics. For *consistent* tasks,
general and content-relevant abilities will be associated with the initial performance individual differences, because controlled processing resources are
required for processing new information. As time-on-task increases, these
abilities will be less associated with performance. Finally, only specific
abilities that tap the skills–processes that overlap with task automatic-
processing components will correlate with late, well-practiced performance.
For predominantly *inconsistent* tasks, initial, intermediate, and late performance individual differences will be associated with both the general and
content-relevant abilities, because controlled processing is required for both
novel and familiar inconsistent information.

In addition to the boundary conditions outlined above, changes in task
difficulty, content domain, and performance-resource characteristics may
be included for predicting other performance–ability relations. (These issues
are discussed in Ackerman, 1984).

PRESENT THEORY AND PREVIOUS LITERATURE

The present theory predicts that transfer-of-training will be determined
by the availability of automatic component skills. Automatic productions
develop with practice. These productions represent specific abilities or skills
to perform consistent processing operations. These specific abilities improve
with training and decay with time. The positive transfer-of-training between
two tasks will be dependent on whether the consistent components trained in
the first task are beneficial to the second task. For example, training to deal
consistently with spatial figures can improve performance on related spatial
tasks (Pellegrino, 1983). In contrast, the controlled-processing resources are
comparatively stable. The differential stability of these processes parallels
Ferguson's (1956) notion that broad general abilities are stable, whereas
more specific abilities are not.

The present theory is consistent with a variety of previous data and
theoretical statements related to individual differences. Fleishman and his
colleagues have examined performance–ability relations in consistent
perceptual–motor tasks (e.g., Morse code, complex coordination). They
found that some broad cognitive abilities (e.g., Verbal, Spatial) correlate
moderately with initial task performance. However, correlations between
these abilities and performance drop to zero or nonsignificant levels late in

practice. On the other hand, motor and related perceptual–motor tests show negligible correlations with early performance but tend to account for moderate proportions of variance as practice proceeds (see Fleishman & Rich, 1963). In factor-analytic studies utilizing a variety of ability tasks, Woodrow (1946) found that initial and final performance after practice identified factors specific to each.

NEW DATA ON INDIVIDUAL DIFFERENCES IN AUTOMATIC/CONTROLLED PROCESSING

PROCEDURAL REQUIREMENTS

Experiments can be designed to obtain fairly pure measures of individual differences in automatic/controlled processing and cognitive abilities. Such experiments must meet special requirements in the (1) initial conditions, (2) procedure, and (3) analytic techniques.

Two sets of initial conditions for the experiment are related to task and test selection, respectively. Tasks must be chosen such that the experimenter can determine the relative differences in task consistency that allow for the automatic/controlled distinction to be made. As for measures of cognitive abilities, tests should be chosen so that a reliable and stable estimation of broad and/or specific abilities may be established. Factor-analytic guidelines suggest using three or four tests per factor to overdetermine ability structures.

Three procedural details are crucial to the success of such an experiment. First, an adequate number of subjects (usually much greater than 30) is necessary for establishing the ability factors as well as for comparing individual differences in abilities with individual differences in performance. The next requirement is a broad distribution of subject ability levels. If subjects come from a homogeneous population, such as college students, restriction-of-range of talent will attenuate any subsequent correlations between abilities and performance (McNemar, 1969). In addition, tasks must include substantial amounts of practice. During the first hour of practice, subjects are in the familiarization stage of performance, and individual differences data are unstable. We typically see between-subject stability of performance after the first 3 hours of training on relatively simple cognitive tasks.

Finally, in order to assess the relations between task performance individual differences and ability individual differences, one must choose an analytic procedure that does not lead to spurious results. For example, putting all test and task data together into a factor analysis to find whether task individual differences load on particular ability factors was a commonly used procedure in the 1950s and 1960s (e.g., Fleishman & Hempel, 1954). One characteristic of learning data is that they are not suitable to common forms of factor analysis (Humphreys, 1960). Instead, one must estimate cognitive ability levels independent of the task data and subsequently make comparisons between abilities and performance (see Fructer & Fleishman, 1967; and the following section for an example).

AN EMPIRICAL INVESTIGATION

We have carried out several studies to examine the applicability of automatic- and controlled-processing concepts for interpretation of practice effects. Here, we describe an initial study examining consistent and inconsistent processing in verbal and spatial tasks. The verbal task was a category search task similar to the one described earlier (see Figure 2.1; Fisk & Schneider, 1983). Subjects searched three probe words to determine which of the words was a member of one of a set of three memory-set categories. Subjects performed in both consistent and varied mapping search conditions.

This experiment was constructed to test whether the performance–ability relations predicted by the theory were consistent with data collected from a broad sample of subjects over what we consider a moderate amount of task practice (5 hours, or 800 trials, per task version). The specific initial predictions were as follows:

1. Normative task performance differences should mirror expectations from automatic and controlled processing theory. That is, the task with predominantly inconsistent, or controlled-processing characteristics will show little improvement after initial strategy selection and familiarity with the task. The task that allows for consistent processing requirements will show much greater improvement as automatic processing development ensues. Consistent task performance will level off much later in practice and may not even reach asymptote after many hours of practice (see Fisk & Schneider, 1983; Schneider & Shiffrin, 1977).

2. Abilities may be represented in a hierarchical arrangement by broadness of content, in accordance with many modern ability theories (e.g., Humphreys, 1979; Vernon, 1961). From the chosen tests, two orders of factors are expected: second order—g; first order—Verbal, Spatial, and Perceptual/Motor Speed.

Given these replications of well-established experimental and psychometric data, we proceed to predictions of performance–ability relations:

3. General and task-relevant broad-content abilities will be highly associated with novel or inconsistent task performance levels.

4. Consistent task characteristics, which allow for automatic processing development, will result in attenuated performance–ability relations with the general and broad-content abilities.

5. Shared processing characteristics, whether consistent or inconsistent, such as encoding or responding components and perceptual–motor requirements of the two task versions, will have no differential effects on performance–ability relations. Therefore, both tasks should be equivalently correlated with a broad perceptual–motor speed ability.

An example of the trial frame sequence for the verbal task is presented in Figure 2.4. On each trial three taxonomic category labels were presented for 5 sec on a terminal screen for memorization. Subsequently the screen cleared and three fixation dots were presented for 0.5 sec. Immediately afterward, three probe words were presented (one target and two distractor words). Subjects responded with buttons indicating the position of the target word. Feedback for correct responses included a character spinning off the screen. For incorrect responses, the appropriate word was displayed and an error tone was presented over the subject's headphones. For the consistent task

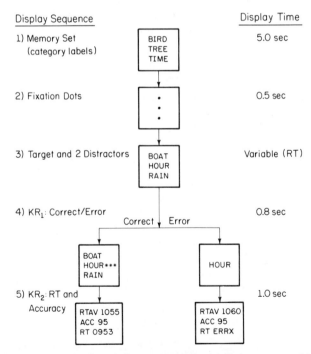

FIGURE 2.4   Example of a verbal category-search trial display sequence. Memory set size = 3. Probe frame size = 3. KR, knowledge of results feedback; RTAV, cumulative average reaction time; ACC, accuracy; RT, reaction time for the present trial (in msec).

version (CM), separate target and distractor lists were used. For the inconsistent or varied mapping version (VM), target and distractor categories were resampled from a common set on every trial.

The experimental data were based on 63 high school and college students (for details, see Ackerman, 1984). In addition to the task practice, several ability tests were administered over the course of the study. The data-analytic procedure and results are presented below.

In order to provide a valid assessment of performance–ability relation differences between tasks, the experimental data must first be consistent with expectations from the normative and individual difference domains (Predictions 1 and 2 above). Figure 2.5 illustrates that normative task performance was consistent with expectations (Prediction 1), the CM condition showing a steeper learning curve and a later asymptote than the VM. Initial performance on both tasks was approximately equal. The VM condition showed little improvement after session 5. The CM condition data show continued improvement, with mean RTs about 50% faster than the VM condition after eight sessions of practice. In addition, the between-subjects' RT standard deviations also reveal data characteristic of consistent and varied conditions. Between-subject variability in the relatively simple, consistent condition attenuates with practice (a 60% decline in standard deviation) as the controlled processing becomes unnecessary (see bottom panel of Figure 2.5). In contrast, the abilities related to varied condition controlled processing maintain influence throughout practice, and between-subject variability remains stable (a 4% increase in standard deviation over eight sessions).

The ability structure was derived by performing a hierarchical factor analysis of the test data (see Table 2.1). Note that the Schmid–Leiman (1957) procedure used for these data provides an orthogonal factor structure in two

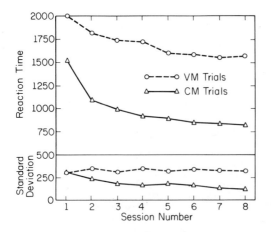

FIGURE 2.5 Verbal task RT means and standard deviations for each practice session (1 session = 5 blocks = 100 trials).

TABLE 2.1

Hierarchical Factor Solution[a]

			Factor		
Tests	g	Verbal	Spatial	Perceptual–Motor Speed	Communality h^2
Finding A's	.561	−.065	.036	.482	.553
Vocabulary	.580	.668	−.081	−.019	.790
Analogies	.671	.513	.042	.101	.725
Space relations	.570	.084	.668	−.032	.779
Cube comparisons	.490	−.044	.688	−.006	.715
Card rotations	.459	−.036	.595	.021	.566
Controlled associations	.578	.602	.076	−.067	.707
Number comparisons	.622	.049	−.092	.521	.669
Letter–number substitution	.632	.051	.112	.397	.572
Raven I & II	.716	.229	.345	.173	.714

[a] Salient scores appear in italics.

orders (see discussion by Carroll in *Individual Differences in Cognition,* 1983, Volume 1, for a description of the method). These data are clearly consistent with the theory of cognitive abilities and previous data on these test measures (Ekstrom, French, Harman, & Dermen, 1976). That is, three first-order factors of Verbal, Spatial, and Perceptual/Motor Speed are well determined by initial factor analysis of the 10 tests (Prediction 2). (We are not concerned with the Spatial factor here, as it pertained to a comparison of spatial task versions.) The positive intercorrelations among these first-order factors provide for the determination of the general, second-order factor. For this limited sample of subjects and test measures, the second-order factor g accounts for about 52% of the total variance.

Finally, factor scores (the subjects' estimated scores on the hypothetical factors) were derived and correlated with the performance measures. The correlations for g, Verbal, and Perceptual/Motor Speed factors and task performance are presented in Figures 2.6, 2.7, and 2.8. Predictions 3 and 4 are confirmed; the task requiring greater use of controlled processing resources shows larger correlations with g and Verbal abilities. Figures 2.6 and 2.7 show that for both the g and Verbal ability factors scores, correlations with the VM condition are larger during practice than correlations with performance in the CM condition. Given the equivalent requirements of the tasks for broad perceptual–motor skills (Prediction 5), the fact that both tasks correlate equivalently with that ability is also consistent with the theory (Figure 2.8). A spatial task that required subjects to classify rigid rotations and reflections of simple dot figures also provided similar data in support of the theory. Individual differences in the varied task version were more highly

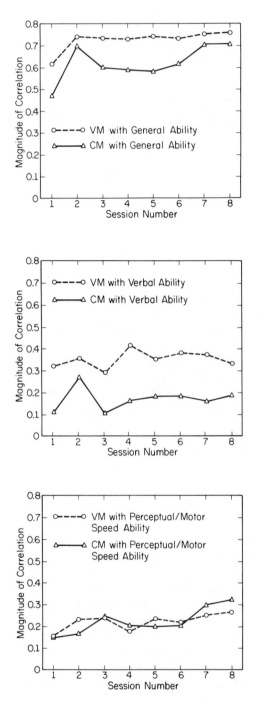

FIGURE 2.6 Verbal task: correlations between derived general ability factor scores and task session performance (RT).

FIGURE 2.7 Verbal task: correlations between derived verbal ability factor scores and task session performance (RT).

FIGURE 2.8 Verbal task: correlations between derived perceptual–motor speed ability factor scores and task session performance (RT).

associated with general and task-relevant content abilities than individual differences in consistent task performance. Further details of the spatial task procedures and results are presented in Ackerman (1984).

The fact that these two task versions shared all characteristics except the stimulus-mapping consistency makes the divergence in correlations a much more impressive finding than the raw performance–ability correlations indicate. Correlations between performance individual differences on equivalent amounts of practice for the two conditions averaged $r = .76$. Therefore, the logical extension is that a more dramatic divergence in correlations could result from sampling tasks that are further separated on the continuum of task characteristics based on controlled and automatic processing requirements.

It is important to note that although these tasks were relatively simple from an integration-of-components viewpoint, 5 hours of practice were not sufficient to establish the attenuation (trend toward zero) of general and content abilities correlations with the CM condition performance levels (i.e., the findings of Fleishman & Hempel, 1955, and Woodrow, 1946). We speculate that further practice and/or the use of simpler tasks would also increase the divergent trend between the consistent and varied conditions.

Two major findings summarize results from this program of research. First, individual differences on tasks that require resource-limited controlled processing are substantially related to individual differences in general and task-relevant content abilities (R approximately .70). Second, when the task dependence on controlled-processing resources is reduced (whether by increasing consistency to allow automatic processing components to develop, or by reducing memory load), the relations between task performance and individual differences on the general and broad content abilities attenuate.

From previous investigations of simple, consistent perceptual/motor task practice, we have already seen the attenuation of broad cognitive abilities correlations with performance over time (e.g., Fleishman & Hempel, 1954, 1955). In addition, such research has indicated that some highly specific abilities/skills *do* maintain association with performance over practice sessions. In order to estimate such associations for more complex tasks, though, we need to consider a number of additional variables.

EXTENSIONS FROM THE THEORY
TO COMPLEX TASKS

To extend the present theory to complex tasks, we must specify how practice affects tasks that include many consistent and inconsistent components. For example, in digital electronic troubleshooting, the expected value of a set of logical gates is a consistent processing requirement. Initially, the trainee would have to maintain the logical rules in memory and effortfully interpret the output state from each input state (see Anderson, 1983, for simulations of interpretive application of knowledge). As practice continues, automatic productions develop for the consistent components such that when a given set of input states is presented, the output state is determined with only minor use of short-term memory and controlled-processing resources.

Complex tasks also include inconsistent and poorly learned components. In electronic troubleshooting, the trainee applies a varied set of strategies (e.g., bracketing, piggybacking, selective shotgunning; see Bond, 1981). The expert troubleshooter must utilize limited controlled-processing resources to activate both strategy and interim state information. Also, if a novel logical element is encountered, controlled-processing resources are required to determine the output state. Note that as more of the logical functions are decoded via automatic processing, additional processing resources are available for maintaining strategy and interim state information (see Schneider & Fisk, 1983, for an illustration of this in the acquisition of musical performance skills). If the task requires the development of many components, years of training may be necessary before the task becomes primarily automatic.

IMPROVING PREDICTIONS

The current state of predicting performance in long-term training programs is modest at best. We have described how practice effects complicate predicting training program success. We believe that standard psychometric procedures typically will be unable to account for more than 20% of the variance when tasks are predominantly consistent. These procedures have been applied now for half a century, and it seems unlikely that new statistical procedures or test questions will greatly increase correlations between test scores and final performance.

Based on our theoretical concepts, normative data, and individual differences data, we suggest new assessment procedures may improve predictions of final performance. These new procedures imply changes in the assessment methodology. First, there must be a task analysis to identify the relevant determinants of performance. For example, the number of automatic productions the trainee must develop and the amount of information that must be actively maintained in memory are two such determinants. Second, research must more directly examine the relations between cognitive/intellectual abilities and the performance determinants. Third, special testing/training procedures must be developed to determine individual differences in the learning rates for critical skills.

Skilled performance in complex tasks is determined by a variety of factors, most of which are not directly measured via standard testing procedures. We briefly mention seven such determinants of performance and propose assessment techniques that more directly assess the performance determinants.

For some tasks, there are *physical system* factors (e.g., visual acuity, muscle strength, auditory sensitivity) that limit performance. Although visual acuity is a minor factor for a pilot in learning basic control of the aircraft, it becomes an important factor in advanced target acquisition. Fleishman and others have contributed a great deal to developing a taxonomy of such factors (see Fleishman, 1972, 1975, for a review). They have found a number of completely physical abilities which are instrumental in practiced performance (such as Dynamic Strength, Equilibrium, and Stamina). Other factors in this domain may be considered physical or perceptual/motor (such as Finger Dexterity, Aiming, and Arm/Hand Steadiness). When individuals are equivalent on other abilities, practiced performance may be greatly determined by such variables.

The *amount of controlled processing resources* devoted to any task will be a function of a subject's relative capacity, moderated by motivational variables. Since the use of controlled processing is crucial to understanding task requirements, this factor is especially important to initial task performance individual differences. In addition, controlled processing resource availability determines performance levels in tasks that involve: allocation of attention, maintenance of temporary information, strategy switching, and incorporation of new information. Few relatively pure measures in the present domain of intellectual abilities (e.g., digit span) are commonly used for predicting performance on complex tasks. If controlled processing resources are differentiated (as Wickens, 1980, suggests), it may be necessary to assess task specific controlled processing resources.

The third factor is *motivation*. The allocation of controlled processing is effortful. Many of our subjects find it difficult to maintain motivation after the first 5 hours of training. Poor motivation reduces the number of trials practiced and the amount learned per trial, thus reducing the development of automatic processes. Superlative performance skills develop over extended practice (e.g., hundreds of hours of training, see Schneider, 1983b). The highly motivated trainee with fewer controlled processing skills may surpass a more intelligent but less motivated trainee. Unfortunately, motivation is generally ignored by classical approaches to ability assessment.

The fourth factor is *automatic component availability*. This determines what procedural skills the trainee brings to the new situation for transfer or integration. For example, in selecting someone for training in copyediting, it is critical to assess basic verbal ability. In order to assess automatic processing components, tests should minimize the degree of controlled processing needed to perform the task. This can be done by making the task exceed controlled processing capacity (e.g., adding four-digit numbers rather than two-digit numbers), occupying controlled processing by having subjects perform a secondary task, or using speed tests (since automatic processing is generally faster than controlled processing).

The fifth factor is *declarative knowledge availability*. Many skills require a specific knowledge base but do not require that all the knowledge be automatic. For example, a historian needs to know many facts but rarely must retrieve them in situations in which the workload is heavy or in which slowing the processing time by a few seconds influences success. This type of general knowledge is frequently assessed in paper and pencil tests (e.g., College Board Entrance Exams).

The sixth factor is *learning rate,* or how fast new declarative information (see Anderson, 1983) and automatic productions are learned. This factor is determined by controlled-processing resources, motivation, and automatic component availability. In general, standard psychometric tests provide too little practice to directly assess learning rate. Since availability of automatic components depends on specific practice, learning rate assessments may have to be examined in the content domain of the target skill (see below).

The seventh factor relates to *strategy use.* Some tasks require the skilled practitioner to change strategies in order to adapt to the situation. For example, an air traffic controller needs to change strategies rapidly in dealing with a single aircraft when weather or traffic patterns change. Tests may have to be designed to assess the ability to change strategies, as most current tests only assess the ability to perform or acquire a given strategy (Kahneman & Gopher, 1971, attention switching task illustrates such a test, 1971).

NEW ASSESSMENT PROCEDURES

The automatic/controlled processing perspective emphasizes the need to assess all seven factors to predict practiced performance. Typical ability tests assess only a small subset of these factors. For example, while some tests assess controlled processing almost uniquely, such as the digit-span test; others measure almost uniquely automatic processes, such as vocabulary tests (i.e., retrieval from long-term store). Still other procedures, such as the digit–symbol substitution test, involve both types of processes (since the test is a novel, but consistent mapping of digits and symbols).

We propose that one way selection procedures can be improved is by unconfounding automatic-processing and controlled-processing demands in ability assessment. Based on our theoretical perspective, final performance derives from stable controlled-processing abilities and changing automatic-processing abilities. The correlation between these two abilities will change depending on the task and amount of practice. Tests which confound automatic and controlled components will optimally predict performance at a given level of practice. Unconfounded measures should provide separate measures of automatic and controlled components. The weighting of these measures in predicting task performance should change with practice. In this manner, it should be possible to establish selection procedures more in tune with the training environment demands. In addition, such test measures could conceivably be used to establish criterion-based cutoff scores once the controlled processing/automatic processing task requirements are established through task analysis. These methods may also make it possible to use the testing procedures as diagnostic tools for tailoring training programs. In the following section we discuss some of the procedures we see as beneficial to this aim.

MEASURES OF CONTROLLED-PROCESSING RESOURCES

To measure controlled-processing resources, we must control or attenuate individual differences attributable to automatic processing. One way of minimizing the role of automatic-processing components is to make use of either extremely novel stimuli or extremely familiar stimuli (when most or all subjects have already internalized stimulus codings). However, when novel stimuli are used, the speed at which subjects develop automatic-processing encoding components may confound measurement of controlled-processing resources.

Another method for deriving estimates of controlled-processing resource availability or efficiency is to construct inconsistent tasks that have limited types of strategies that may be employed. For example, in Chase and Ericsson's (1981) study of digit-span performance, one subject was able to impose a consistent strategy of categorization that ultimately raised his performance from 9 to 80 items. The strategy the subject employed was based on utilization of a network of well-established categories of running times (the subject was an avid runner). However, the strategy would only be effective in dealing with numeric information. By changing the type of stimuli from numbers to letters, the authors were able to show that the subject's short-term memory based on controlled processing capacity was no different than that of other subjects. Test constructors should examine strategy use via methods such as protocol analysis and comparisons between different measures representing similar constructs (e.g., letters and numbers in the Chase and Ericsson study).

Finally, another possible confounding of content-specific controlled-processing resource measurement occurs when subjects use strategies that bring other content resources into use for a specific task or test. For example, some evidence exists for proposing that some subjects more efficiently encode spatial stimuli by using verbal resources to provide names to stimuli (see relationship of spatial figures and verbal naming data, Glanzer & Clark, 1964). Investigators may be able to preclude such extra-content controlled processing by loading memory with a secondary task in the appropriate alternative domain. These dual-task procedures may ultimately be used for assessment of specific controlled-processing resource "pools," enabling more accurate measurement of particular content-based processing abilities (see Wickens, 1980).

MEASURES OF AUTOMATIC-PROCESSING DEVELOPMENT RATES

In order to predict individual differences in ultimate success or failure after practice or training on a complex but consistent task, it is important to assess both the controlled-processing resources available for the initial performance of the task and the rate at which subjects will build the automatic-processing components. Note that controlled-processing resource levels serve as the first hurdle for skilled-performance levels to be approached. If it is necessary to maintain, say, eight rules in memory for successful task performance, subjects with insufficient resources to perform the task successfully may show little improvement with practice. If the demands of the task involve integrating several automatic-processing components, the rate at which such components are established will influence performance both during and after training.

Several methods of assessing learning rate have been reported in the literature over the years, but they have been rarely utilized. Probably the simplest and most straightforward estimate of learning rate, or achievement, is by the partial regression estimate of final performance, with initial performance differences partialled out (see Cohen & Cohen, 1975, p. 380):

$$\text{Achievement}_{(Est.)} = \text{Final performance} - r_{\text{initial, final}} \left(\frac{\text{SD}_{\text{final}}}{\text{SD}_{\text{initial}}} \right)(\text{Initial performance})$$

A second, more sophisticated procedure involves estimating scores for subjects on different components of individual learning curves (e.g., initial, intermediate, and asymptotic portions of the learning curve). This is accomplished by use of three-mode factor-analytic techniques (Tucker, 1966). Although this method of assessing the learning-curve patterns of subjects involves considerable calculational complexities, the procedure provides much richer data than just one overall achievement value. Other factor-analytic approaches to estimation of learning-curve parameters have been used successfully in short-term learning experiments but not for conditions of extended practice (Allison, 1960; Stake, 1958).

Proficiency at complex tasks involves not just the development of automatic processing components but also the integration of components at various levels of development. So, in addition to assessing learning rate for automatic processing components, one should assess the rate at which subjects integrate components of performance. This may be accomplished by measuring achievement levels for new (integrated) components after subjects have been given either initial component training of short (less than 50 trials) or long (greater than 1,000 trials) duration. One way of assessing the integrative abilities of subjects involves partialling out individual differences on initial-component performance from second-component performance measures. Another method for examining this type of ability is to train all subjects to an arbitrary criterion and then measure subsequent component-building performance in isolation.

Finally, some rough estimation of learning rates may be possible by obtaining learning-history information from subjects. That is, by examining subjects' experiential successes in other learning situations that are based on automatic processing, such as high school grades, facility at video games, technical skill at musical instrument playing, typing skill, and so on, we can get an estimate of how likely it is that a subject will develop similar efficiency at other automatic-processing task components. Note that this measure does confound many of the variables that determine final performance, such as controlled-processing resource capacity, motivation, transfer-of-training opportunity, and so on. However, used in combination with measures of these component variables, this type of data may contribute significantly to prediction of later performance after an extended practice period.

By using purer measures of controlled-processing resource availability and automatic-processing development rates, researchers should be able to obtain not only more valid predictors of practiced complex task performance differences, but also information useful for diagnostic purposes. These abilities, along with the other instrumental factors mentioned above, can be used to estimate the proportion of subjects that will be able to learn the task in a given training environment. Further, the diagnostic information can be used for restructuring the program in accordance with deficiencies in critical elements of the task. This type of procedure has been used by Fredericksen, Weaver, Warren, Gillotte, Rosebery, Freeman, and Goodman

(1983) to remediate learning skills for complex-task training and by Schneider, Vidulich, and Yeh (1982) for restructuring an air-intercept training environment.

CAUTIONS REGARDING NEW ASSESSMENT PROCEDURES

At this stage, there is little evidence for the applied value of our suggested approach. For instance, there is no direct information that refined measures of controlled and automatic processing can improve predictions of practiced performance. We do not know whether such measures are stable or can be estimated during practical testing periods. Automatic process learning rate may vary within an individual depending on the context domain (e.g., it is possible that rates of declarative knowledge learning poorly predict spatial learning). Estimates of motivation in an artificial testing situation may poorly predict the motivation of some trainees in the real situation. These all represent unanswered research questions.

CLOSING COMMENTS

The foundation of data and theory of automatic and controlled processing and individual differences in performance–ability relations presented in the preceding pages yields a cautious optimism regarding the future success of selection research and applications. Several final points must be made in concluding our remarks on individual differences and practice.

First, we have little encouragement for investigations aimed at predicting individual differences after practice on simple, initially data-limited, consistent tasks (such as knob adjustment, discrimination RT tasks, two-hand coordination, etc.; see Jones, 1970; Fleishman & Hempel, 1954, 1955). Our theoretical perspective and the data both indicate that individual differences are greatly attenuated in such situations. Variables such as memory limitations, strategy selection, integration of automatic-processing components, and transfer of training are important only on the first several trials of these simple tasks and have little influence subsequent to that. Therefore, the only predictions of individual differences in performance for these tasks must come from highly specific physical and perceptual–motor control abilities. Even so, the limited amount of stable individual-differences variance (relative to random or transient variability) in those tests sets an upper limit of association between performance measures and those abilities (probably around $r = .2-.4$ in relatively broad samples of subjects).

Second, when the cognitive processing requirements of a task are increased, even to the limited extent shown in our examples of category-search tasks, presently available ability-test measures can predict substantial variance in practiced tasks (e.g., the .7–.8 correlations that we have found). Tasks that require additional allocation of controlled-processing resources or integration of new automatic-processing components are expected to correlate even higher with these standard paper and pencil measures.

Third, extended task practice (in excess of 30 hours) with predominantly consistent requirements attenuates performance–ability relations when standard test measures are employed. This set of circumstances is representative of many training requirements, such as air traffic control, electronic troubleshooting, technical adequacy on musical instruments, and so on.

Fourth, for extended practice in consistent task situations, a new generation of ability-assessment procedures may substantially improve predictions. The procedures should focus on learning rates and automatic-processing integration rates. We propose that assessment procedures must be expanded beyond the 2–30 minute limitations of current psychometric conventions. Standard psychometric testing should be used in initial selection as the first hurdle; then, a secondary selection procedure should be used to assess learning rate, motivation, and strategy use within the skill domain. We feel properly designed secondary selection procedures would substantially increase predictive validity. It is important to note that a 20-hour subsequent selection test that can reduce the number of washouts by 1% in a 1-year training program would be cost-effective in many domains.

Finally, data that are based on controlled processing individual differences and in automatic processing may be used diagnostically in the development of training or teaching procedures. By analyzing the information-processing demands of the criterion task and the initial performance requirements, investigators can undertake appropriate restructuring of the program to accommodate the student or trainee characteristics. For example, if the applicant pool has members with insufficient abilities for part-task integration of components with short training times, remediation (by expanding training) or tailored training may be instituted. In this way, the selection process reduces influence as more applicants can reach appropriate criterion performance levels. Procedures of this type are currently under way, based on this automatic- and controlled-processing framework and are detailed elsewhere (see Fredericksen et al., 1983; Schneider, Vidulich, & Yeh, 1982).

Even though individual differences in learning and practice have been investigated from many perspectives over the past 70 years, a fundamental change in approach may produce substantial progress. At this stage of investigation, many questions concerning the heuristic and applied value of the present approach are unanswered. However, new theoretical developments provide an interpretation of the qualitative changes with practice, and new assessment procedures may be able to track these changes and better predict final performance.

REFERENCES

Ackerman, P. L. *A theoretical and empirical investigation of individual differences in learning: A synthesis of cognitive ability and information processing perspectives.* Unpublished doctoral dissertation, University of Illinois, Urbana–Champaign, 1984.

Adams, J. A. *The prediction of performance at advanced stages of training on a complex psychomotor task* (Research Bulletin 53–49). Lackland AFB, TX: Air Research and Development Command, Human Resources Research Center, 1953.

Allison, R. B. *Learning parameters and human abilities* (Office of Naval Research Technical Report). Princeton, NJ: Educational Testing Service, 1960.

Anastasi, A. The influence of specific experience upon mental organization. *Genetic Psychology Monographs,* 1936, *18*(4), 245–355.

Anderson, J. R. *The architecture of cognition.* Cambridge, MA: Harvard University Press, 1983.

Bennett, G. K., Seashore, H. G., & Wesman, A. G. *Differential Aptitude Tests.* New York: Psychological Corp., 1977.

Bond, N. A. Troubleshooting in the commercial computer industry: A success story. In J. Rasmussen & W. B. Rouse (Eds.), *Human detection and diagnosis of system failures.* New York: Plenum Press, 1981.

Burt, C. The structure of the mind, a review of the results of factor analysis. *British Journal of Educational Psychology,* 1949, *19,* 110–111, 176–199.

Carroll, J. B. *Individual difference relations in psychometric and experimental cognitive tasks* (Tech. Rep. No. 163). Chapel Hill: University of North Carolina, The L. L. Thurstone Psychometric Laboratory, 1980.

Carroll, J. B. Studying individual differences in cognitive abilities: Through and beyond factor analysis. In R. F. Dillon & R. R. Schmeck (Eds.), *Individual differences in cognition* (Vol. 1). New York: Academic Press, 1983.

Chase, W. G., & Ericsson, K. A. Skilled memory. In J. R. Anderson (Ed.), *Cognitive skills and their acquisition.* Hillsdale, NJ: Erlbaum, 1981.

Cohen, J., & Cohen, P. *Applied multivariate regression/correlation analysis for the behavioral sciences.* Hillsdale, NJ: Erlbaum, 1975.

Crossman, E. R. F. W. A theory of the acquisition of speed-skill. *Ergonomics,* 1959, *2,* 153–166.

Ekstrom, R. B., French, J. W., Harman, H. H., & Dermen, D. *Kit of factor-referenced cognitive tests.* Princeton, NJ: Educational Testing Service, 1976.

Ferguson, G. A. On transfer and the abilities of man. *Canadian Journal of Psychology,* 1956, *10,* 121–131.

Fisk, A. D., & Schneider, W. Category and word search: Generalizing search principles to complex processing. *Journal of Experimental Psychology: Learning, Memory, & Cognition,* 1983, *9,* 177–195.

Fisk, A. D., & Schneider, W. Memory as a function of attention, level of processing, and automatization. *Journal of Experimental Psychology: Learning, Memory, and Cognition,* 1984, *10,* 181–197.

Fleishman, E. A. Human abilities and the acquisition of skill. In E. A. Bilodeau (Ed.), *The acquisition of skill.* New York: Academic Press, 1966.

Fleishman, E. A. On the relation between abilities, learning, and human performance. *American Psychologist,* 1972, *27,* 1017-1032.

Fleishman, E. A. Toward a taxonomy of human performance. *American Psychologist,* 1975, *30,* 1127-1149.

Fleishman, E. A., & Hempel, W. E., Jr. Changes in factor structure of a complex psychomotor test as a function of practice. *Psychometrika,* 1954, *19,* 239-252.

Fleishman, E. A., & Hempel, W. E., Jr. The relation between abilities and improvement with practice in a visual discrimination reaction task. *Journal of Experimental Psychology,* 1955, *49,* 301-316.

Fleishman, E. A., & Rich, S. Role of kinesthetic and spatial-visual abilities in perceptual-motor learning. *Journal of Experimental Psychology,* 1963, *66,* 6-11.

Frederiksen, J. R., Weaver, P. A., Warren, B. M., Gillotte, H. P., Rosebery, A. S., Freeman, B., & Goodman, L. *A componential approach to training reading skills* (Report No. 5295, Final Report). Cambridge, MA: Bolt, Beranek and Newman, Inc., 1983.

Fructer, B., & Fleishman, E. A. A simplical design for the analyses of correlational learning data. *Multivariate Behavioral Research,* 1967, *2,* 83-88.

Glanzer, M., & Clark, H. W. The verbal-loop hypothesis: Conventional figures. *American Journal of Psychology,* 1964, *17,* 621-626.

Gopher, D., & Kahneman, D. Individual differences in attention and the prediction of flight criteria. *Perceptual and Motor Skills,* 1971, *33,* 1335-1342.

Guilford, J. P. *The nature of human intelligence.* New York: McGraw-Hill, 1967.

Horn, J. L. *Fluid and crystallized intelligence: A factor analytic study of the structure among primary mental abilities.* Unpublished doctoral dissertation, University of Illinois, Urbana, 1965.

Horn, J. L., & Cattell, R. B. Refinement and test of the theory of fluid and crystallized general intelligences. *Journal of Educational Psychology,* 1966, *57,* 253-270.

Humphreys, L. G. Investigation of the simplex. *Psychometrika,* 1960, *25,* 313-323.

Humphreys, L. G. The organization of human abilities. *American Psychologist,* 1962, *17,* 475-483.

Humphreys, L. G. The fleeting nature of the prediction of college academic success. *Journal of Educational Psychology,* 1968, *59,* 375-380.

Humphreys, L. G. The construct of general intelligence. *Intelligence,* 1979, *3,* 105-120.

Humphreys, L. G. The hierarchical factor model and general intelligence. In N. Hirschberg & L. G. Humphreys (Eds.), *Multivariate applications in the social sciences.* Hillsdale, NJ: Erlbaum, 1982.

James, W. *Principles of psychology.* New York: Holt, 1890.

Jones, M. B. Rate and terminal processes in skill acquisition. *American Journal of Psychology,* 1970, *83,* 222-236.

Kahneman, D. *Attention and effort.* Englewood Cliffs, NJ: Prentice-Hall, 1973.

Kennedy, R. S., Jones, M. B., & Harbeson, M. M. Assessing productivity and well-being in Navy workplaces. *Proceedings of the 13th Annual Meeting of the Human Factors Association of Canada,* 1980, 8-13.

LaBerge, D. Acquisition of automatic processing in perceptual and associative learning. In P. M. A. Rabbitt & S. Dornic (Eds.), *Attention and performance V.* New York: Academic Press, 1975.

McNemar, Q. *Psychological statistics* (4th ed.). New York: Wiley, 1969.

Newell, A., & Rosenbloom, P. S. Mechanisms of skill acquisition and the law of practice. In J. R. Anderson (Ed.), *Cognitive skills and their acquisition.* Hillsdale, NJ: Erlbaum, 1981.

Norman, D. A., & Bobrow, D. B. On data-limited and resource-limited processes. *Cognitive Psychology,* 1975, *7,* 44-64.

Pellegrino, J. W. *Individual differences in spatial ability: The effects of practice on components of processing and reference test scores.* Paper presented at AERA Meetings, Montreal, Canada, April 1983.

Posner, M. I., & Snyder, C. R. R. Attention and cognitive control. In R. L. Solso (Ed.), *Information processing and cognition: The Loyola Symposium.* Hillsdale, NJ: Erlbaum, 1975.

Rabbitt, P. Visual search. In C. R. Puff (Ed.), *Handbook of research methods in human memory and cognition.* New York: Academic Press, 1982.

Schmid, J., & Leiman, J. M. The development of hierarchical factor solutions. *Psychometrika,* 1957, *22,* 53–61.

Schneider, W. *A simulation of automatic/controlled processing predicting attentional and practice effects.* Paper presented at the meeting of the Psychonomic Society, San Diego, CA, November 1983a.

Schneider, W. *Training high performance skills: Fallacies and guidelines.* Manuscript submitted for publication, 1983b.

Schneider, W., Dumais, S. T., & Shiffrin, R. M. Automatic and control processing and attention. In R. Parasuraman & D. R. Davies (Eds.), *Varieties of attention.* New York: Academic Press, 1984.

Schneider, W., & Fisk, A. D. Concurrent automatic and controlled visual search: Can processing occur without resource cost? *Journal of Experimental Psychology: Learning, Memory, and Cognition,* 1982a, *8,* 261–278.

Schneider, W., & Fisk, A. D. Degree of consistent training: Improvements in search performance and automatic process development. *Perception & Psychophysics,* 1982b, *31,* 160–168.

Schneider, W., & Fisk, A. D. Attention theory and mechanisms for skilled performance. In R. A. Magill (Ed.), *Memory and control of action.* New York: North-Holland, 1983.

Schneider, W., & Fisk, A. D. Automatic category search and its transfer. *Journal of Experimental Psychology: Learning, Memory, and Cognition,* 1984, *10,* 1–15.

Schneider, W., & Shiffrin, R. M. Controlled and automatic human information processing: I. Detection, search, and attention. *Psychological Review,* 1977, *84,* 1–66.

Schneider, W., Vidulich, M., & Yeh, Y. Training spatial skills for air-traffic control. *Proceedings of the 26th Annual Meeting of the Human Factors Society,* 1982, 10–14.

Shiffrin, R. M., & Schneider, W. Controlled and automatic human information processing: II. Perceptual learning, automatic attending, and a general theory. *Psychological Review,* 1977, *84,* 127–190.

Simrall, D. V. *The effects of practice on the factorial equations for perceptual and visual-spatial tests.* Unpublished doctoral dissertation, University of Illinois, Urbana, 1946.

Spearman, C. General intelligence objectively determined and measured. *American Journal of Psychology,* 1904, *15,* 201–293.

Stake, R. E. *Learning parameters, aptitudes and achievements* (Office of Naval Research Technical Report). Princeton, NJ: Educational Testing Service, 1958.

Stroop, J. R. Studies of interference in serial verbal reactions. *Journal of Experimental Psychology,* 1935, *18,* 643–662.

Tucker, L. R. Learning theory and multivariate experiments: Illustration by determination of generalized learning curves. In R. B. Cattell (Ed.), *Handbook of multivariate experimental psychology.* Chicago: Rand McNally, 1966.

Vernon, P. E. *The structure of human abilities.* New York: Wiley, 1961.

Wickens, C. D. The structure of attentional resources. In R. S. Nickerson (Ed.), *Attention and performance VIII.* Hillsdale, NJ: Erlbaum, 1980.

Woodrow, H. The ability to learn. *Psychological Review,* 1946, *53,* 147–158.

Woodworth, R. S. *Experimental psychology.* New York: Holt & Co., 1938.

3

Spatial Aptitude*

Lynn A. Cooper and Randall J. Mumaw

INTRODUCTION

The ability to use spatial information is clearly a fundamental aspect of human cognition. Real-world tasks, such as learning to locomote through the environment or correctly anticipating the trajectory of an approaching object, as well as more intellectual endeavors, such as solving complex problems in engineering, physics, or topology, all seem, intuitively, to require some degree of spatial skill. Yet despite the centrality of spatial aptitude to an understanding of human behavior, surprisingly little is known about the underlying cognitive processes that contribute to spatial ability or about the nature and locus of individual differences in spatial skill. To take an everyday example, it is not uncommon to encounter individuals who have no difficulty succeeding in academic situations that seem to require skill in dealing with spatial material but who, nonetheless, appear unable to generate even the most rudimentary internal representation of the environment in which they work and live. (One of the authors is such an individual.) Are these two aspects of processing spatial material to be considered manifestations of a single underlying construct of *spatial aptitude,* or are they more appropriately to be analyzed as products of separable cognitive processes that may be dissociable within a given individual?

In this chapter, we systematically discuss existing and ongoing research designed to elucidate the nature of the elusive concept of spatial aptitude. Our analysis is based on work on individual differences in spatial ability, and

*The preparation of this paper was funded in part by Contract N00014–81–C–0532 from the Office of Naval Research to the first author.

we consider three distinct research traditions in turn. First, we selectively review the psychometric work on spatial aptitude, which has proceeded vigorously since the development of tests of mental abilities (e.g., Thurstone, 1938). In this research tradition, the goal is to describe the nature of spatial aptitude without reference to underlying cognitive operations. Second, we consider research characteristic of the traditional information-processing approach. Here, the goal is to generate a model of cognitive processes underlying spatial performance and to locate the processing stages that distinguish individuals with high spacial aptitude from those lower in spatial ability. The implicit assumption of this view is that a single basic model is adequate to describe performance and that individuals differ primarily in the efficiency with which they carry out one or more of the operations specified by the model. Third, we discuss a research approach that emphasizes possible qualitative differences between individuals and explores the relationship between strategy variation and spatial aptitude. Finally, we conclude with a consideration of persisting problems and promising research directions.

THE FACTOR-ANALYTIC WORK:
CORRELATIONAL INDIVIDUAL DIFFERENCES

Factor analysis is a set of statistical techniques developed to determine the number and nature of underlying intelligence or personality factors that account for a given set of performance measures. In practice, correlational analyses are applied to a set of performance measures from a large group of subjects to derive a set of factors and to determine how well each measure reflects, or "loads on," each factor. The assumption is made that the set of factors is quite small in comparison to the number of measures and that any performance measure can be expressed in terms of these factors. Factors characterized as spatial–mechanical appeared in the earliest factor-analytic work (e.g., Thurstone, 1938; McFarlane, 1925) and were independent of verbal and quantitative factors of intelligence. In the last 60 years, the tests that have been found to load on these factors have varied from tests of perceptual speed to tests of spatial reasoning. In this section we discuss the utility of measures of spatial aptitude, the theoretical bases of the spatial factors, and methodological weaknesses that limit the factor-analytic approach.

Spatial aptitude tests (measures that have high loadings on spatial factors) are reliable predictors of performance in both scholastic and industrial settings. A review by McGee (1979) provides a comprehensive survey of the literature on the predictive ability of measures of spatial aptitude. This

literature can be summarized as follows: For academic curriculae and voca-
tional-technical training programs, spatial tests correlate most strongly with
course grades in mechanical drawing, shop courses, art, mechanics,
mathematics, and physics. In the area of job performance in industry, where
productivity and supervisor ratings are the criterion measures, spatial tests
have been most useful in predicting success in engineering, drafting, design,
and other mechanically oriented areas. More importantly, the predictive
validity of a general intelligence or verbal measure for these criteria is
generally much lower than that of the spatial measure. The extensive
literature is clear in showing that spatial aptitude tests measure a component
of real-world skills that is not measured by other types of aptitude tests.

In the remainder of this section, we discuss the process of identifying em-
pirically determined factors as components of intelligence. This theoretical
factor-analytic work attempts to define the mental processes that contribute
to individual differences in spatial aptitude. The wide variety of tasks that
load on spatial factors suggests that, instead of a unitary factor, several correlated subfactors may exist. However, theorists disagree on the number of
subfactors sufficient to describe spatial aptitude. Two reviews of the
literature on spatial aptitude (Lohman, 1979; McGee, 1979) illustrate this
lack of convergence in the interpretation of the factor-analytic work. In addition, Carroll (1983) and Lohman (1979) cite several reasons for this situation, and they stress the need for the reanalysis of data from the major
studies. Some of the issues are (1) the use of different factoring methods can
lead to different interpretations of the factor structure, (2) changes in the
format or administration of a test (e.g., the use of time or accuracy as the
dependent measure and the complexity of the items) can affect the resultant
factor structure, and (3) the combination of tests included in the battery can
affect the number and the nature of the factors obtained.

In order to resolve some of these inconsistencies, Lohman (1979)
reanalyzes most of the major U.S. factor-analytic work that includes spatial
aptitude. He attempts to reinterpret this work in terms of a broadly defined
spatial factor with several correlated subfactors. There were three subfactors
that were consistently produced by his reanalyses. The first, Spatial Relations, represents the ability to solve simple mental rotation items quickly.
The second subfactor, Spatial Orientation, represents the ability to imagine
how a stimulus array will appear after a reorientation of the body. This is
similar to what has been referred to as a *kinesthetic* factor by others (e.g.,
Thurstone, 1951). The third subfactor described by Lohman is Visualization. He provides no concise description of this subfactor but states that the
tests that best define it are relatively unspeeded and contain the most complex items.

Lohman (1979) extends this reanalysis by applying multidimensional scaling and cluster analysis to the entire set of factors and subfactors related to spatial aptitude. Factors related to visual information-processing, such as perceptual speed, closure speed, visual memory, and left–right discrimination or kinesthetic ability are related to spatial aptitude tasks and referred to as *primary factors*. These secondary analyses were done for the purpose of determining the psychological processes that underlie the differences among subfactors. In addition, the results suggest a theoretical structure for organizing these spatial subfactors by conceptualizing them in terms of a speed–power or simple–complex dimension. This structure depicts Visualization and Spatial Orientation as composits of several elementary mental processes required for spatial problem solving. Included are such processes as matching, identification, transformation, and memorial representation. Tests that represent each of these processes are often highly speeded and load on the separate primary factors described above. As the test items become more complex—that is, as the number of elementary processes required for solution increases—tests tend to be less speeded and more highly related to tests of reasoning. The Spatial Relations subfactor is depicted as more similar to the primary factors than to either of the other two subfactors. Similar conceptualizations of the spatial subfactors have been made by other theorists. Zimmerman (1954) hypothesizes that the complexity of test items can be manipulated to produce tests that would load on different factors. As item complexity increases, the importance of speed of response is minimized, and tests load on progressively more power-related factors, perceptual speed, spatial relations, visualization, and, ultimately, reasoning. Attempts by Lohman and Zimmerman to confirm this hypothesis have been partially successful. Lohman uses a speed index (average solution time per item) to provide evidence that supports a weak form of the hypothesis. He shows that higher factor tests are more difficult than tests that measure the primary factors and require more time per item. Zimmerman's direct manipulation of complexity to produce loadings on higher-order factors was successful for the higher spatial factors, though he was unable to produce tests that loaded on reasoning.

Lohman's conceptualization of the spatial subfactors in a unidimensional or quasi-hierarchical manner effectively organizes the results from the reanalyses and the multidimensional scaling work. He admits, however, that this conceptualization can be misleading. It seems to suggest that proficiency in Visualization is related to the efficiency of iteratively executing component mental processes. However, the evidence shows that the correlations between high- and low-level factors are not substantial. Thus, proficiency in Visualization requires something that is not captured by individual differences in the primary factors. Several factor analysts (see Lohman, 1979; Smith, 1964) have argued on a rational basis that the quality and control of the visual representation is an important determinant of Visualization ability. There is converging evidence for this hypothesis from the information-processing work that is addressed in more detail in the next section.

The reviews of the factor-analytic work reveal two implicit methodological assumptions. First, the process of interpreting factors incorporates the implicit utilization of rational models of processing for a variety of aptitude tests. That is, theorists attempt to characterize factors with mental processes assumed to be common to the tests that load highly on a particular factor. These processes are presumed to be the loci of individual differences. However, this approach provides no techniques to validate the rational process models that drive the factor interpretation. The lack of such validation weakens the theoretical contributions that factor analysis can make. In the next section we discuss current methods for the validation of rational process models of aptitude tasks.

ʼ The second implicit assumption made by this methodology is that solution strategies for any test are consistent across subjects. However, differences in the solution strategies utilized by a group of subjects can significantly alter the factor structure that is obtained. This assumption is especially suspect for the more complex tests that represent the Visualization and Spatial Orientation subfactors. Indeed, it is often difficult to identify both subfactors in a single study since the Spatial Orientation tests are often susceptible to Visualization strategies. That is, subjects may mentally manipulate an object depicted on a test item instead of imagining themselves moving in relation to that object. The detection of alternative strategies is not possible without the supplemental use of additional dependent measures or of an accompanying verbal protocol, neither of which characterizes the typical factor-analytic work. At present, too little is known about the variability of solution strategies, the best means of detecting that variability, or the effect that variability may have on factor-analysis solutions. The measurement of individual differences in strategy selection is addressed in a later section of this chapter.

In summary, the spatial aptitude literature is quite clear in showing that a broadly defined spatial factor exists independently of verbal and quantitative factors and that this spatial factor is more effective than other measures of intelligence in predicting success in certain academic and industrial areas. Also, Lohman's (1979) reanalyses of the major U.S. factor—analysis studies suggest that the speed–power or simple–complex dimension is important in describing the structure of spatial subfactors. However, despite the practical utility of the factor-analytic approach, two methodological difficulties have limited its contributions to the theory of individual differences in spatial aptitude. The first is the implicit use of untested rational process models of aptitude tests. The second is the questionable assumption that all individuals consistently use the same solution strategies.

THE INFORMATION-PROCESSING APPROACH: QUANTITATIVE INDIVIDUAL DIFFERENCES

The factor-analytic approach provides no models of task performance or difficulty but makes inferences about a task's processing requirements based solely on correlations with other unmodeled tasks. The information-processing approach, on the other hand, implements a rationally determined model of processing that defines the elementary processes that are required to perform a task. The assumption is made that each subject's performance is best described by these same elementary processes in the same sequence. The goal of this approach is to isolate the subset of processes that best reflect individual differences in task performance. This is accomplished by deriving latency estimates for subsets of processes and correlating them with aptitude test scores. The basic premise is that variation across individuals in the speed or efficiency of executing processes that are highly related to spatial ability should be correlated with variation across individuals in spatial aptitude test scores. In addition, variation in processes that are not related to spatial ability should not be correlated with variation in test scores. We refer to this approach as *the identification of quantitative individual differences,* since individual differences are defined in terms of relative speed or efficiency of elementary information processes.

This approach incorporates the building and validation of information-processing models of spatial tasks. A detailed information-processing model of a task provides several advantages for research on intelligence and individual differences. One advantage is the identification of task components defined in terms of basic cognitive processes. Measurements of these components can be used to evaluate cognitive skills, to suggest instructional techniques appropriate for those cognitive skills, and to indicate cognitive deficits that may require remediation. Second, if a process is determined to be an important contributor to individual differences for several tasks, it can be assumed that there will be a strong correlation between those tasks. This cross-task validation serves as a type of factor analysis. That is, factors can be defined by observing the presence of certain important task components instead of by the correlational analysis of a set of aptitude tests. Given a tested process model, it may be possible to predict which factors a new task will load on or to create tasks that load on certain factors.

The origins of the information-processing approach to spatial cognition can be traced to experimental techniques developed in connection with the theoretical work of Shepard and his colleagues (e.g., Cooper & Shepard, 1973; Shepard & Feng, 1972; Shepard & Metzler, 1971). These investigators have constructed process models for laboratory tasks that seem to require the same type of spatial transformations that are used in paper and pencil tests of spatial aptitude. In an initial experiment, Shepard and Metzler required subjects to determine as rapidly as possible whether pairs of perspective drawings of three-dimensional block figures were the same in shape or were mirror images of each other. The major finding of this study is that the time required to make the same–different judgment is a linear function of the angular disparity between the two figures. This finding and similar findings have been interpreted as evidence that mental representations of objects and transformations on those representations can have properties that are analogous to the properties of corresponding external objects and spatial transformations. Shepard and Metzler interpreted these initial results as suggesting that subjects performed the task by "mentally rotating" one object into the same orientation as the other object and then comparing the transformed internal representation with the second object.

The information-processing models developed from this research can be utilized without making assumptions about the nature of the underlying internal representations or processes. Indeed, the Shepard and Metzler paradigm has been used since 1971 to study individual differences in spatial tasks because it allows the chronometric measurement of several processing parameters for each individual. The processes commonly included in the models of spatial tasks are (1) encoding a visual stimulus, (2) transforming the representation of the stimulus, (3) comparing the transformed representation with an external stimulus, (4) and producing a response. In most experiments, the degree of spatial transformation required is varied, and two parameters—the slope and intercept of the latency function—are identified in the data. The processes that are dependent on the spatial manipulation (e.g., angular disparity) of the stimuli are represented by the slope parameter; the processes independent of the spatial manipulation in the stimuli are represented by the intercept. These are processes common to every item. The parameter estimates, slope and intercept, provide a measure of processing speed or efficiency for each subject. To determine which parameters are important for describing individual differences, these measures must be linked to measures of aptitude. Since 1975, a literature has developed around the information-processing approach, and two distinct methodologies have evolved. Pellegrino and Glaser (1979), in a review of that literature, refer to these two methodologies as cognitive correlates and cognitive components.

The cognitive correlates analysis, though not used in the spatial aptitude literature, has been important for studies of verbal aptitude. It is used to determine the general information-processing abilities that are differentially related to high and low levels of aptitude. Individuals are initially classified as high or low ability by their performance on a standard aptitude test. Next, standard cognitive laboratory tasks are administered to all subjects. The parameters obtained from the laboratory tasks are used to define several measures of cognitive ability, such as speed of retrieval or probability of retention. These two types of measures, information-processing parameters and aptitude test scores, are then submitted to a correlational analysis. If basic processing differences exist, the correlations should show patterns that differentiate the two groups.

The work of Hunt and his colleagues illustrates this method. In one well-known study (Hunt, Lunneborg, & Lewis; 1975), the verbal composite score from a university precollege test was used to define two subgroups of individuals. These subgroups represented the upper and lower quartiles of the distribution of that university's students. Hunt et al. brought the individuals from these subgroups into the lab to obtain processing measures from several traditional cognitive tasks. The processing measures were then ranked in terms of their ability to discriminate between the two subgroups. The investigators were able to summarize the set of best discriminators with two process-oriented factors: the ability to retrieve the name of an item rapidly and the ability to hold information in short-term memory for a brief period.

The cognitive components analysis, on the other hand, proceeds from a task analysis, usually in the form of an information-processing model. The goal is to create models of performance for items actually used on aptitude tests and to use those models to determine the locus of individual differences. In this way, the measures are more refined than accuracy scores, which are the traditional measures of aptitude, yet they are derived from the same task in a laboratory format. The laboratory task items that are created are generally designed to vary the spatial transformation systematically while holding item elements constant. This form of the information-processing approach is strongly associated with the work of Sternberg (1977) on inductive reasoning tasks and the body of work on spatial aptitude.

Two examples from the recent literature on individual differences in spatial aptitude illustrate the development of the cognitive components method and show how the measurement of processes can be refined to provide better models of task performance. The first example is a study by Egan (1978) that deals with the relationships between accuracy and latency measures of spatial ability. Initially, Egan had a group of Navy aviation candidates complete three spatial aptitude tests and four spatial laboratory tasks, three of which were modified versions of the aptitude tests. Accuracy scores were collected from the aptitude tests, and both an accuracy score and a mean latency to respond were collected from each of the laboratory tasks. A correlational analysis of these data revealed that the accuracy scores were highly intercorrelated and the latency measures were highly intercorrelated but that each measured a different aspect of spatial ability. A factor analysis produced two distinct factors, one with high loadings for accuracy and one with high loadings for latency.

In a second experiment, Egan derived new latency measures: slope and intercept parameters for two of his laboratory tasks. Mean latency to respond and accuracy scores were also collected for each individual. A correlational analysis showed that two of the latency measures, mean latency and the slope parameter, were not related to accuracy measures. Laboratory task accuracy scores were correlated with aptitude test scores and also showed predictive validity for measures of pilot training performance. The third latency parameter, the intercept, was much more similar to the accuracy scores, both in its intercorrelations and its predictive validity. Egan concludes from this that spatial ability, as traditionally defined, is related primarily to accurate performance and to speed of encoding and decision processes. This speed difference may reflect individual differences in the ability to form accurate mental representations. The major source of variation in mean latency measures, on the other hand, is the speed of transformation, and this latency measure reflects a different aspect of spatial processing. Thus, Egan eliminates what may be the most intuitive candidate for explaining individual differences: the speed of transformation.

Egan initially attempted to characterize the general relationships between accuracy and latency without depending heavily on an information-processing model that isolated single processes. The latency parameters that he derived were unrefined, and each reflected the combined effects of several processes. Indeed, even his two slope parameters were not composed of the same processes. More recent work has placed emphasis on task modeling and on the measurement of single processes. The next example (Mumaw, Pellegrino, & Glaser, 1980) also utilizes the cognitive components analysis for this purpose.

Mumaw et al. (1980) first developed an information-processing model for a Visualization task: the Minnesota Paper Form Board (MPFB; Quasha & Likert, 1937). Figure 3.1 shows the five laboratory versions of the MPFB that were created. In this form, the subject's task is to determine whether the array of pieces on the right can be used to assemble the completed puzzle on the left. If a mismatching piece is present, the item is "different." The process model that was developed represents a piece-by-piece processing loop that is iterated until a mismatching piece is located or until all pieces are checked. The processes included in the loop are (1) encoding a piece in the completed puzzle, (2) searching for that piece in the array (based on the

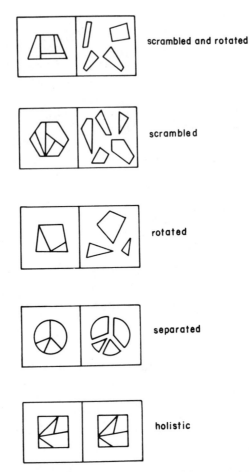

FIGURE 3.1   The five item types created for the laboratory version of the Minnesota Paper Form Board.

global features of the piece), (3) mentally rotating the piece until it has the correct orientation, and (4) comparing the transformed mental representation with the puzzle piece for verification. The investigators systematically manipulated the number of pieces, from two to six, and the complexity of the items. Five levels of complexity were created by manipulating the number of processes that were required to solve an item.

Reaction time and accuracy data were collected from 34 subjects who had taken the MPFB and represented a wide range of spatial ability. Figure 3.2 shows the group latency functions for "same" trials. Note that the functions are linear and reflect the effects of both independent variables—num-

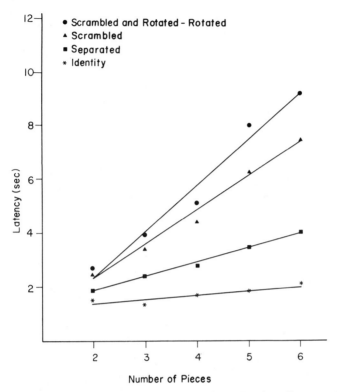

FIGURE 3.2   Mean group latency for "same" trials as a function of item complexity and the number of item pieces for the laboratory Minnesota Paper Form Board.

ber of pieces and complexity. The data from the scrambled-and-rotated and rotated conditions were identical and have been combined in Figure 3.2. This result implies that when rotation is introduced, an item is, subjectively, as complex as it can become and search is required. Four parameters—search, rotate, encode and compare, and prepare–respond—were derived from the "same" trial data by simultaneously solving the "same" trial reaction-time equations. This information-processing model successfully accounted for 97% of the variance in the group latency "same" trial data and was almost equally effective for individual data.

In addition to the success of the information-processing model, the process parameter estimates were quite reliable. These latency parameter estimates and "same" and "different" error rates were entered into a multiple regression for the individual-differences analysis with scores on the MPFB as the criterion measure. Four of the six measures—the search parameter, the encode and compare parameter, and the two error rates, accounted for 63% of the variance in the MPFB scores. The simple correlations revealed that "same" and "different" error rates and the speed of search were most strongly correlated with MPFB performance. The intercorrelation of error rates was zero, but "different" trial errors were significantly correlated with the speed of search. This pattern of results suggests that there are two independent sources contributing to high ability on this task. One is the quality of the mental representation, as reflected by the speed of search, speed of encoding and comparison, and errors on "different" trials (inability to detect a mismatch). The second contributing factor is the ability to rotate pieces accurately, as reflected by errors on "same" trials (most of which came from the most complex items). High-ability subjects tended to be proficient in both aspects of performance, while low-ability subjects tended to be deficient in one or the other though seldom in both.

In summary, the work of Mumaw et al. (1980) and Egan's (1978; see also Egan, 1979) suggests that traditional measures of spatial aptitude are not closely related to the speed of mentally transforming an internal representation of a visual form but are more closely related to the speed and quality of encoding and comparison processes. However, other researchers in the past few years have provided evidence that the speed of transformation can be effective in explaining individual differences in spatial aptitude.[1] This apparent inconsistency may be the result of changing task-demands over a wide variety of tasks. The results mentioned here seem to indicate that there are differences between tasks defined as simple and complex within Lohman's (1979) factor structure described above. In other words, tasks representing the Spatial Relations factor, with high emphasis on speed, could be best explained by the speed of transformation, especially when the objects that must be rotated are familiar, codable forms. Individual differences for more complex tasks could be best explained by encoding and comparison processes. As the task becomes more complex and more transformations are applied to a single representation, the quality and stability of that representation should become more important. Although this scenario is appealing and much of the current evidence supports it, the results are not entirely consistent (e.g., Lansman, 1981).

[1] Most notably, Lansman (1981) found a strong correlation between scores on a Visualization factor and the slope parameter from a Shepard–Metzler task. Using a similar mental rotation task, Pellegrino and Mumaw (1980) also found that speed of transformation, as reflected by a slope parameter, was strongly related to scores on a paper and pencil spatial aptitude test. In addition to this individual differences work, several studies have indicated that speed of transformation is associated with sex differences (Petrusic, Varro & Jamieson, 1978; Tapley & Bryden, 1977) and age differences (Kail, Carter & Pellegrino, 1979; Kail, Pellegrino & Carter, 1980) in spatial aptitude.

The empirical work reviewed above shows how process parameters can be derived from latency data. A methodological advance—the use of eye movement protocols—has allowed investigators to refine information-processing models further. Just and Carpenter (1976) recorded both the durations and patterns of eye fixations of subjects who were solving Shepard–Metzler items. Figure 3.3 illustrates the sequence of fixations of one subject for a "same" trial in which the angular disparity is 80°. Just and Carpenter's analysis of these fixation patterns suggests that there are three stages of processing. The first stage, search, is defined as the initial few fixations that are used to locate corresponding segments (1–4) of the block figures. The next stage, transform-and-compare, is used to rotate the two segments into congruence and is identified by the repeated fixation of corresponding segments (5–8). The final stage, confirmation, is a check to verify that the other segments of the two figures will also be brought into congruence by the rotation process. This stage is indexed by fixations on the segments not fixated during the transform-and-compare stage (9–12).

The durations of these three stages are obtained by combining the durations of the fixations that define each stage. Figure 3.4 shows that when the durations of each stage are plotted as a function of angular disparity, linear increases in each stage are revealed. This implies that the slope parameter derived from the Shepard–Metzler task is actually composed of these three individual processes. Thus, it is possible that individual differences that are located in the slope parameter reflect all three of these processes or any subset of them. More specifically, individual differences in the slope

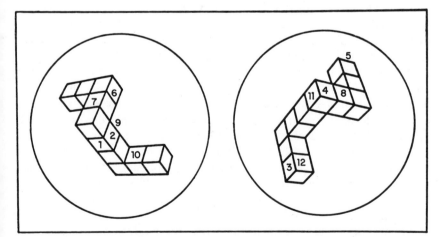

FIGURE 3.3   The sequence of eye fixations on a correct "same" trial in which the disparity was 80° (from Just & Carpenter, 1976).

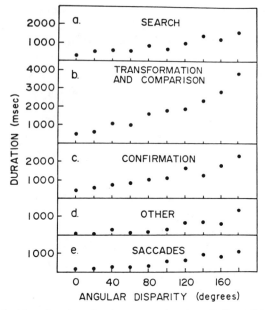

FIGURE 3.4   Mean duration of various processing stages in "same" trials as a function of angular disparity (from Just & Carpenter, 1976).

parameter could reflect differences in search time and not differences in the transform-and-compare stage as is usually assumed. This would clearly cast doubt upon conclusions that have been made about individual differences from previous work. Most importantly, it presents a strong argument for developing methodology and process models that provide a detailed enough picture of spatial problem solving to isolate quantitative differences.

Finally, there are two issues within the information-processing work that must be considered in future investigations. First, although the process parameters that have been identified are, in most cases, more reliable than, or as reliable as, spatial aptitude tests, these measures have not been related to real-world criteria and, therefore, lack necessary external validation. This is true not only for research in spatial aptitude, but for all of the quantitative individual-differences work. Rather than relating parameters solely to scores on aptitude tests, which are collections of items selected for their discriminability, real-world criteria should be used to evaluate the interpretation of these parameters. If successful, such an effort would provide a more meaningful test of their theoretical value. In addition, if these parameters are stable characteristics of an individual's processing ability, they should be identifiable in several spatial tasks, especially when the tasks are strongly correlated. Too few attempts have been made to do this type of cross-task validation (see Pellegrino & Kail, 1982). Early in this section, we described these two validation processes as being advantages of using information-processing models. The current cognitive-components litera-ture, however, has not exploited them.

The second important issue concerns the conclusion reached by several investigations (e.g., Carpenter & Just, in press; Mumaw et al., 1980) that in-dividual differences in the richness or quality–stability of the mental representation of spatial figures is of major importance for individual dif-ferences in spatial tasks. The evidence for this has been indirect, stemming from measures such as the speed of search, speed of encoding and com-parison, error patterns, and the duration of processing stages determined from eye movements. In actuality, there can be no direct measures of the quality of a mental representation, but more specific hypotheses concerning the nature and locus of representational differences can be generated and tested. Several possible hypotheses come to mind. High-ability subjects may be able to form mental representations that maintain more detail and, therefore, preserve more information following any transformations. Similarly, high-ability subjects may form more stable representations and, therefore, preserve more information over time. Both of these explanations suggest that individual differences are attributable to inherent traits of the perceptual-memory system. However, there are several studies that suggest that training can be effective in improving spatial aptitude scores (e.g., Blade & Watson, 1955). An alternative explanation, then, is that the quality of the mental representation is determined by active encoding processes used by the subject. High-ability subjects may be more efficient at encoding visual–spatial information or may have more knowledge about identifying meaningful spatial configurations and transformations. These skills may be affected by experience and may be trainable. Currently, we know of no published work that speaks directly to this issue.

STRATEGY SELECTION: QUALITATIVE INDIVIDUAL DIFFERENCES

Neither the psychometric work nor the approach through information pro-cessing has considered the possibility that individuals may differ qualita-tively in the strategies used for spatial problem solving and that such strategy differences may be related to differences in spatial aptitude. The psychometric approach strives to describe components of spatial ability without reference to underlying processes, and the information-processing approach assumes that all individuals carry out the same basic operations in spatial problem solving. Under this view, individual differences in aptitude are located in the efficiency with which one or more elementary processes are carried out. In this section, we evaluate the notion that differences in aptitude may be related to global strategy differences and flexibility in strategy selection, as well as to efficiency of underlying processing operations.

The idea that strategies—or methods for approaching a task or solving a problem—may be important components of aptitudes is not a new one; however, it has received very little experimental attention until recently. Hunt (1974) provides an analysis of two rather different strategies for completing items on the Raven Progressive Matrix Test of general intelligence, one based on analytical skills and the other based on Gestalt-like perceptual factors. However, he has not produced any experimental evidence that either or both strategies are in fact used. Baron (1978), too, argues for the importance of strategies in ability differences, and Sternberg (1977) emphasizes the contribution of strategy differences (conceived of as differences in the order in which processing operations are combined) in his analysis of the solution of analogy items.

Recently, experimental evidence for a relationship between strategies and aptitudes has come from a variety of different sources. For example, MacLeod, Hunt, and Mathews (1978) show that individual subjects' relative levels of verbal and spatial abilities may predict the nature of the strategies they select for performing a sentence–picture verification task (Clark & Chase, 1972). In this experimental paradigm, subjects must determine as rapidly as possible whether or not a particular sentence is true or false of a simple visual display. One model for performance on this task holds that the sentence–picture comparison is made by converting the picture into an underlying symbolic representation and then verifying whether this representation is congruent with a linguistic representation of the sentence (see, for example, Carpenter & Just, 1975). Another potential model for performance holds that the comparison is made by generating a spatial representation of the sentence and by then directly comparing this representation with the picture (see, for example, Glushko & Cooper, 1978). The two models make quite different latency predictions. What MacLeod et al. demonstrate is that subjects relatively high in spatial ability perform in a manner consistent with the visual strategy, while subjects with lower spatial ability scores (but verbal ability scores equal to those of the first group) perform in a fashion consistent with the more symbolic strategy. Sternberg and Weil (1980) report a similar finding of relationships between relative levels of verbal and spatial abilities and strategies selected for solving problems in the form of linear syllogisms. Subjects high in spatial aptitude were those identified as using a spatial strategy to solve the problems, and the data of subjects identified as using a linguistic strategy were correlated with level of verbal ability but not with spatial aptitude measures.

The correlational studies discussed above provide insight into the relationship between spatial–verbal ability structure and strategy selection. Recent research in our own laboratory has taken the further step of attempting to identify qualitatively different strategies used by individual subjects in performing what might be regarded, intuitively, as "purer" spatial tasks. In one of these projects, strategy differences in a simple visual information-processing situation and strategy flexibility are examined (see Cooper, 1982, for a summary of this research program). No attempt has yet been made to relate the strategy differences to differences in spatial aptitude. Another research project examines directly the relationship of spatial aptitude to strategies for solving complex visual problems.

The first set of studies (Cooper, 1976, 1980, 1982; Cooper & Podgorny, 1976) concerns individual differences in performance on a same–different visual comparison task. Subjects are shown a visual shape, and they must compare a memory representation of the initial shape as rapidly as possible with a test shape varying in similarity to the initial shape. Two basic patterns of performance emerge that are termed *holistic* and *analytic* strategies for visual memory comparison. Subjects characterized as holistic show no effects of similarity on "different" reaction times, show "same" times faster than "different" times, and respond rapidly overall. Subjects characterized as analytic show a monotonic decrease in "different" reaction times with increasing dissimilarity between the initial and the test shapes, "same" times of intermediate speed, and slower responses overall than the holistic subjects. However, the two groups exhibit virtually no differences in either the pattern or magnitude of errors. For both groups, error rates decrease monotonically with increasing dissimilarity between the initial and test shapes.

The thrust of this research program has been to examine how flexible these strategies are in the face of stimulus manipulations and task modifications that are designed to favor one processing strategy over the other. Cooper (1980, 1982) reports that holistic subjects can adopt the analytic mode when task-demands naturally draw on that strategy. However, only under unusual conditions can analytic subjects adopt the holistic mode. Furthermore, when analytic subjects are induced to switch strategies, they use the holistic mode less efficiently than do the "natural" holistic individuals. Thus, it appears that holistic processors are more flexible and efficient than analytic processors. An ongoing phase of this research program consists of an attempt to relate the holistic–analytic strategy difference to individual differences in spatial aptitude. This approach seems promising, for to the extent that strategy differences appear in simple visual information-processing situations, there is reason to believe that such differences contribute as well to differences in performance on more complex problems, such as items on tests of spatial aptitude.

A second research project investigates more directly the relationships among spatial aptitude, strategy selection, and skill in solving complex visual problems for students who have completed a beginning course in mechanical engineering. The problem-solving skill being analyzed is the comprehension and comparison of different three-dimensional objects in two-dimensional drawings. The problem format is of the sort typically encountered in courses in mechanical engineering and design graphics. An example of the type of drawing used in this research is shown in Figure 3.5. At the bottom of the

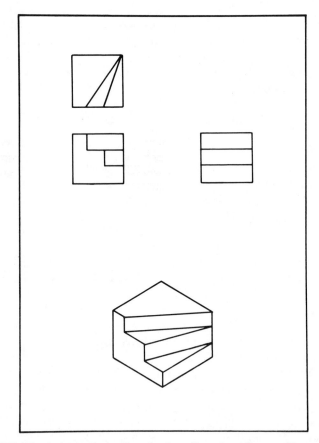

FIGURE 3.5 An isometric drawing of a three-dimensional figure and its corresponding orthographic projections.

figure, an isometric drawing of a three-dimensional object is shown. In this form of pictorial representation, the object is illustrated in perspective approximately as it would be seen by the eye. At the top of Figure 3.5, an alternative way of representing the three-dimensional object—three orthographic projections—is shown. In this form of representation, separate projections of the front, top, and one side view of the object are depicted as an observer would see each view if looking directly at each of the appropriate surfaces of the object. The actual problems that were used are laboratory versions of problems encountered in courses in mechanical engineering. Although a variety of problem types have been studied, only one type, illustrated in Figure 3.6, is discussed here. In this sort of problem, a judgment of the compatibility of various orthographic projections of an object must be made.

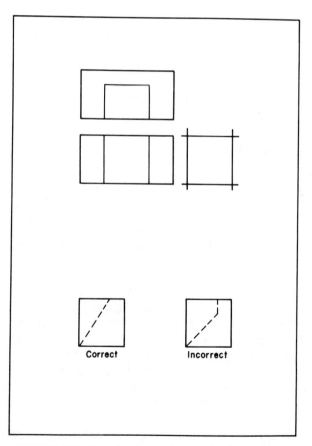

FIGURE 3.6   Example of an engineering drawing problem.

That is, given two orthographic projections of an object and a placeholder for the third (such as those shown at the top of Figure 3.6), the correctness or compatibility of a third orthographic view (such as that shown at the bottom left of Figure 3.6, incorrect third view shown at bottom right) must be determined.

In the actual experimental situation, subjects controlled both the rate of sequential presentation of the two partial orthographic views of a given object and the duration of each presentation. Each was presented on a slide. Thus, in addition to accuracy of problem solution, dependent measures included the number of looks or alternations after initial viewing of the first projection, total time taken for problem solution, duration of first look at the first slide, duration of first look at the second slide, and average duration of subsequent looks at both the first and the second slide. Subjects were questioned extensively during and after each experimental session concerning how they thought they solved the problems. That is, retrospective verbal protocols were collected concerning alternative solution strategies. In addition to these laboratory measures, each subject was tested on a battery of psychometric tests, including tests of spatial aptitude. On the basis of these tests, subjects were categorized in terms of level of spatial ability.

The basic question to which this study was addressed is whether success in solving the engineering items is related to psychometric measures of spatial aptitude. Two possible relationships were considered in advance. First, it could be that there is one basic method for solving these problems and that high-aptitude subjects are more efficient in using that method than are low-aptitude subjects. A second and more interesting possibility is that aptitude could be related the type of strategy used to solve these complex spatial problems. That is, high- and low-aptitude subjects could be using qualitatively different solution methods, determined by the nature of their ability profiles. We have termed the two possible strategies for solving these problems *constructive* and *analytic*.

How might the use of these alternative strategies be reflected in the data? A constructive or *pure* spatial strategy might involve the generation of an internal representation of a possible three-dimensional object as a mediator between the first and the second presentation of orthographic views. The second orthographic projection could then be compared directly with the appropriate side of the mentally constructed representation to determine whether that projection could combine with the first two to make a possible object. This strategy should be revealed by a relatively long time taken to inspect the first set of orthographic views—in order to generate an appropriate spatial model—but relatively few alternations between the first and second slides once the representation had been constructed. An analytic or *feature-oriented* strategy might consist of sequential comparisons between features or parts of the two partial representations, rather than the generation of a mediating internal spatial model. The use of this strategy should result in many alternations between the first and second views but relatively brief inspection times. Furthermore, we reasoned that subjects high in spatial aptitude would tend to favor the constructive strategy, while low-aptitude subjects would be inclined to select a more analytic approach.

The results of this study are complex, but they reveal clear, if surprising, relationships between spatial aptitude and selection of solution strategies. Classification of subjects into constructive or analytic strategy groups was first done on the basis of the verbal protocols. In addition, for a subject to be categorized as using a constructive strategy, the average number of alternations between the two views had to be small (2.2 or less) and the percentage of total time spent on the first inspection of the first view had to be large (35% or more). For a subject to be categorized as using an analytic strategy, the reverse trends had to hold (i.e., a large number of alternations between the two views and a small percentage of total time spent inspecting the first view). Using these joint criteria, almost all of the subjects could be classified in terms of strategy selection.

Figure 3.7 presents average solution time and overall solution accuracy as a function of both strategy type and level of spatial aptitude. Several features of these data deserve emphasis. First, our initial hypothesis concerning the relationship between aptitude level and type of strategy selected was clearly incorrect. In the high-ability group, more subjects opted for analytic strategy than for a constructive mode of processing. In the low-ability group, more subjects selected the constructive mode than the analytic mode. That is, the majority of subjects fail to use the strategy that we reasoned was most compatible with their ability level.

It is important to note that there were clear consequences of this surprising pattern of strategy use. For subjects using a constructive strategy who were also high in spatial aptitude, performance was relatively fast and accurate, compared with the other subjects in Figure 3.7. However, subjects low in spatial aptitude who selected a constructive strategy suffered performance decrements in one of two ways as a result of their strategy choice. Either these subjects required twice as much time as the high-aptitude subjects for problem solution, with an equivalent level of accuracy, or they matched their high-aptitude counterparts in solution speed, with accuracy plummeting to below chance. Thus, these data suggest that one consequence of adopting a strategy inconsistent with one's spatial aptitude is an overall loss in efficiency in terms of either speed or accuracy.

Note, however, that this deterioration in performance cannot be attributed to generally inferior problem-solving skills in the low-aptitude subject. The low-aptitude subjects using an analytic strategy performed almost

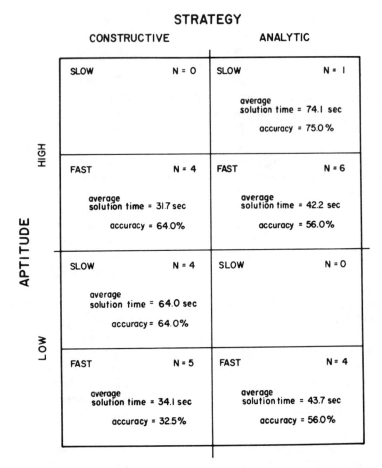

FIGURE 3.7 Average solution time and accuracy for groups defined by strategy, aptitude, and response latency.

as rapidly and accurately as the high-aptitude subjects using a constructive strategy, presumably because the analytic strategy was more appropriate to their aptitude structure. Finally, the subjects high in spatial aptitude who selected the analytic strategy performed almost as efficiently as the high-aptitude subjects using the constructive strategy, although their times are slightly longer and accuracy slightly poorer.

In summary, the results of this preliminary study demonstrate interpretable, if complex, relationships between spatial problem-solving strategies and level of spatial aptitude. One general conclusion is that performance is most efficient when selected strategies are compatible with relative degree of aptitude. The near equivalence of performance for the high-ability subjects using either processing strategy suggests additional possibilities. First, one component of high spatial aptitude may be a high degree of flexibility in strategy selection. Second, the high-aptitude individual may also be characterized by efficiency in the use of any processing strategy he or she adopts for a spatial task. These possibilities remain open issues for future research.

A rather different approach to analyzing the relationship between aptitudes and strategies is exemplified by the work of Snow and his associates (Kyllonen, Woltz, & Lohman, 1981; Snow, 1978). These investigators distinguish among three possible relationships between aptitude and strategies and report experiments specifically designed to test these possibilities. A Case I relationship holds when strategy choice is determined by aptitude level. In a Case II relationship, aptitude is not reflected in initial strategy choice; however, efficiency in the use of any strategy is aptitude related, with abler individuals performing more efficiently. A Case III relationship allows for both possibilities. Aptitude level not only constrains strategy selection but also determines efficiency in use of the chosen strategy.

For one spatial task, Kyllonen et al. (1981) found evidence for Case II and Case III relationships at different stages of the task. Subjects were required to view a simple geometric figure, encoding it in memory, then to synthesize that figure mentally with two additional shapes presented after encoding. Finally, a test display (an integrated figure) was presented, and subjects had to determine as rapidly and accurately as possible whether the three initially presented shapes combined to match the test display. The results of the study are complex, and a variety of models are fit to each of the three stages of the task (encoding, synthesis, and comparison). For the encoding and synthesis stages, a Case III relationship holds. Subjects high in spatial ability tended both to select the most appropriate strategy for the task and to use it efficiently. For the comparison stage, a Case II relationship was found. Individuals high in spatial aptitude were able to use a number of strategies more efficiently than their low-aptitude counterparts. Another important finding of this study is that aptitude is related to the occurrence of strategy shifting. The data of high-aptitude subjects were better fit to shift models than were the data of low-aptitude subjects, and sometimes these shifts appeared to occur in response to item types. This result led the investigators to suggest that an important component of aptitude level may be strategy flexibility, a suggestion quite similar to our own.

Snow (1978) and his associates also used eye fixation data to make qualitative assessments of strategy use in both verbal and spatial aptitude tasks. The central finding appears to be that the eye movement patterns of high-aptitude individuals are more orderly than those of low ability persons.

The eye fixation methodology was exploited by Carpenter and Just (in press) in an elegant series of studies suggesting relationships between spatial aptitude and strategies for solving spatial problems. Their analysis is essentially the same as that described in the previous section, but in this research the specific aim was to observe eye movement protocols of subjects differing in spatial aptitude. The two tasks that they examined intensively are the mental rotation task and a cube comparison task. In their modification of the Cube Comparisons Test, introduced by Thurstone (1938) and found in his Primary Mental Abilities Test, subjects were shown a line drawing of a pair of cubes each having three sides visible and displayed in different orientations. Symbols were shown on these three sides and subjects were required to determine as rapidly and accurately as possible whether the configuration of elements on the cubes would be consistent if the cubes were rotated into congruence. Variables manipulated included the number of 90° rotations required to bring the cubes into congruence and the number of mismatching symbols (if any).

The analysis of eye fixations in the cube comparison task, in conjunction with the dependent measures of latency and errors, revealed consistent differences in the strategies employed by high- and low-spatial subjects. Most of the subjects appeared to use a series of mental rotations in performing the task, but they differed in both the nature and the efficiency with which that strategy was employed. Subjects high in spatial aptitude sometimes imagined the cube rotated in depth about an axis corresponding to the long diagonal of the cube. In contrast, low spatial subjects imagined a series of rotations or single "flips" of the cube from one face to the other. An intriguing difference was found in the patterns of errors made by the two groups. Low-aptitude subjects showed high error rates on trials in which a symbol on the cube "disappeared from mental view." This suggests the possibility that high- and low-aptitude groups differ not only in processing strategies, but also in the richness of their spatial representations and their ability to maintain complex spatial structures in memory. Low-aptitude individuals used a larger number of rotations than high spatials, and the duration of an individual rotation was longer for lows than for highs. Again, this suggests a failure on the part of the subject low in spatial aptitude to generate a complex spatial representation that remains intact during mental transformation. Carpenter and Just's (in press) analysis of differences between persons high and low in spatial aptitude on the standard Shepard–Metzler rotation task is similar to their assessment of behavior on the cube comparison task.

Carpenter and Just report another interesting feature of their data. One subject classified as high in spatial aptitude claimed to have matched features of the symbols on the various faces of the cubes rather than performing a mental rotation, and the subject's data were consistent with this claim. This is reminiscent of a Case II relationship between strategies and aptitudes (cf., Kyllonen et al., 1981) in which aptitudes are not particularly instrumental in determining strategy choice, but they become important in determining the efficiency with which a chosen strategy is executed. These data also suggest that one characteristic of the high-aptitude individual may be the availability of a larger repertoire of strategies to apply in solving spatial problems.

In summary, we view the analysis of relationships between spatial aptitude and spatial problem-solving strategies as promising and as providing a useful complement to the psychometric and information-processing approaches. The available data base is meager at present, but a number of researchers are pursuing this question with a variety of different methodologies. Currently, the existing literature suggests the following potential characterization of an individual high in spatial aptitude: First, that individual may have a diverse set of available strategies and be flexible in strategy application. Second, that individal may be highly efficient in carrying out a particular strategy once it is selected for the spatial task at hand.

CONCLUDING REMARKS

Our discussion of spatial aptitude has looked at three distinct but related directions of research. First, we considered the factor-analytic tradition, pointing to what is known from 60 years of work and to methodological limitations. Second, we reviewed work stemming from the information-processing approach. Here we considered the logic of the approach and presented several examples of studies suggesting the possibility of quantitative differences between individuals in the speed or efficiency with which one or more elementary operations contributing to spatial aptitude is carried out. Finally, we evaluated the possibility of qualitative or strategic differences between individuals as determinants of measured differences in spatial aptitude, highlighting our own work on constructive and analytic strategies in complex spatial problem solving.

We view as particularly promising for future research the role of strategies and aptitudes in performance on spatial items. This is particularly true in that neither the factor-analytic approach, which makes little attempt to model task performance, nor the information-processing approach, which assumes that a particular model underlies performance of all subjects, is capable of uncovering strategic variation as it contributes to aptitude. Still another topic that we see as ripe for research concerns the possible heterogeneity of spatial skills. We return to a question that we posed at the beginning of this chapter: To what extent do common processes and representations underlie skill in dealing with large-scale space and spatial ability as measured by standard aptitude tests? Some investigators have begun to address questions such as this (e.g., Thorndyke & Stasz, 1980), but future advances await the development of richer process models that will capture the nature of both quantitative and qualitative sources of individual differences for a variety of forms of spatial skill. Finally, several investigators have suggested that differences in the quality or richness of a subject's mental representation contribute to the level of spatial aptitude. We view this as an intriguing possibility that should also receive increased attention.

REFERENCES

Baron, J. Intelligence and general strategies. In G. Underwood (Ed.), *Strategies in information processing*. London: Academic Press, 1978.

Blade, M. F. & Watson, W. S. Increase in spatial visualization test scores during engineering study. *Psychological Monographs*, 1955, *69* (12, Whole No. 397).

Carpenter, P. A., & Just, M. A. Sentence comprehension: A psycholinguistic processing model of verification. *Psychological Review*, 1975, *82*, 45–73.

Carpenter, P. A., & Just, M. A. Spatial ability: An information processing approach to psychometrics. In R. Wu & S. Chipman (Eds.), *Learning by eye.*, in press.

Carroll, J. B. Studying individual differences in cognitive abilities: Through and beyond factor analysis. In R. F. Dillon & R. R. Schmeck (Eds.), *Individual differences in cognition* (Vol. 1). New York: Academic Press, 1983.

Clark, H. H., & Chase, W. G. On the process of comparing sentences against pictures. *Cognitive Psychology*, 1972, *3*, 472–517.

Cooper, L. A. Individual differences in visual comparison processes. *Perception & Psychophysics*, 1976, *19*, 433–444.

Cooper, L. A. Spatial information processing: Strategies for research. In R. Snow, P-A. Federico, & W. E. Montague (Eds.), *Aptitude, learning, and instruction: Cognitive process analyses*. Hillsdale, NJ: Erlbaum, 1980.

Cooper, L. A. Strategies for visual comparison and representation: Individual differences. In R. J. Sternberg (Ed.), *Advances in the psychology of human intelligence* (Vol. 1). Hillsdale, NJ: Erlbaum, 1982.

Cooper, L. A., & Podgorny, P. Mental transformations and visual comparison processes: Effects of complexity and similarity. *Journal of Experimental Psychology: Human Perception & Performance*, 1976, *2*, 503–514.

Cooper, L. A., & Shepard, R. N. Chronometric studies of the rotation of mental images. In W. G. Chase (Ed.), *Visual information processing*. New York: Academic Press, 1973.

Egan, D. E. Characterizing spatial ability: *Different mental processes reflected in acccuracy and latency scores* (Research Rep. No. 1224). Pensacola, Florida: Naval Aerospace Medical Research Laboratory, August, 1978.

Egan, D. E. Testing based on understanding: Implications from studies of spatial ability. *Intelligence*, 1979, *3*, 1–15.

Glushko, R. J., & Cooper, L. A. Spatial comprehension and comparison processes in verification tasks. *Cognitive Psychology*, 1978, *10*, 391–421.

Hunt, E. Quote the Raven? Nevermore! In L. Gregg (Ed.), *Knowledge and cognition.* Hillsdale, NJ: Erlbaum, 1974.

Hunt, E., Lunneborg, C., & Lewis, J. What does it mean to be high verbal? *Cognitive Psychology,* 1975, *7,* 194–227.

Just, M. A., & Carpenter, P. A. Eye fixations and cognitive processes. *Cognitive Psychology,* 1976, *8,* 441–480.

Kail, R., Carter, P., & Pellegrino, J. The locus of sex differences in spatial ability. *Perception and Psychophysics,* 1979, *26,* 182–186.

Kail, R., Pellegrino, J. & Carter, P. Developmental changes in mental rotation. *Journal of Experimental Child Psychology,* 1980, *29,* 102–116.

Kyllonen, P. C., Woltz, D. J., & Lohman, D. F. *Models of strategy and strategy-shifting in spatial visualization performance* (Tech. Rep. No. 17). Aptitude Research Project, School of Education, Stanford University, 1981.

Lansman, M. Ability factors and the speed of information processing. In M. P. Friedman, J. P. Das, & N. O'Connor (Eds.), *Intelligence and learning.* New York: Plenum Press, 1981.

Lohman, D. F. *Spatial ability: A review and reanalysis of the correlational literature* (Tech. Rep. No. 8). Aptitude Research Project, School of Education, Stanford University, 1979.

MacLeod, C. M., Hunt, E. B., & Mathews, N. N. Individual differences in the verification of sentence–picture relationships. *Journal of Verbal Learning and Verbal Behavior,* 1978, 493–508.

McFarlane, M. A. A study of practical ability. *British Journal of Psychology Monograph Supplement,* 1925, *8*(1, Whole No. 8).

McGee, M. G. Human spatial abilities: Psychometric studies and environmental, genetic, hormonal, and neurological influences. *Psychological Bulletin,* 1979, *86,* 889–918.

Mumaw, R. J., Pellegrino, J. W., & Glaser, R. *Some puzzling aspects of spatial ability.* Paper presented at the annual meeting of the Psychonomic Society, St. Louis, MO, November, 1980.

Pellegrino, J. W., & Glaser, R. Cognitive correlates and components in the analysis of individual differences. *Intelligence,* 1979, *3,* 187–214.

Pellegrino, J. W., & Kail, R. Process analyses of spatial aptitude. In R. J. Sternberg (Ed.), *Advances in the psychology of human intelligence* (Vol. 1). Hillsdale, NJ: Erlbaum, 1982.

Pellegrino, J. W., & Mumaw, R. J. Multicomponent models of spatial ability. Unpublished manuscript, University of California at Santa Barbara, 1980.

Petrusic, W. M., Varro, L., & Jamieson, D. G. Mental rotation validation of two spatial ability tests. *Psychological Research,* 1978, *40,* 139–148.

Quasha, W. H., & Likert, R. The Revised Minnesota Paper Form Board Test. *Journal of Educational Psychology,* 1937, *28,* 197–204.

Shepard, R. N., & Feng, C. A chronometric study of mental paper folding. *Cognitive Psychology,* 1972, *3,* 228–243.

Shepard, R. N., & Metzler, J. Mental rotation of three-dimensional objects. *Science,* 1971, *171,* 701–703.

Smith, I. M. *Spatial ability.* San Diego: Knapp, 1964.

Snow, R. E. Eye fixation and strategy analyses of individual differences in cognitive aptitudes. In A. M. Lesgold, J. W. Pellegrino, S. D. Fokkema, & R. Glaser (Eds.), *Cognitive psychology and instruction.* New York: Plenum Press, 1978.

Sternberg, R. J. *Intelligence, information processing and analogical reasoning: The componential analysis of human abilities.* Hillsdale, NJ: Erlbaum, 1977.

Sternberg, R. J., & Weil, E. M. An aptitude x strategy interaction in linear syllogistic reasoning. *Journal of Educational Psychology,* 1980, *62,* 226–236.

Tapley, S. M., & Bryden, M. P. An investigation of sexual differences in spatial ability: Mental rotation of three dimensional objects. *Canadian Journal of Psychology/Review of Canadian Psychology,* 1977, *31,* 122–130.

Thorndyke, P. W., & Stasz, C. Individual differences in procedures for knowledge acquisition from maps. *Cognitive Psychology,* 1980, *12,* 137–175.

Thurstone, L. L. Primary mental abilities. *Psychometric Monographs,* 1938, *1.*

Thurstone, L. L. An analysis of mechanical aptitude (Rep. No. 62). Chicago: University of Chicago, Psychometric Laboratory, 1951.

Zimmerman, W. S. The influence of item complexity upon the factor composition of a spatial visualization test. *Educational and Psychological Measurement,* 1954, *14,* 106–119.

4

Predicting A Child's
Preschool Language Performance
from Perinatal Variables

Victoria J. Molfese and Dennis L. Molfese

INTRODUCTION

Since the mid-1970s, researchers have become increasingly interested in developing assessment tools that predict developmental status in childhood for individual children from measures obtained at birth or in early infancy. This interest has been sparked by the belief that if investigators could identify early a child's potential for language and cognitive development, the opportunities for intervening to correct developmental problems could be moved back earlier in time. Early intervention, then, might increase the likelihood of success in treating these problems. Although there have been a number of attempts to predict accurately a child's preschool language and cognitive skills based on prenatal, perinatal, and postnatal tests, the results have generally been disappointing. While sometimes statistically significant, the results usually show low correlations between scores obtained in early infancy and cognitive scores obtained in later childhood. When regression models are constructed, it becomes clear that traditional prenatal, perinatal, and postnatal measures accurately identify individual differences in only relatively small proportions of the children tested. This accuracy does not improve even when the tests attempt to distinguish between a child who is classified as at risk (e.g., who has respiratory distress or is premature) and a child not identified with this problem. The review that follows divides the traditional studies into two groups: attempts to predict a child's cognitive and language scores from perinatal measures (i.e., measures obtained before, during, and within a few days after birth) and attempts to predict those scores from measures obtained in later infancy. For each study, the characteristics of the subjects, the specific tests and measurements obtained, and the results of statistical analyses are reviewed to provide information on the types of approaches traditionally employed. With the results of previous research as a contrast, an alternative approach utilizing electrophysiological measures is then described. The success achieved using an electrophysiological approach is used as the basis for developing a model of the relation between early auditory processing of language-relevant stimuli and later language and cognitive performance.

PREDICTIONS BASED
ON PERINATAL MEASURES

Past studies have evaluated the relative values of a large number of perinatal measures as predictors of general mental development in the preschool period. These studies usually included measures of the prenatal characteristics of the mother, labor and delivery events, the postnatal status of the infant, scores on the Brazelton Neonatal Assessment Scale (Brazelton, 1973), and demographic characteristics. Mental development was typically measured in these studies by the Bayley Scales of Infant Development (Bayley, 1969), the Stanford–Binet Test of Intelligence (Terman and Merrill, 1973), the Cattell Infant Intelligence Scale (Cattell, 1960), or the Gesell Developmental Schedules (Knobloch & Pasamanick, 1974). Only a few studies, however, have examined the influence of those perinatal variables on specific types of mental development such as language abilities. In one such study, Field, Dempsey, and Shuman (1981) report on the development from birth to 2 years of age of a sample of 59 normal, full-term infants and 46 respiratory-distressed, low birthweight infants. All the subjects were assessed as newborns on several perinatal variables: the Obstetric Complications Scale (Littman & Parmelee, 1978); weight, length, head circumference; 5-minute Apgar scores (Apgar, 1953); the Postnatal Complications Scale (Littman & Parmelee, 1978); and the Brazelton Scale. At 2 years of age the subjects were assessed on the Vineland Social Maturity Scale (Doll, 1965), physical development, mother and child language production, the Behavior Problem Checklist (Quay & Peterson, 1975), the Bayley mental, motor, and behavioral subscales, and the Pediatric Complications Scale (Littman & Parmelee, 1978). Significant group differences were noted from birth through 2 years of age on most variables including Bayley mental and motor subscale scores and language measures of verbosity, mean length of utterance (MLU), and working vocabulary (total number of novel words). Unfortunately, only group—and not individual—differences are reported at each age. No specific information is provided on the predictability of second-year mental development and language scores from the perinatal measures.

Siegel (1982) also investigated the relationship between perinatal characteristics and cognitive and language scores measured at 3 years of age. Siegel reports on the usefulness of three types of perinatal risk variables: reproductive (i.e., gravidity, amount of maternal smoking, and number of spontaneous abortions), perinatal (i.e., birthweight, 1- and 5-minute Apgar scores, hyperbilirubinemia, gestational age, respiratory distress, asphyxia, and apnea), and demographic (i.e., socioeconomic status, sex, and maternal and paternal educational levels). In addition, scores on the 12-month Bayley mental subscale and the 12-month scores on the HOME (Home Observation for Measurement of the Environment; Bradley & Caldwell, 1977) Inventory were used to predict Stanford–Binet IQ and Reynell Developmental Language Scale scores (Reynell, 1969) obtained at 3 years of age. The subjects were 52 premature and 51 full-term infants participating in a longitudinal study. The correlations between individual independent variables and the dependent variables were generally low for both subject groups (r values of .05–.36 for premature and .16–.42 for full-term infants). However, some improvement was made in determining predictive models utilizing stepwise linear multiple regression analyses. Regression models were constructed with the perinatal risk variables as the independent variables and scores on the Stanford–Binet IQ Test and the Rcynell Language Comprehension and Language Expression Scales as the dependent variables. For the premature infants the multiple correlations for the three dependent variables were .59, .47, and .48, respectively. For the full-term infants the multiple correlations were .63, .45, and .38, respectively. Better predictions were obtained from regression models using 12-month scores on the Bayley scales, the HOME scale, and socioeconomic status as the independent variables to predict Stanford–Binet and Reynell Comprehension and Expression scores. Multiple correlations for the premature infants for the three dependent variables were .72, .68, and .65 respectively, and for full-term infants the multiple correlations were .58, .68, and .41. Unfortunately, the results of a regression model utilizing all the perinatal and infancy variables is not reported in much detail. There is a note that "infant test scores added very little to [the] multiple correlations" involving the reproductive, perinatal and demographic variables alone (p. 966). While the infant variables may not add much to the predictability using the perinatal variables, the elimination of the perinatal variables from the regression models and the use of the infant and social–environmental variables alone increased the predictability for both the premature and the full-term infants. These same findings are also reflected in the results using linear discriminant function analyses to classify individual subjects into categories (true positives, false positives, true negatives, and false negatives) with either perinatal variables or infant and social–environmental variables as the predictors. Classification accuracy was generally better using the infant variables rather than the perinatal variables. Classification accuracy using the perinatal variables only for premature infants ranged from .67 to .73 across the dependent variables and for full-term infants ranged from .71 to .84. Using the infant and social–environmental variables the range for prematures was .68–.90 and for full terms was .75–.87. Although the classification accuracy looks good, the most accurate classifications tended to be for nondelayed children. There was also a high false positive rate (children classified as delayed who were not delayed). In a follow-up, Siegel (1983) identified socioeconomic status for full-term infants and socioeconomic status, sex of infant, and maternal education for preterm infants as important characteristics involved in predicting 5-year Peabody Picture Vocabulary (Dunn, 1965) scores. Again, it is largely social–environmental and maternal factors which are important rather than infant perinatal factors.

Using a different set of perinatal and infant variables, Bee, Barnard, Eyres, Gray, Hammond, Spietz, Snyder, and Clark (1982) investigated the predictability of 3-year IQ and language scores in a sample of 193 normal, healthy infants. A large number of perinatal and infant variables were assessed at different ages. The variables were gestational age, weight, length, head circumference, 5-minute Apgar, sex, minor congenital anomalies, the Brazelton scale, the HOME Inventory, scores on the Bayley mental and motor subscale, the Denver Developmental Screening Test (Frankenberg & Dodds, 1967), the motor subscale of the McCarthy Scales of Children's Abilities (McCarthy, 1972), Preschool Behavior Questionnaire (Behar & Stringfield, 1974), the Neonatal Perception Inventory (Broussard & Hartner, 1970), assessments of physical health, socioeconomic and family stress, observations of mother–infant interactions, and receptive and expressive language scores (using the Sequenced Inventory of Communication Development, Hedrick, Prather & Tobin, 1975; Fluharty Speech and Language Screening Test, Fluharty, 1974; and language items from the

Bayley mental subscales). A range of 8 to 22 of the variables were assessed at birth and ages 4, 12, 24, 36, and 48 months. These variables were used in multiple regression analyses to predict 36-month receptive and expressive language scores and 48-month Stanford-Binet IQ. The variables that were part of the strongest predictive models were those related to the child's 12-, 24-, and 36-month test scores, mother-infant interaction and social-environmental variables. Perinatal and infant status variables obtained prior to 12 months of age were very weak predictors.

The Siegel (1982) and the Bee et al. (1982) studies share a number of similarities in their findings despite differences in the variables assessed and in the ages and characteristics of the subjects tested. First, both studies found perinatal variables to be either as helpful or less helpful than infant and child variables in the prediction of preschool cognitive and language scores. Second, in both studies, the social-environmental variables were found to be important predictors of later cognitive and language scores. Infants reared in poorer social-environmental conditions performed at a lower level on the cognitive and language tests compared to infants reared in better social-environmental conditions. Third, both studies found that the infant-child variables, together with the social-environmental variables, produced the best predictive models. These similarities are striking, especially in light of the subjects sampled in the two studies. Half of Siegels' subjects were premature infants, which might introduce sources of physiological, maturational, and pathological variance absent in the Bee et al. study. However, the characteristics that predicted best for the premature infants were similar to those found for healthy full-term infants in both studies. Clearly, prematurity per se did not affect the measures under study by these researchers.

In general, despite the use of a variety of measures, the accuracy of the perinatal measures alone in predicting subsequent developments in the preschool period and in identifying normal versus delayed children has not been good—certainly not as good as perinatal measures need to be in order to accurately identify individual infants at risk for developmental deviations. Other researchers, in coming to similar conclusions concerning traditional perinatal measures, have sought to identify alternative measures. Sigman (1983) has noted that while traditional perinatal measures such as gestational age, number of medical complications, and length of hospitalization following birth are related to length of fixation duration in a visual preference task, it is the length of fixation measure obtained at age 4 months that is most predictive of intelligence at 18 months, 25 months, and 5 years (Fagan and McGrath, 1981). Infants who fixate on a stimulus long enough to process the stimulus but do not fixate too briefly nor too long are more likely to perform better on cognitive tests in the preschool period. Thus, it seems clear that traditional perinatal measures can be used to identify individual differences in birth characteristics, but these individual differences do not in themselves seem to be as important for predicting performance on tests of cognition and language as are measures obtained in infancy and childhood.

PREDICTIONS BASED ON INFANT MEASURES

Several researchers have looked at the relationship between measures of infant development obtained in later infancy (4–18 months of age) and cognitive and language scores obtained in the second and third year. For example, in an earlier report of her longitudinal study, Siegel (1981) used 4-, 8-, 12-, and 18-month scores on the Bayley mental and motor subscales, the Uzgiris–Hunt Scale (Uzgiris & Hunt, 1975) and the HOME Inventory to predict 2-year-old scores on the Bayley Scales and on the Reynell Language Development Scales. The correlations in the various comparisons are often significant but are generally low (ranging from .20 to .65). The disappointment in identifying strong predictors from these variables is further underscored when, at best, less than 40% of the variance could be accounted for in the correlations. This study, together with the second report of the Siegel study, allows for the comparison of correlations between the 12-month Bayley Scale scores and 2- versus 3-year-old language scores. There were generally low but significant correlations at 2 years (ranging from .45 to .55). At 3 years, however, the only significant correlation was between 12-month Bayley mental subscale scores and language comprehension for the premature infants ($r = .38$).

The Siegel (1981, 1982) findings resemble to some extent the findings reported by Nelson (1973). The subjects in her study were 18 infants between the ages of 10 and 30 months. Nelson examined the correlations between measures of specific language abilities (ages at which the child acquired 10 words, 50 words, 10 phrases; vocabulary at 24 months and 30 months; MLU at 24 months and 30 months; and rate of word acquisition), which were obtained between the ages of 10 and 30 months, and measures of cognitive development (Bayley mental subscales; the Concept Familiarity Index, Palmer & Rees, 1969; and the Peabody Picture Vocabulary Test), which were obtained at 2 and $2\frac{1}{2}$ years. The correlations between the Bayley scores and the language measures were all significant (r ranging from .42 to .62). All of the correlations between the Concept Familiarity Index and the language measures were significant except those with the age at which the child had 10 words and vocabulary at 30 months. The range of the significant correlations was .38–.54. For the Peabody Picture Vocabulary Test, only the correlations with vocabulary at 24 and 30 months and MLU at 30 months were significant (ranging from .48 to .60). Similar to Siegel's findings, the results of the Nelson study show stronger correlations between first-year measures of development and 2-year-old language measures than 3-year-old language measures. Children who had the best language abilities tended to be the same children who performed best on the other cognitive tests.

Ramey, Campbell, and Nicholson (1973) also used measures obtained in infancy to predict cognitive and language scores. The subjects were 24 infants. Significant positive correlations were found among the independent variables of 6- to 8-month Bayley motor subscale scores, 9- to 12-month Bayley mental subscale scores, 13- to 16-month Bayley mental scale scores and the dependent variables of 36-month Stanford–Binet scores and the 36-month Illinois Test of Psycholinguistic Abilities (Kirk, McCarthy, & Kirk, 1968). The 9- to 12-month Bayley motor subscale scores also correlated significantly with the Illinois Test of Psycholinguistic Abilities. The correlations ranged from .68 to .90. Interestingly, none of the correlations between Bayley Scale scores obtained at 6–8 months, 9–12 months and 13–16 months with the 24-month Stanford–Binet scores was significant. In this case, contrary to the results of the Siegel (1981, 1982) studies and those of the Nelson (1973) study, correlations between infant measures and 2-year-old scores were not significant, while those between infant measures and the 3-year-old scores were significant. Bee et al. (1982) also found that correlations between 24-month Bayley mental subscale scores and the 36-month receptive and expressive language scores were nearly double (r values were .51 and .30, respectively) the magnitudes of the correlations involving 12-month Bayley mental subscale scores and the 36-month language scores (r values were .28 and .13, respectively).

SUMMARY AND IMPLICATIONS OF FINDINGS FROM PREDICTIVE STUDIES

The aforementioned studies, summarized in Table 4.1, illustrate a number of research issues that need to be addressed. First, the perinatal variables that have been used have not produced accurate predictions of cognitive and language scores obtained at ages 3 and 4 years. Indeed, simple correlations, multiple correlations, and attempts to classify individual subjects using discriminant function analyses have rarely shown the perinatal variables to be as powerful as the infant variables. Studies of Brazelton Scale scores obtained in the newborn period and measures of general mental development obtained in the first year (e.g., scores on the Bayley mental, motor, and infant behavioral record subscales and on the Cattell Infant Intelligence Scale) also report generally low correlations (.47–.49, Sostek & Anders, 1977; .47–.67, Powell, 1974; .30–.70, Scarr & Williams, 1971; .13–.30, Vaughn,

TABLE 4.1
Predictive Results from Studies of Infant Variables with Cognitive and Language Variables

Studies	Subjects and testing ages	Measures	Analyses	Findings
		PERINATAL		
Siegel (1982)	52 prematures, 51 full-terms. Tested at 4, 8, 12, 18, 24, and 36 months.	Independent variables: reproductive, demographic, Bayley mental, HOME. Dependent variables: Stanford–Binet, Reynell Scales.	Correlation, stepwise, linear multiple regression, discriminant function analysis	Significant correlations ranged .05–.42 between dependent and independent variables. Best regression models involved infant and social-environmental factors. Classification accuracy: using perinatal measures, .67–.84; using infant and social-environmental measures, .68–.90.
Bee, Barnard, Eyers, Gray, Hammond, Spietz, Snyder and Clark (1982)	193 normals. Tested at birth, 4, 12, 24, 36, and 48 months.	Independent variables: perinatal and infant status; child mental, motor, and language behaviors; family ecology and parent perception; parent–infant interaction and environmental quality. Dependent variables: Stanford–Binet, 36-month receptive and expressive language.	Correlation, multiple, regression	Significant correlations ranged .16 to .62 between dependent and independent variables. Best regression models involved 12-, 24-, and 36-month child scores, mother–infant interactions and social-environmental variables. Correlations between 24-month and 36-month variables stronger than those between 12-month and 36-month variables.

Vaughn, Taraldson, Crichton, and Egeland (1980)	243 infants. Tested at birth, 3, 6, and 9 months.	Independent variables: Brazelton Scale—four dimensions, Bayley mental, Bayley motor, Bayley Infant Behavioral Record.	Correlation, ANOVA	Few significant correlations or ANOVA results between dimensions scores and Infant Behavioral Record. Significant correlations of dimension scores with mental scores ($r < .20$). ANOVA significant for two dimensions with mental scores.
Sostek and Anders (1977)	18 infants. Tested at birth, 51-94 days ($\bar{x} = 68.8$ days)	Dependent variables: Brazelton Scale—four dimensions. Independent variables: Bayley mental, Bayley motor.	Correlation	Significant correlations only between state dimension and total score and Bayley mental ($r = .47$ and $.49$)
Powell (1979)	13 low birthweight infants. Tested at birth, 2-, 4-, 6-months	Independent variables: Brazelton Scale—two dimensions. Dependent variables: Bayley Infant Behavior record, Bayley mental, Bayley motor.	Correlation	Significant correlations between two dimensions and Bayley Scales ($r = .47$-$.67$)
Scarr and Williams (1971)	30 low birthweight infants. Tested at birth, 4-6 weeks, and 1 year	Dependent variables: Brazelton Scale. Independent variables: Cattell Infant Intelligence Test.	Correlation	Significant at birth ($r = .30$-$.55$ including birthweight; $.30$-$.70$ excluding birthweight). At 4 weeks, fewer significant correlations ($r = .40$-$.43$).

(*Continued*)

TABLE 4.1 (*Continued*)

Studies	Subjects and testing ages	Measures	Analyses	Findings
		INFANT		
Siegel (1981)	148 prematures and full-terms. Tested at 4, 8, 12, 18, and 24 months.	Independent variables: Bayley mental and motor, Uzgiris and Hunt, HOME. Dependent variables: 2-year Bayley mental and motor, 2-year Reynell comprehension and expression.	Correlation	Significant correlations ranged .20 to .65. Correlations significant at 2 years are not significant at 3 years.
Nelson (1973)	18 normals. Tested at 19–25 months and 30 months.	Independent variables: Specific language measures. Dependent variables: Bayley mental, Concept Familiarity Index, Peabody Picture Vocabulary Test.	Correlation	Significant correlations ranged .38 to .60. Correlations with 2 year scores slightly stronger than with 3 year scores.
Ramey, Campbell, and Nicholson (1973)	24 normals. Tested at 6–8 months, 9–12 months, 13–16 months.	Independent variables: Bayley mental & motor. Dependent variables: 3-year Stanford Binet, 3-year Illinois Test of Psycholinguistic Abilities.	Correlation	Significant correlations ranged .68 to .90. Correlations significant at 3 years, not significant at 2 years.

Taraldson, Crichton, & Egeland, 1980). This problem of low correlations between perinatal variables and later infancy and preschool variables seems to be due to the specific perinatal variables used rather than to a lack of predictability of cognitive and language scores from measures obtained so early in infancy. As discussed in the next section, auditory-evoked response measures of neonatal subjects do predict with a high degree of accuracy the subjects' language scores at age 3 years.

Second, infant variables, like perinatal variables, have not been consistent predictors of preschool performance variables. Half of the studies reviewed report that the variables that were the significant predictors of performance at age 2 years are no longer significant predictors at age 3; the other half of the studies note the reverse. When one looks at specific infant measures, a rather complex set of relationships is revealed. For example, in most cases the mental and motor subscale scores of the popularly used Bayley Scales also do not show consistent correlations with cognitive and language scores. The correlations do not seem to indicate a lack of relationship between Bayley Scale scores and later language skills, since quite respectable correlations have been reported by some researchers (Ramey et al., 1973; Bee et al., 1982). On the other hand, the Bayley scores do not reliably predict later language skills across studies. The significant correlations may simply reflect the degree of similarity between the language items on the Bayley Scale and items on the specific language-assessment tests used in various studies. The inconsistencies found in the predictions of preschool performance from infant variables may be due to the degree of relatedness of the items on the infant scales and those on the preschool scales.

Third, replicability of findings has been absent. There have been no reports of attempts to determine if the independent variables found to be significant predictors with one sample are also significant predictors using another sample. The generalizability of the findings is also difficult since subjects are often selected because they possess abnormal characteristics (e.g., prematurity, low birthweight, or respiratory distress). Except in the Bee et al. (1982) study, relatively few normal subjects have been studied. Comparisons of findings across studies, therefore, have been largely speculative due to differences in subject characteristics. In addition, except in the Siegel (1982) study, little attempt has been made to determine the classification accuracy or homogeneity of the data sets on which significant predictions have been based.

As described above, researchers have attempted to develop predictive tests that, when administered in early infancy, could accurately identify infants at risk for abnormal cognitive or language development during the preschool years. To date, no predictive tests with meaningful success rates (measured in terms of predictive accuracy) have been developed based on measures obtained in the perinatal period. Results based on measures obtained during later infancy are only slightly better. Because of the need to develop measures that can be utilized in early infancy and that have high predictive accuracy, researchers have been turning toward other types of measures that might converge with the traditional measures to build better predictive models for individual children.

ELECTROPHYSIOLOGY AND LANGUAGE

One area that has attracted researchers is electrophysiology. Studies utilizing evoked brain responses have provided new information concerning the structural integrity of the brain and insights into brain functioning and the development of hemispheric involvement in cognitive and language abilities (Calaway, Tueting, & Koslow, 1978; Corballis, 1983; Segalowitz, 1983). Although electrophysiological methods have been applied extensively in the study of various cognitive abilities, much of the recent work has centered on brain and language relations.

Interest in biologically related influences on language acquisition can be traced to a number of research findings reported over the last two decades. Lenneberg (1967) argues that a biological substrate exists, which subserves language abilities. Evidence for such a view, he notes, can be seen at a number of levels in humans. For example, even at the gross morphological level of the vocal tract, humans (unlike other primates) are structured in a certain way to produce a wide variety of speech sounds (Lieberman, 1977). The pinna itself is structured to favor the perception of sound frequencies that characterize the majority of important speech cues. Lenneberg (1967) argues that at the neurological level, language acquisition is linked to brain organization. For Lenneberg, lateralization of brain functions is a biological sign of language ability (p. 67). Although investigators have challenged some of Lenneberg's specific hypotheses on lateralization and language development (Molfese, 1972; Molfese, Freeman, & Palermo, 1975), his general view that there are specific biological underpinnings for language that may facilitate language development continues to be supported (Dennis & Whitaker, 1975; Molfese & Molfese, 1979a, 1979b, 1980; Segalowitz, 1983; Segalowitz & Gruber, 1977).

Since 1975, our laboratory has studied the importance of lateralization and brain organization for language development in groups as well as in individuals. In addition to investigating changes in the developmental patterns of lateralization across the lifespan, these studies attempt to isolate and identify the electrophysiological correlates of various speech-perception cues across and within a number of developmental periods. The perceptual cues studied include place of articulation and voice onset time (VOT). The place cue is important for discriminating between consonants such as /b/ and /g/, which are produced in different portions or places of the vocal tract. The consonant /b/, on one hand, is referred to as a front consonant because it is produced in the very front of the vocal tract with the two lips. The consonant /g/, on the other hand, is produced in the back of the vocal tract and is labeled a back consonant. When the following vowel sounds are the same, the second formant transition, as depicted in a sound spectrograph, signals the place of articulation of the consonant. In the case of the syllable, /ba/, the second formant transition rises. This formant transition falls, however, for the initial /g/ of the syllable /ga/. In general, our studies have noted that patterns of electrical activity recorded from different areas of the scalp change as a function of place of articulation. Furthermore, these patterns of discrimination do not appear to change to any great extent from early in infancy (Molfese & Molfese, 1979a, 1979b, 1980) into adulthood (Molfese, 1978, 1980, 1983; Molfese & Schmidt, 1983).

Studies with adults note that portions of the average evoked response (AER) that occur 300 msec after stimulus onset and that are recorded from electrodes placed over the left hemisphere discriminate between consonants such as /b/ and /g/. That is, the amplitude of this portion of the waveform as measured from the positive peak occurring at 300 msec to the following negative peak at 400 msec is reliably larger for the AERs elicited by the /b/ initial syllables than for the /g/ initial syllables (Molfese, 1978, 1980, 1983; Molfese & Schmidt, 1983). In studies with adults in which electrodes are placed at multiple sites over the two hemispheres (Molfese, 1980, 1983; Molfese & Schmidt, 1983), a second portion of the AER located at approximately 100 msec following stimulus onset varies reliably when evoked by a /b/- versus a /g/-initial syllable. This second component behaves in a fashion similar to the one occurring at 300 msec with the exception that it occurs simultaneously over both hemispheres. In this way the AERs elicited by speech syllables reliably produce changes in two portions of the waveform in response to the /b/ and /g/ syllables. One area of waveform change discriminates between place differences at one point in time only over the left hemisphere electrode sites, while a second portion of the AER changes systematically over both hemispheres in response to place changes. A similar pattern of lateralized and bilateral responses are elicited in response to a different speech cue, VOT, with the exception that the lateralized response occurs over the right hemisphere rather than the left hemisphere (Molfese, 1978, 1980; Molfese & Hess, 1978). These right-hemisphere findings have been discussed in depth elsewhere in terms of their reliability and similarity to findings in the clinical literature (Molfese, 1983; Molfese & Molfese, 1983).

Building on this work with adults, several papers have reported comparable findings with newborn infants. Molfese & Molfese (1979a), reported that, based on tests with 16 newborn infants, the initial large negative deflection or peak of the newborns' AERs that occurred approximately 230 msec following stimulus onset was larger in size when evoked by /b/-initial syllables than by /g/-initial syllables. This response difference occurred only over the left-hemisphere electrode site. As with adults, however, a second portion of the AERs detected at electrodes placed over both hemispheres were also noted to discriminate between the /b/- and /g/-initial syllables. A later study with preterm infants (Molfese & Molfese, 1980) reports comparable lateralized and bilateral responses that discriminated place cues. This pattern of bilateral and lateralized discrimination of the place of articulation cues as reflected in different portions of the AERs occurs, then, in both young infants as well as adults.

PREDICTIONS OF PERFORMANCE BASED ON BRAIN RECORDINGS

A major issue raised concerning the implications of these lateralized and bilateral patterns of responses to speech sounds concerns their implications for later language development (Corballis, 1983; Molfese, 1983). Do these patterns of responses have any implications for later language development for individual children or do they reflect some basic patterns of auditory processing in the brain that have little relation to language development? Given Lenneberg's (1967) notion that lateralization is a biological sign of language, could such early patterns of lateralized and bilateral discrimination of speech sounds predict later language outcomes? Theoreticians have long speculated that the absence of hemisphere differences in a child indicates that the child is at risk for certain cognitive or language deficits. While the data have not generally supported such a position, it is possible that when hemisphere differences are considered in light of specific ability differences, predictions concerning later performance will be enhanced. One major aim of a longitudinal study by Molfese and Molfese carried out between 1978 and 1982 with funding from the National Foundation/March of Dimes was to establish the predictive validity of demographic variables, behavior scales, and auditory-evoked potentials for identifying developmental deviations for particular children in language abilities. Sixty low birthweight and normal weight infants were tested at birth, at 6-month intervals thereafter until age 2 years and again at age 3 years. For each child the following information was obtained: sex, birthweight, length, and gestational age; the ages, income level, education and occupation of both parents; and scores on the Obstetric

Complications Scale (Littman & Parmelee, 1978), on the Brazelton Neonatal Assessment Scale (using scores on each of four a priori dimensions, Als, Tronick, Lester, & Brazelton, 1977, and on the overall profile based on ratings for the 26 items of the scale), on the mental subscale of the Bayley Scales of Infant Development, and on two language tests administered at 36 months (the Peabody Picture Vocabulary Test and the subscales of the Mc-Carthy Scales of Children's Abilities). Auditory-evoked responses were recorded at each testing period using scalp electrodes placed over left and right temporal locations (T_3 and T_4) and referred to linked ears. The auditory stimuli were speech (normal formant) and nonspeech (sine wave formant) synthetic consonant-vowel syllables (/bi/, /bæ/, /bɔ/, /gi/, /gæ/, /gɔ/). These stimuli are described in detail in papers by Cutting (1974) and Molfese (1980). Stimuli were presented at 80 db (A) with varied interstimulus intervals, with 16 random orderings of the 12 stimuli, while the subjects were quiet and awake.

Analyses of the electrophysiological data were developed for four general purposes: (1) to identify the electrophysiological response correlates of specific stimulus features, (2) to predict later language performance from brain responses recorded early in development and from behavioral responses, (3) to evaluate the contribution of individual perinatal and infant variables to the prediction of language performance, and (4) to evaluate the brain responses of infants found to perform normally and below normal on language tests.

SPECIFIC STIMULUS FEATURES IDENTIFIED FROM BRAIN RESPONSES

The AERs recorded at birth from each infant were averaged separately for each stimulus at 8 msec intervals for 88 points (704 msec). These 768 averages (32 subjects × 12 stimuli × 2 hemisphere leads) were normalized and then input to a principal-components analysis having a covariance matrix and utilizing varimax rotation. Factor analysis of the AER data produced 10 factors that accounted for 90% of the total variance. Subsequent analyses of variance for Hemispheres × Consonant × Vowel × Formant Structure identified these factors as systematically reflecting hemisphere responses that differentiated between specific speech and nonspeech sounds. Only those factors of the brain waves that were subsequently found to contribute significantly to the predictive models are described here. A Formant × Vowel × Consonant interaction characterized Factor 2 and reflected changes in the area of the AER that discriminated the normal formant syllable /bi/ from /gi/. Factor 3 differentiated between the general responses of the left and right hemispheres. A Formant × Vowel × Consonant interaction occurred for Factor 8, which discriminated the speech formant structure syllables /bi/ from /gi/ and /bæ/ from /gæ/.

In other analyses of the AER data obtained from 6 months through 3 years of age, it has been possible to identify correlates of specific stimulus characteristics. Portions of the brain response have been found to discriminate consonant sounds, stimulus bandwidth, and vowel differences. Also found, and consistent with earlier published reports (Molfese & Molfese, 1979a, 1980), have been the presence of brain responses reflecting hemisphere differences that are present at birth and continue through 36 months of age.

PREDICTING LANGUAGE PERFORMANCE AT AGE 3 YEARS FROM AERs OBTAINED AT BIRTH

Sixteen infants were included in a subsample of subjects who were available for testing at age 3 years on the Peabody Picture Vocabulary Scale and on the McCarthy Scales of Children's Abilities. The subsample of subjects did not differ significantly at birth from the corresponding untested subjects on the independent variables under study. The subsample tested at 3 years of age had mean Peabody scores of 51.0 (*SD,* 31.9) and mean McCarthy verbal scores of 45.0 (*SD,* 33.1).

Stepwise multiple regression models were constructed using Peabody scores and McCarthy scores as the dependent variables and the AER factor scores obtained at birth for those factors that discriminated between consonant speech sounds (Factors 2, 3, and 8) as the independent variables. One model included the responses of both hemispheres for each infant to the syllable /bi/ (Factors 2 and 8) and /gi/ (Factor 8), as well as the hemisphere differences noted for Factor 3. Seventy-eight percent of the total variance was accounted for in predicting McCarthy scores, while 69% of variance was accounted for in predicting Peabody scores.

As a test of the internal consistency of this data set and the stability of the findings independent of the principal components-analysis of variance procedure, classification functions were developed for the averaged AERs based on the digitized time points for each waveform. Results were cross-validated by means of the jackknifed procedure. In this application there were 16 classes to be discriminated: two subject groups (formed by a median split between the high and low language performers) composed of 8 infants each, the two consonant sounds (/b/ and /g/), two formant bandwidths (speech and sine wave), and the two electrode sites (T_3 and T_4). The stepwise discriminant analysis selected two points in order of their effectiveness in classifying each of the original averaged AERs for each infant into these 16 conditions.

For the high language group this classification was successful at above chance levels for the left-hemisphere site for the normal formant /b/ and the normal formant /g/ stimuli. The left-hemisphere site also correctly classified AERs for sine wave formant /b/ and sine wave formant /g/. Significant levels of classification for the low language group occurred for only the normal formant /g/ AERs recorded from the T_4 site. When jackknifed classifications were used, the classification accuracy for the high language group for the four conditions was still significantly above chance, but the classification accuracy for the low language group dropped to chance levels. The discriminant function analyses, using discrete AER data points rather than factor scores, correctly classified the same stimuli found to be important in the regression model for the high language group.

THE CONTRIBUTION OF PERINATAL AND INFANT VARIABLES TO THE PREDICTION OF LANGUAGE PERFORMANCE

Although the primary focus of this project was to determine the validity of AERs recorded at birth for predicting language performance at age 3 years, the contributions of the behavioral measures were also assessed. As was generally found in the studies reviewed earlier, the correlations between the perinatal variables and the infant and child variables were low. In this case, few of the correlations reached significance. Significant correlations were found between Brazelton Neonatal Assessment Scale scores and 6-month (.41) and 12-month (.53) Bayley mental subscale scores. Obstetric Complication Scale scores were significantly correlated with Bayley mental subscale scores at 6 months (.66) but not at other ages. The Bayley mental subscale scores from age 18 months on showed stronger correlations with the 3-year language measures. The 18-month and 24-month Bayley mental subscale scores correlated significantly (.71 and .58, respectively) with the 36-month Peabody score. The 18- and 24-month Bayley scores significantly correlate at .63 and .73, respectively, with the 36-month McCarthy Scale scores. The Peabody scores and the McCarthy Scale scores significantly correlate at .64.

Demographic characteristics were not significant correlates of infant development and language-performance scores. This finding may be due to the relatively homogeneous nature of the families and infants involved in the study and the small number of characteristics measured. The families were middle class with average incomes of $20,000 to $25,000, and both parents had at least completed high school.

Regression models were constructed to test hypotheses concerning the usefulness of perinatal, demographic, and infant development tests to predict language performance at 36 months. The models showed that Mc-Carthy scores can be predicted from the following variables, individually and in combinations: birthweight, length, gestational age, labor length, 18- and 24-month Bayley scores and Peabody scores. (The best full model is birthweight, length, gestational age, and 18-month Bayley). In general, infants whose birthweights and length were appropriate for full-term gestational age, who were products of normally long labors, and who had average or better Bayley and Peabody scores performed best on the McCarthy scales. Peabody scores can be predicted from the following variables, individually and in combinations: labor length, Bayley at 18 and 24 months, McCarthy scales. (The best models are Bayley-18 and McCarthy, and Bayley-24 and McCarthy). In general, infants whose Bayley and McCarthy scores were average or better performed best on the Peabody scale. However, the amount of variance accounted for by both models is, at best, 57%. When only birth scores (i.e., Brazelton Neonatal Assessment Scale, birthweight, gestational age, length, and obstetrical events and complications) were used to predict language scores at three years of age, the regression models were not significant.

Regression models were also constructed to test hypotheses concerning the usefulness of all the independent variables (i.e., perinatal, demographic, and infant measures, and AER factor scores) to predict the language-performance scores. The only regression model that was significant involved predicting McCarthy Scale scores from Brazelton scores (lower scores were better), Obstetric Complication scores (lower scores were better), and AER factor scores. This regression model accounts for 81% of the variance, which is only 3% more accounted for using perinatal measures and AER factor scores than was accounted for by using AER factor scores alone.

BRAIN RESPONSE DIFFERENCES IN HIGH AND LOW LANGUAGE-PERFORMING CHILDREN

In an effort to identify the specific characteristics of individual children who show high and low language performance, subsequent analyses were undertaken. In these analyses, a median split was used to separate the children into two groups: those who scored above 50 on the verbal subscale of the McCarthy Scales of Children's Abilities and those who scored below 50. The perinatal characteristics, as measured by the Obstetrical Complication Scale (Littman & Parmelee, 1978), birthweight, gestational age, and Brazelton Neonatal Behavioral Assessment Scale scores of these two groups showed no differences. There were major differences, however, in the newborn brain responses to speech sounds produced by the subjects in these two groups.

Only the high language-performance group produced brain responses at birth that showed the presence of bilateralized and lateralized processes that discriminated between consonants independent of the following vowel (i.e., /b/ from /g/). While the low language-performance group did not produce brain responses that reflected the discrimination of consonants independent of the following vowel, they did discriminate differences between consonants in different vowel environments (i.e., discriminations among /bi/, /bæ/, /bɔ/, /gi/, /gæ/, and /gɔ/) in a manner similar to high language-performance group. However, the brain responses of the high language-performance infants contained an additional component that reflected discrimination of consonants in different vowel environments. For the high language group, the portions of the brain responses that discriminated between consonants as a function of their vowel environment occurred at later points in time than those that discriminated consonant sounds independent of their vowel sounds. This is the reverse of what has been found with adults. Such adult versus infant differences in the timing of brain responses reflect maturity differences, but it is as yet unclear if other variables are also involved.

The differential responsivity shown by the high language-performance group to the consonants alone and to the consonants in different vowel environments indicates that the nervous system of these infants is more sensitive to the various cues that are important to later language development. The earlier an infant can detect and discriminate among patterns of sounds in the language environment, the better able that infant will be able to utilize such information as the extensive process of language acquisition begins. Infants who are less responsive or less sensitive to such relevant speech cues face a more difficult task mastering the discriminations involved in later word differences. These early discrimination difficulties may be reflected in language performance at age 3 years.

IMPLICATIONS

Based on the previous predictive studies using traditional medical and behavioral measures and based on studies using electrophysical procedures, it seems clear that predictive statements of cognitive and language development based on perinatal data are still far from perfect. There are, however, several signs of progress. First, while studies utilizing both perinatal measures and measures obtained in later infancy report that perinatal measures are less helpful predictors than infant measures, perinatal electrophysiological measures have been shown to have a high predictive accuracy. Children who at age 3 years were the better performers on language tests produced brain responses to speech sounds at birth that reflect abilities in discriminating between speech stimuli and in hemisphere responsiveness that are distinctly different from those of children who did not perform as well. The predictive accuracy achieved using the AER factor scores exceeded by far the predictive abilities of the other perinatal measures. The AER factor scores apparently reflect the more important distinctions between early individual differences and later language performance. Second, as can be seen by the large variety of variables measured in the studies described above, researchers' perspectives on the types of variables that can be used in predictive research are broad but parochial. There seem to be few attempts to develop novel combinations of methodologies to address the issues involved in assessment. However, several theoretical and methodological works (Knopp & Parmelee, 1979; Parmelee, Knopp & Sigman, 1976; Sameroff, 1979) address the importance of multivariate approaches to predictive modeling in cognitive and developmental research. In addition, Sameroff (1979) presents examples of statistical models useful for evaluating and analyzing these multivariate approaches. These works should facilitate the development of more diverse assessment methodologies, perhaps utilizing more extensive and individualized medical, behavioral, and electrophysical measures, for the purpose of developing models that more accurately predict and classify individual children's performance. Third, with the use of more-complex multivariate research designs, there will have to be an increase in the sample sizes used. Certainly, based on the research reviewed in this chapter, there is ample evidence that the sample sizes are increasing. There is a move away from the sample sizes of under 30 employed in older research to samples of over 100 subjects used in more recent reports. Such increases are necessary to assure the reliability and stability of the analyses for the subject groups and identified subgroups. Ideally, there should be a 10:1 ratio of number of subjects to number of measures. Finally, although the predictions of developmental status have not yet been extended to individuals, there is evidence that research is moving closer to individual applications. Researchers are reporting on the characteristics of identified subgroups that are predictive of later outcome (Bee et al., 1982; Molfese & Molfese, 1983; Siegel, 1982). If these characteristics are shown to be reliable in other subject samples, it should be possible to apply the characteristics to identify individuals according to predicted developmental outcome. Such an identification process might involve a screening system whereby specific perinatal and infant characteristics that have good predictive records would be used in examining individual infants during periodic infant health checks.

Infants who are identified as at risk for cognitive disabilities can be targeted for follow-up care. If such a screening scale can be developed and if it is not prohibitively expensive and lengthy, then a decade of work to develop assessment tools with high predictive accuracy will have reached a long-awaited goal.

REFERENCES

Als, H., Tronick, E., Lester, B., and Brazelton, T. The Brazelton Neonatal Behavioral Assessment Scale (BNBAS). *Journal of Abnormal Child Psychology,* 1977, *5,* 215-231.

Apgar, V. A proposal for a new method of evaluation of the newborn infant. *Anesthesia and Analgesia: Current Research,* 1953, *32,* 260-267.

Bayley, N. *Bayley scales of infant development: Birth to two years.* New York: Psychological Corps, 1969.

Bee, H., Barnard, K., Eyres, S., Gray, C., Hammond, M., Spietz, A., Snyder, C., & Clark, B. Prediction of IQ and language skills from perinatal status, child performance, family characteristics and mother–infant interaction. *Child Development,* 1982, *53,* 1134-1156.

Behar, L., and Stringfield, S. A behavior rating scale for the preschool child. *Developmental Psychology,* 1974, *10,* 601-610.

Bradley, R., and Caldwell, B. Home observation for measurement of the environment: A validation study of screening efficiency. *American Journal of Mental Deficiency,* 1977, *81,* 417-420.

Brazelton, T. B. *Neonatal Behavioral Assessment Scale.* Philadelphia: Lippincott, 1973.

Broussand, E., and Hartner, M. Maternal perception of the neonate as related to development. *Child Psychiatry and Human Development,* 1970, *1,* 16-25.

Calaway, E., Tueting, P., & Koslow, S. *Event-related brain potentials and behavior.* New York: Academic Press, 1978.

Cattell, P. *Cattell Infant Intelligence Scale.* New York: Psychological Corp., 1960.

Corballis, M. *Human laterality.* New York: Academic Press, 1983.

Cutting, J. Two left-hemisphere mechanisms in speech perception. *Perception and Psychophysics,* 1981, *16,* 601-612.

Dennis, M., & Whitaker, H. Hemispheric equipotentiality and language acquisition. In S. Segalowitz and F. Gruber (Eds.), *Language development and neurological theory.* New York: Academic Press, 1975.

Doll, E. *Vineland Social Maturity Scale.* Circle Pines, MN: American Guidance Service, 1965.

Dunn, L. *Peabody Picture Vocabulary Test.* Circle Pines, MN: American Guidance Service, 1965.

Fagan, J., and McGrath, S. Infant recognition memory and later intelligence. *Intelligence,* 1981, *5,* 121-130.

Field, T., Dempsey, J., and Shuman, H. Developmental follow-up of pre- and posterm infants. In S. L. Friedman and M. Sigman (Eds.), *Preterm birth and psychological development.* New York: Academic Press, 1981.

Fluharty, N. The design and standardization of a speech and language screening test for use with preschool children. *Journal of Speech and Hearing Disorders,* 1974, *39,* 75-88.

Frankenberg, W., and Dodds, J. The Denver Developmental Screening Test. *Pediatrics,* 1967, *71,* 181-191.

Hedrick, D., Prather, E., and Tobin, A. *Sequenced inventory of communication development.* Seattle: University of Washington Press, 1975.

Kirk, S., McCarthy, J., and Kirk, W. *The Illinois Test of Psycholinguistic Abilities* (Rev. Ed.). Urbana: University of Illinois Press, 1968.

Knobloch, H., and Pasamanick, B. (Eds.). *Gesell and Amatruda's developmental diagnosis* (3rd Ed.). New York: Harper and Row, 1974.

Knopp, C., & Parmelee, A. Prenatal and perinatal influences on infant behavior. In J. Osofsky (Ed.), *Handbook of infant development.* New York: Wiley, 1979.

Lenneberg, E. *Biological foundations of language.* New York: Wiley, 1967.

Lieberman, P. *On the origins of language.* New York: MacMillan, 1977.

Littman, B., and Parmelee, A. Medical correlates of infant development. *Pediatrics,* 1978, *61,* 470–474.

McCarthy, D. *Manual for the McCarthy Scales of Children's Abilities.* New York: Psychological Corp., 1972.

Molfese, D. *Cerebral asymmetry in infants, children and adults: Auditory evoked responses to speech and noise stimuli.* Doctoral dissertation, The Pennsylvania State University, 1972.

Molfese, D. Left and right hemispheric involvement in speech perception: Electrophysiological correlates. *Perception and Psychophysics,* 1978, *23,* 237–243.

Molfese, D. Phoneme and the engram: Electrophysiological evidence of the acoustic invariant stop consonant. *Brain and Language,* 1980, *9,* 372–376.

Molfese, D. Event related potentials and language processes. In A. Gailliard and W. Ritter (Eds.), *Tutorials in ERP research: Endogenous components.* Amsterdam: Elsevier Press, 1983.

Molfese, D., Freeman, R., & Palermo, D. The ontogeny of lateralization for speech and non-speech stimuli. *Brain and Language,* 1975, *2,* 356–368.

Molfese, D., and Hess, T. Speech perception in nursery school age children: Sex and hemisphere differences. *Journal of Experimental Child Psychology,* 1978, *26,* 71–84.

Molfese, D., and Molfese, V. Hemisphere and stimulus differences as reflected in the cortical responses of newborn infants to speech stimuli. *Developmental Psychology,* 1979, *15,* 505–511. (a)

Molfese, D., and Molfese, V. Infant speech perception: Learned or innate. In H. Whitaker and H. Whitaker (Eds.), *Advances in Neurolinguistics* (Vol. 4). New York: Academic Press, 1979. (b)

Molfese, D., and Molfese, V. Cortical responses of preterm infants to phonetic and non-phonetic speech stimuli. *Developmental Psychology,* 1980, *16,* 574–581.

Molfese, D., & Molfese, V. Electrophysiological indices of auditory discrimination in newborn infants: The bases for predicting later language development? *Infant Behavior and Development,* in press.

Molfese, D., & Schmidt, A. An auditory evoked potential study of consonant perception. *Brain and Language,* 1983, *18,* 57–70.

Nelson, K. Structure and strategy in learning to talk. *Monographs of Society for Research in Child Development, 38,* (Nos. 1 and 2).

Palmer, F., and Reese, A. Concept training in two-year-olds: Procedures and results. Paper presented at the biennial meeting of the Society for Research in Child Development, Santa Monica, California, March 1969.

Parmelee, A., Knopp, C., & Sigman, M. Selection of developmental assessment techniques for infants at risk. *Merrill–Palmer Quarterly,* 1976, *22,* 177–199.

Powell, L. The effect of extra stimulation and maternal involvement on the development of low birth weight infants and on maternal behaviors. *Child Development,* 1974, *45,* 106.

Quay, H., and Peterson, D. *Manual for the behavior problem checklist.* Unpublished manuscript (available from the H. Quay, Mailman Center for Child Development, Miami, FL 33152), 1975.

Ramey, C., Campbell, F., and Nicholson, J. The predictive power of the Bayley scales of infant development and the Stanford–Binet intelligence test in a relatively constant environment. *Child Development,* 1973, *44,* 790–795.

Reynell, J. *Reynell Developmental Language Scales.* Windsor, Berkshire: NFER, 1969.

Sameroff, A. *The etiology of cognitive competence: A systems perspective.* New York: Erlbaum, 1979.

Scarr, S., and Williams, M. The assessment of neonatal and later status in low birthweight infants. Paper presented at the biennial meeting of the Society for Research in Child Development, Minneapolis, MN: April 1971.

Segalowitz, S. *Language functions and brain organization.* New York: Academic Press, 1983.

Segalowitz, S., & Gruber, F. *Language development and neurological theory.* New York: Academic Press, 1977.

Siegel, L. Infant tests as predictors of cognitive and language development at two years. *Child Development,* 1981, *52,* 545–557.

Siegel, L. Reproductive, perinatal, and environmental factors as predictors of the cognitive and language developments of preterm and full term infants. *Child Development,* 1982, *53,* 963–973.

Siegel, L. The prediction of possible learning disabilities in preterm and full-term children. In T. Field and A. Sostek (Eds.), *Infants born at risk.* New York: Grune and Stratton, 1983.

Sigman, M. Individual differences in infant attention: Relations to birth status and intelligence at five years. In T. Field and A. Sostek (Eds.), *Infants born at risk.* New York: Grune and Stratton, 1983.

Sostek, A., and Anders, T. Relationships among the Brazelton Neonatal Scale, Bayley Infant Scales, and early temperament. *Child Development,* 1977, *48,* 320–323.

Terman, L., and Merrill, M. *Stanford–Binet Intelligence Scale—Manual for the third revision form L–M.* Boston: Houghton–Mifflin, 1973.

Uzgiris, I., and Hunt, J. McV. *Assessment in infancy: Ordinal scales of psychological development.* Urbana: University of Illinois Press, 1975.

Vaughn, B., Taraldson, B., Crichton, L., and Egeland, B. Relationships between neonatal behavioral organization and infant behavior during the first year of life. *Infant Behavior and Development,* 1980, *3,* 47–66.

5

From Hemispheric to Perceptual Asymmetry: From Where Has All the Variance Come?

Ovid J. L. Tzeng and Daisy L. Hung

THE LOCALIZATION VIEW AND HEMISPHERIC ASYMMETRY

The belief that the brain is the center of the mind is not necessarily and historically universal. In ancient Greece, although both Pythagoras and Plato held the view that the brain is the chief organ of the mind, Aristotle assigned the mental functions primarily to the heart. In the Orient, the ancient Chinese in general also ascribed thought to the heart. However, Hua Tuo, one of the most eminent Chinese medical scholars in the late Han Dynasty, commented on Emperor Tsao-Tsao's illusory thinking and occasional seizures as probably due to the tumors in the brain. But the comments were intended to be a joke rather than any serious cerebral localization of cognitive function (Huang, 1983); it was Descartes (1650/1931) who localized the interaction between the soul and body at the pineal gland in the brain.

From Descartes we skip to Gall (1825), who, in the first two decades of the nineteenth century, localized more than 30 mental faculties at specific regions or spots in the brain and on the skull. Gall was much criticized later on and the school of phrenology gradually dwindled. However, with respect to language, the idea of a speech center in the brain has been prevalent throughout history. In fact, written records of aphasia go back at least 4,500 years to the Ebers papyrus of Egypt, in which a man who suffered a head injury was described as having lost his ability for speech without paralysis of his tongue (Hécaen & Albert, 1978). Nevertheless, it was the French neurologist Paul Broca (1861) who took the brain of a man who had lost the ability to speak and had died from an infection shortly after Broca had thoroughly examined him to the Société d'Anthropologie and convinced its members that the speech loss was due to deterioration in the third convolution of the left frontal lobe.

But Broca was by no means the first person to make the connection between left hemisphere lesion and resulting speech difficulty. In 1836, 25 years before Broca's first observation, Marc Dax assembled a mass of evidence to show that aphasia was related to disease of the left hemisphere. However, he did not make his discovery known to the public except through the distribution of copies of his paper, ''Lesions of the left hemisphere coinciding with forgetfulness of the signs of thought,'' to two or three friends. The paper was finally published in 1865 by his son, and the controversy over who should be credited with the discovery of left-hemisphere dominance for speech soon followed. Nevertheless, the reality of cerebral localization was established, and now Broca's aphasia is neurologically accepted. The syndrome includes slow and hesitant speech accompanied by effort and poor articulation; a tendency to omit articles, connective words, auxiliaries, and inflections, resulting in telegraphic or agrammatic utterances; and finally, a tendency to rely heavily on nouns and, to a lesser degree, on verbs (Zurif, 1980).

Soon after Broca's discovery of the posterior portion of the third, or inferior, frontal gyrus as the location of the expressive, or motoric, types of speech disorder, a young German neuropsychiatrist, Carl Wernicke (1874) demonstrated another major type of aphasic disorder. He described a patient who had apparently lost his memory for the auditory images of words. The crucial lesion associated with this amnesic type of aphasic disorder was identified to be situated in the hinder portion of the superior temporal convolution, the first temporal gyrus on the parietal–temporal junction of the left hemisphere. The key features of Wernicke's aphasia are fluent but disordered speech with apparently intact grammar and syntax but lack of meaning, analogous disturbances in writing, and impaired comprehension in speech and in both oral and silent reading.

Wernicke's contribution is by no means limited to this discovery. The theory he advanced not only accounted for known aphasic syndromes but also correctly predicted the existence of an as-yet-undescribed form of aphasia. Based upon what he already knew about the two existing types, Wernicke predicted that patients with the inability to repeat what they heard would be found with a lesion that interrupted the connections between the two areas that subserved speech comprehension and production. Such a syndrome, now known as *conduction aphasia* was subsequently confirmed in patients with damage around the arcuate fasciculus, the connecting tract between Broca's and Wernicke's areas.

Following these leads, Geschwind (1965) published his seminal paper in which agnosic, apraxic, and aphasic disorders are interpreted as products of neural disconnection, providing the impetus for intense investigation of functional localization in both animals and humans. Since then, more types of aphasias and their various linguistic deficits have been described. These include transcortical sensory aphasia, transcortical motor aphasia, global aphasia, anomic aphasia, alexia with agraphia, alexia without agraphia (pure alexia), pure word deafness, and atypical aphasia (for reviews, see A. Damasio, 1981; H. Damasio, 1981).

The idea of left hemispheric specialization of linguistic behavior has been confirmed with new clinical techniques such as the Wada test (an injection of the barbiturate sodium amytal into one of the carotid arteries, right or left, that supplies an ipsilateral hemisphere) and electroconvulsic therapy (its unilateral application produces effects similar to the Wada test except that the effects are more durable). Based upon clinical and neurological data, it has been frequently claimed that virtually all right-handers (95–99%) are left-hemisphere dominant for language (for reviews see Blumstein, Goodglass, & Tartter, 1975; Levy & Reid, 1978. Chen, Hung, & Chen, 1983, also report 99% for Chinese patients with Wada test).

Evidence of left hemispheric specialization for language also comes from studies of commissurotomized (split-brain) patients (Gazzaniga, Bogen, & Sperry, 1962). Split-brain surgery involves surgically cutting some of the fibers that connect the two cerebral hemispheres. The first such operations to relieve epilepsy were performed in the early 1940s on approximately 25 patients. However, these early operations failed to reveal any obvious psychological consequences of the commissurotomy. It was not until the 1960s that Sperry's group, which studied patients with complete commissurotomies, was able to dramatically confirm that in most persons control of speech is localized in the left hemisphere. Intensive investigations, coupled with ingeneous testing procedures, of these patients have yielded many important insights into the dominance and specialization of the two cerebral hemispheres. There is dispute as to whether the right hemisphere is capable of any linguistic function except general comprehension. A review of studies of spilt-brain patients in the last 20 years suggests that the occurrence of right-hemisphere language is very infrequent (Gazzaniga, 1983).

The left cerebral hemisphere is generally considered specialized for *spoken* language, and, in fact, the major language-mediating areas of the brain are intimately connected with the vocal auditory channel. The right hemisphere has a complementary specialization for processing visual–spatial relationships. It seems appropriate to raise a question at this point: Can the left-hemispheric language center be modified by variations in the mode of linguistic expression? That is, Is it possible to obtain a different pattern of cerebral asymmetry in a visual–spatial language, such as American Sign Language? The answer is no. Bellugi, Poizner, and Klima (1984) provide a much-needed systematic analysis of aphasia for a visual–gestural language. They conclude that damage to the left hemisphere in deaf patients clearly produced sign aphasia, indicating left-hemispheric specialization for sign language.

We can push the issue of visible language a little further and ask whether or not learning to read Chinese logographs produces a different pattern of cerebral asymmetry. The question is by no means an unreasonable one. Since Chinese characters are complex in their visual–spatial layout and since their grapheme–sound relationship is opaque in nature, one might expect a greater involvement of right-hemisphere activity in processing them. Furthermore, Zaidel (1983) claims that the right hemisphere of his split-brain patients seemed to be able to read English words ideographically. Thus, it seems plausible to expect right-hemisphere processing of Chinese logographs. However, after an extensive review of literature on reading Chinese characters, Tzeng and Hung (1983) conclude that there is little evidence that Chinese characters are read by the right hemisphere. Therefore, clinical as well as neurological data suggest a very strong left-hemisphere specialization for speech, script, and sign language (the three S's) of human communication.

PERCEPTUAL ASYMMETRY
IN NORMAL SUBJECTS

Hemispheric asymmetries with respect to language have also been supported with perceptual asymmetries in normal right-handed subjects. In visual hemifield experiments, stimuli are presented briefly one by one via a tachistoscope onto the right visual field (RVF) or the left visual field (LVF) relative to a center fixation point. Since the optic fibers from the nasal hemiretinae cross at the optic chiasm and project contralaterally, and those from the temporal hemiretinae project ipsilaterally to the hemisphere on the same side, stimuli on each visual half-field are projected first to the contralateral hemisphere. With careful control of central fixation and the avoidance of scanning eye movements (exposure durations of 150 msec or less are usually employed), and with words as stimuli, a RVF advantage over the LVF is inferred to demonstrate the expected left-hemispheric specialization for language. The first such study was carried out by Mishkin and Forgays (1952), who demonstrated that normal right-handed subjects were better at identifying English words flashed briefly in the RVF than they were at identifying words presented in the LVF. However, this early study also suggests that directional scanning plays a major role in generating RVF superiorities with words. In the years that followed, hundreds of studies with similar procedures but with better control for the habits of directional scanning produced results showing that the magnitude of the RVF superiority had little to do with the habitual scanning pattern. It is now a fairly well established fact that visual half-field experiments generally produce the RVF superiority across languages as well as across writing systems (Hung & Tzeng, 1981). This is exciting, for it suggests that hemispheric asymmetry observed in clinical and split-brain patients has reality for the normal brain as well.

In the early 1960s when psychologists were interested in studying the problems of selective attention and information-processing capacity with normal human subjects, the dichotic-listening technique was invented to lateralize auditory input information. The technique involved essentially the simultaneous presentation to paired materials, one to each ear. With this technique, Kimura (1967) was able to demonstrate a right-ear advantage (REA) for verbal materials and a left-ear advantage (LEA) for nonverbal materials. At first glance, such findings are surprising because each ear in fact sends information from all its receptors to both hemispheres. However, there is neurophysiological evidence that the contralateral auditory pathway has more fibers than the ipsilateral auditory pathway and that contralateral stimulation results in greater cortical activity (Berlin, 1977). Thus, with the additional assumption that when two different stimuli are presented simultaneously to each ear, the difference in the strength of the pathways may be exaggerated so that information sent along the ipsilateral route is suppressed, Kimura proposes a structural account of hemispheric asymmetry in which laterality differences reflect privileged access, via superior contralateral pathways, to hemispheres uniquely specialized for processing a given type of information.

Although Kimura's functional prepotency model can and should be criticized on empirical as well as theoretical grounds (see Bradshaw & Nettleton, 1983, for a comprehensive review), the possibility of using the dichotic-listening technique to test further theoretical implications of hemispheric asymmetry with normal human subjects represents a major step toward understanding the relationship between brain and language. Indeed, following Kimura's (1961) pioneer work, many dichotic-listening experiments have been successfully carried out to specify the exact nature of the REA in normal human subjects.

THE DISCREPANCY AND VARIOUS APPROACHES TO ITS RESOLUTION

In comparing the clinical data of hemispheric asymmetries to normal right-handed subjects' perceptual asymmetries, one discrepancy becomes immediately apparent. While the former usually shows above 95% cases favoring the left hemisphere, the latter typically shows only 70% (Hellige & Wong, 1983; Levy, 1974; Porter & Hughes, 1983; Searleman, 1977). In other words, there is evidently much variance being added to the perceptual asymmetries. Given the established fact of hemispheric asymmetries in the clinical population, where has all the additional variance come from? Of course, estimates of the frequency of left-hemisphere specialization for language obtained from clinical studies may not be appropriate as estimates for studies of perceptual asymmetries. For example, the former usually involves production and the latter perception. But still, this difference cannot account for all the added variance. We need to look for something subtle but suggestive. One possibility is that perceptual asymmetry is not a pure measure of hemispheric asymmetry and that other factors, such as individual differences at various levels of the language activities, are certainly involved. It is generally agreed that language is not a unitary cognitive process for either production or comprehension (Hellige & Wong, 1983). Individual differences with respect to the laterality of many of the subprocesses should be addressed to account for the discrepancy between hemispheric and perceptual asymmetries. In the following, we examine several different positions that deal with the issue of individual differences at different levels of conceptualization.

DIFFERENCES IN ANATOMICAL STRUCTURES

It is now well known that the surface of the left temporal planum is larger than that of the right temporal planum in adults (Geschwind & Levitsky, 1968) as well as in infants (Wada, Clarke, & Hamm, 1975; Witelson & Pallie, 1973). It is also believed that differential neuroanatomical characteristics of the two hemispheres may lead to a wide range of specific consequences for cognition. In addition, there is a growing list of physical and functional cerebral differences that may result from variations in early experience

(Ojemann & Whitaker, 1978; Rosenzweig, 1979). As Segalowitz and Bryden (1983) cogently put it, "Given this scope for inconsistencies across individuals, it is not surprising that attempts to provide relatively direct measures of linguistic representation often produce nonunanimous results" (p. 342).

The idea that early experience may have important influence on hemispheric specialization has led to investigations concerning patterns of cerebral specialization in cogenitally deaf adults (Naville & Bellugi, 1978) and in various types of bilinguals (Vaid, 1982). It has also generated a whole series of studies that attempt to establish relations between brain organization and experience in learning to read different types of written scripts (Hung & Tzeng, 1981; Tzeng & Wang, 1983). The issue here is, of course, whether any of these differences in the cognitive processes involved in language use create varying intrahemispheric and interhemispheric relationships that result in the large variance observed in perceptual asymmetries.

Another factor that may contribute part of the variance in perceptual asymmetries is individual differences in the relative superiority of ipsilateral and contralateral auditory pathways in dichotic-listening situations. For example, a case reported (Damasio, Lima, & Damasio, 1975) in which a patient with right hemispherectomy showed a LEA for recognizing digits, words, and nonverbal sounds in dichotic-listening experiments. Given our knowledge of the anatomy, this could only occur when the patient's ipsilateral projection from the left ear to the left hemisphere overtook the contralateral projection from the right ear to left hemisphere. This and other considerations have led Teng (1981) to the conclusion that some individuals may really have such a reversed dominance pattern of ipsilateral over contralateral input. In fact, she even suggests that dichotic ear difference is a poor index for the functional asymmetry between the cerebral hemispheres.

DIFFERENCES IN HEMISPHERIC AROUSAL

An interesting and promising account of individual differences in laterality studies is offered by Levy (1983). Her proposal is simply that much of the variance in perceptual asymmetries among right-handed subjects on standard behavioral measures of laterality results from their characteristic and habitual patterns of asymmetric hemispheric arousal, which may magnify or counteract perceptual asymmetries arising from hemispheric dominance. The notion that individuals may differ in the relative arousal levels of the left and right hemispheres, with task performance tending to be better for a more highly aroused hemisphere, is consistent with observations of the effects of dopamine on animal behavior. Dopamine is a central neurotransmitter that is critically involved in the maintenance of general arousal and activity (Iversen, 1977). Asymmetries of dopamine level are usually an indication of asymmetries of arousal. Animal studies have demonstrated that there are asymmetries of dopamine levels on the two sides of the nervous system, and turning responses have been found to show bias toward the side of space that is contralateral to the hemisphere with higher dopamine level (Glick, Jerussi, & Zimmerberg, 1977).

A similar relationship has also been observed with human subjects. In fact, a massive neurological literature shows that asymmetries of hemispheric arousal usually result in concomitant lateral orientation reflexes of attention and movement toward the side of space that is contralateral to the hemisphere with higher degree of arousal (Gur & Gur, 1980; Heilman & Watson, 1977; Trevarthen, 1972). Clinical data with depressed patients show that asymmetrically low arousal in the right hemisphere is associated with a selective deficit on tasks specialized to the right hemisphere. Moreover, the deficit reduces when the depression is alleviated (Bruder & Yozawitz, 1979).

All this physiological and clinical evidence led Levy (1983) to suspect that much of the variance observed in perceptual asymmetry experiments with normal right-handed subjects might be mediated by such individual differences in characteristic patterns of arousal asymmetries between hemispheres. In order to verify the suspected correlation, she and her associates (Levy, Heller, Banich, & Burton, 1983) performed an experiment in which right-handed subjects having a large RVF advantage on a tachistoscopic syllable-identification task (a left-hemisphere specialized task) were compared on a variety of dimensions with those having weak or no asymmetries. Several hypotheses were advanced according to the arousal asymmetries account. First, because characteristic arousal asymmetries are expected to generate individual differences in perceptual asymmetries, right-handed subjects with strong RVF advantage on the syllable task (by definition, these subjects are presumed to have higher arousal in the left hemisphere) should outperform those with weak or no asymmetries (these are presumed to have high right-hemisphere arousal and low left-hemisphere arousal). Second, the types of errors made in the RVF and LVF should manifest respective linguistic and nonlinguistic natures, and both groups of subjects should show the same special types of errors in the two visual fields. Third, with respect to the ability to discriminate performance in the two visual fields (a metalinguistic process), the pattern of asymmetry should follow the pattern obtained with the syllable identification task itself for both groups. That is, confirmation of this hypothesis would rule out the possibility that for the weak group, metalinguistic processes are specialized to the right hemisphere and that the dissociation between linguistic and metalinguistic processes somehow interfere with performance in the RVF.

Lastly, due to the correlation between right-hemisphere arousal and the dysphoric or euphoric mood, it was hypothesized that the strong group should show pessimistic mood and the weak group should show optimistic mood in rating their own performance, particularly for the LVF. All these hypotheses were confirmed by the experimental results.

Given that the arousal levels were not experimentally manipulated, any single analysis of Levy et al.'s (1983) data can be offered alternative interpretations, as they themselves freely admit in the article. However, it is the whole set of hypotheses and the confirming evidence that point impressively to the arousal model as the underlying mechanism for the individual differences observed in the perceptual asymmetry experiments with normal subjects. Unfortunately, Levy et al. did not make any attempt to tie the inferred differential arousal levels of their two groups to psychometric scales in order to reinforce their arguments. If the arousal asymmetries of the two hemispheres are assumed to be characteristic and habitual of the subjects, then their influence should have shown up on many occasions and across many tasks. Thus, establishing interactive relationships between treatments (e.g., verbal versus spatial tasks) and a psychometric scale (e.g., cognitive styles and manic versus depressive) would certainly make their argument more convincing.

In Levy's (1983) arousal account, two independent concepts are required in the evaluation of any perceptual asymmetry experiment. That is, experimental observations of any laterality task are simultaneously sensitive, first, to hemispheric specialization, which is referred to as *hemispheric competence* and is reflected in the average asymmetry for a group of right-handers, and, second, to individual differences in characteristic patterns of asymmetric hemispheric arousal, which is referred to as *hemispheric dominance* and is reflected in diversities among subjects in the magnitude, and even the direction, of perceptual asymmetries (Levy et al., 1983). If we accept this account, then much of the variance observed in perceptual asymmetry experiments cannot be treated as error variance, and a reevaluation of much laterality research is necessary. In the past, most research in the investigation of cerebral lateralization has emphasized the concept of competence, and research has been directed toward identifying the differential specializations within each hemisphere. Under the competence model, variance arises due to the presence or absence of a particular specialization in the two hemispheres or to the migration of specialization into the nonspecialized hemisphere. Individual differences, in a sense, are a nuisance factor with respect to the identification of hemispheric specializations. Levy's account led to defining the concept of dominance in terms of the arousal asymmetries in the two hemispheres. Under the dominance model, individual differences are an index of the characteristic patterns of asymmetric arousal. In other words, even though each of the two hemispheres is uniquely specialized for processing a given type of information, variance can still result from the characteristic patterns of asymmetric hemispheric arousal.

DIFFERENCES IN MENTAL STATES AND ATTENTIONAL SHIFTS

Levy's (1983) arousal model is intended to be an interpretation of individual differences in the perceptual asymmetries at the neurological, as opposed to the psychological, level; that is, cerebral arousal is related, but definitely not equivalent, to attention. Attention may be one of the consequences of arousal, but it is by no means the only one. Furthermore, attention can be induced in a certain location in which the cue validity for predicting a certain event is high. At the psychological level of interpretation, a biased attention for one field (visual or auditory) will tend to enhance performance for that field and to reduce performance for the other. Several theorists have attributed part of the observed variance in the perceptual asymmetries to such an attention bias.

According to Kimura's (1966, 1967) structural account of hemispheric asymmetry, different laterality effects reflect differential specializations of the two hemispheres. This is the view that there is a fixed lateralization that a person can do little to change. However, many investigators disagree: They regard hemispheric specializations as relative and quantitative rather than absolute and qualitative. For them, the dynamic and changing aspects of lateral superiorities in perceptual asymmetries argue against the inflexibility of Kimura's model.

One of the earlier challenges to Kimura's structural model came from research of conjugate lateral eye movements (CLEM). The observation of consistent individual differences in the direction of CLEM led Bakan (1969) to postulate that people who habitually look to the left are activating their right hemispheres and, therefore, should be more spatial and holistic and less verbal in their thinking. In contrast, the right-lookers are activating their left hemispheres and should be more verbal in their thinking. Thus, one is either a left-hemisphere person or a right-hemisphere person, and one's hemispheric preference may influence career goals. Indeed, group differences, as measured by university major chosen (Kocel, Galin, Ornstein, & Merrin, 1972) or by clinical diagnosis (Smokler & Shevron, 1979), have been reported. Dabbs (1980) found significant group differences between English and architecture majors in terms of the resting blood flow to the left and right sides of the head, measured by temperature change at the inside corner of each eye. As a group, the English majors showed greater left-hemisphere flow whereas the architecture majors showed greater right-hemisphere flow. Hence, the postulated relationship between mental states and hemispheric activation seems to have some empirical support. The problems with this view are that the reliability of these types of group differences needs to be established and that the postulated mental states do not seem to transfer to other personality variables. As far as we can tell, there is only one personality trait, the so-called field-independent scale, that seems to show a slight relation to the functional asymmetries of the two hemispheres. For example, several studies reported that high field-dependent subjects had weaker asymmetry patterns (Oltman, Ehrlichman, & Cox, 1977; Zoccolotti, Passafiume, & Pizzamiglio, 1979). However, even these differences may simply reflect strategy differences and have nothing to do with hemispheric asymmetries (Arndt & Berger, 1978). We totally agree with Ehrlichman and Weinberger's (1978) conclusion that there is little evidence for the notion of preferred hemisphere as a stable personality trait and that classifying people into either right-hemisphere persons or left-hemisphere persons does not serve any useful function in the theorization of cerebral asymmetries.

At a more theoretical level, Kinsbourne (1970) put forth a rather radical view about perceptual asymmetry. Instead of focusing on personality traits as a reliable indicator of an individual's activated hemisphere, his attentional account emphasizes the momentary shifts of hemisphere activation. In this view, laterality differences result from activation of one or the other hemisphere as a function of context in which a particular task is to be performed. That is, hemispheric activation can be internally primed by expectancies as to the likely nature (verbal or spatial) of the processing that a particular task may require. Accordingly, perceptual asymmetries (regardless of hemifield studies or dichotic-listening studies) arise not as described by the structural determinant account, but rather as a consequence of such momentary attentional or activation biases.

Kinsbourne's (1970) attention-activation account has led to two different areas of research. One area concentrates on the activation aspect, and its experimental paradigm is to look for CLEM pattern as a function of types of elicited questions. Kinsbourne (1972) provides some supporting evidence. He found that verbal questions elicited greater right-eye movements and that spatial questions elicited greater left-eye movements. This result has been replicated by other investigators (e.g., Gur, Gur, & Harris, 1975). However, there might be an equal number of failures to replicate Kinsbourne's original findings (see Ehrlichman & Weinberger, 1978, for a rather pessimistic review).

A much more encouraging piece of evidence supporting the notion of activation came from a series of studies by Ley (1980). In three separate experiments, he administered a lateralization task, a verbal dichotic-listening task, a musical dichotic-listening task, and a visual half-field face-recognition task, before and after subjects were exposed to a list of words they were instructed to remember. The words to be remembered were either high or low in imagery and either high or low in emotionality. The results showed a reliable LVF or left-ear superiority in reporting high imagery and high emotionality words. Somehow the memory tasks induced different mental states that resulted in a shift toward the right hemisphere. But, Why did memory tasks induce such a subtle change in the activation state of the two hemispheres? To answer this question, we need to examine the second area of intensive research brought about by Kinsbourne's (1970) attention-activation theory.

One tenet of the attention-activation theory is that ongoing verbal activities should increase left-hemisphere performance, whereas ongoing spatial or musical thought should prime the right hemisphere and thus, improve performance on tasks presented in the LVF or left ear in a dichotic-listening experiment. Kinsbourne (1970) again provides supporting evidence for this view. In a task requiring subjects to detect a threshold-size gap on the side of a square, he obtained a RVF advantage only when the subjects were concurrently holding a verbal memory load, which presumably activated the left hemisphere. This observation was consistent with the results of Spellacy and Blumstein (1970) in which a REA was obtained in a dichotic-listening task of vowel detection only when subjects were expecting speech. Morais and Landercy (1977) also reported that a REA for dichotically presented nonsense syllables decreased when subjects concurrently stored short musical passages. However, the initial success of Kinsbourne's account was followed by a number of studies that have failed to support the predictions generated from his model (see Bryden, 1982, for a critical review on parameters that may contribute to the success or failure of attempting to replicate earlier supporting experiments).

Among those studies that failed to support a direct relationship between concurrent activities and their selective activation of hemispheres, two aspects turned out to be of theoretical importance. First, several studies (Geffen, Bradshaw, & Nettleton, 1972; Goodglass & Calderon, 1977; Kallman, 1978) demonstrated that two hemispheres could concurrently and independently process that component of a complex stimulus for which each is uniquely specialized. This result is of course contrary to the predictions of the Kinsbourne model. More importantly, it suggests that the processing system is not unified and that the subsystems draw their own independent resources. Second, Hellige and his associates (Hellige, 1978; Hellige & Cox, 1976; Hellige, Cox, & Litvac, 1979; Hellige & Wong, 1983) found that complex effects of verbal memory load on laterality differences such that light loading did prime a particular hemisphere, enhancing its superiority, whereas heavier loading actually overloaded it, depressing its performance. Furthermore, they also failed to find any systematic effects of a nonverbal memory load on laterality effects, in direct contrast to what would be expected from Kinsbourne's original proposal. The notion that a heavy concurrent verbal memory load can overload the left hemisphere and thus produce the reversal of laterality patterns is not new (see Geffen, Bradshaw, & Nettleton, 1972). The further confirmation by the systematic investigation of Hellige and his associates leads to an important point: dual task manipulations may have little to do with selectively priming one or the other hemisphere; rather, their results seem to indicate capacity interference. In fact, it is this idea that led to the proposal of the Dual Processor Model by Friedman & Polson (1981).

DIFFERENCES DUE TO RESOURCE COMPOSITIONS

In the 1970s, a number of information-processing models focused on the notions of limited capacity and resource allocation strategies (Kahneman, 1973; Kantowitz & Knight, 1976; Norman & Bobrow, 1975; Posner & Snyder, 1975; Shiffrin & Schneider, 1977). A basic experimental paradigm employed to develop these ideas involves the comparison between single- and dual-task performance. After an intensive review of the earlier literature, Navon and Gopher (1979; see also Gopher, Brickner, & Navon, 1982) come to the conclusion that the single-capacity assumption is probably too simplistic and advance a theory of allocation based upon the notion of multiple resources that are not mutually accessible. Friedman and Polson (1981) immediately saw the usefulness of the notion of multiple resources in explaining why the cerebral specialization literature has been plagued with the "apparent capriciousness of the phenomena" (p. 1031). They propose that the two cerebral hemispheres should be regarded as two separate, limited-capacity pools of undifferentiated resources that are not mutually accessible. Each hemisphere is capable of performing any task required of it by using its own mechanisms and resources, but performance differences may be present between hemispheres. These differences should be viewed from the perspective of performance-resource functions, which are affected either by resource limitation or by data limitations (Norman & Bobrow, 1975). Friedman and Polson successfully applied these performance-resource functions to a variety of data from experiments involving perceptual and cognitive information processing, control of motor performance, and changes in electrical activities of the brain. But perhaps the best support of their hemisphere-as-separate-resource model is their ability to account for results from the dual-task experiments of Hellige and his associates (Hellige & Cox,

1976; Hellige, et al., 1979). Friedman, Polson, Dafoe, & Gaskill (1982) provide further support for this model. Using dual-task methodology in which subjects were induced to pay different amounts of attention to the two tasks, they found that left-hemisphere resources became scarce because of increasing memory loads, such that subjects who had maintained a consistent RVF advantage for naming nonsense syllables when that task was performed alone showed greater decrements from single-task to dual-task performance. In fact, under the heavier memory load, visual-field advantage switched from RVF to LVF.

According to this multiple resource model, variance obtained in the perceptual asymmetry experiments results from the fact that subjects can use a variety of resource compositions, drawn from the two hemispheres, to meet the requirements of any given task. For better control of individual differences, Freidman and Polson (1981) urge that investigators use populations that show the largest and most consistent laterality differences and try to employ within-subjects designs. These suggestions are well intended. However, as Hardyck (1983) cogently observes, "It is not clear how the careful subject selection they advocate will control for the problems of subjects using different resource compositions to achieve solutions to the task. . . . What criteria do we use to insure that the tasks we choose draw primarily on one hemisphere?" (p. 232). Even so, Friedman and Polson have done an excellent job in the attempt to bring together two seemingly different areas into a coherent theoretical framework. As for the source of variance in any perceptual asymmetry experiment, we now have another level of control—the resource compositions drawn from the two hemispheres—to worry about.

DIFFERENCES OF TEMPORAL RESOLUTION IN THE TWO HEMISPHERES

So far we have been describing various theoretical accounts that, in general, attribute variance in the perceptual asymmetries to nonhemispheric factors such as differences in auditory neuropathways, in arousal asymmetries, in attention shifts, and in resource compositions of the two hemispheres. None of these positions addresses the question of what it means to be highly verbal in the left hemisphere. In a strictly information-processing sense, the question becomes, What is the basic mechanistic ability (or the basic information-processing ability) that is the building block of verbal ability? The answer to such a question may eventually help us to understand why language came to reside in the left hemisphere. Moreover, differences with respect to this particular ability may account for part of the variance observed in perceptual asymmetries. This is exactly the position taken by Tzeng and Wang (1984) in their account of some anomalous effects in perceptual asymmetries. Since their approach is a bit unusual, let us take a closer look at their arguments.

Central to their argument is the assumption that from an evolutionary viewpoint, a certain advantage in the left hemisphere at the *sensory* level must have enabled the elaboration of a basic feature at the *cognitive* level that is essential to the development of human language. This assumption led them to search for the most elementary requirement in the development of language, a requirement that could be better fulfilled by the left hemisphere. They start their argument by identifying such a required feature in language development, a feature called *duality of patterning* by Hockett (1960). They then show that this feature makes possible the mapping of an immense complex cognitive world onto a simple set of no more than several dozen motor gestures and that the expressive power of language lies in part in the large number of possibilities with which these gestures may be sequenced. Given the important feature of duality of patterning and the need to resolve the order of elements within a linear array, it is suggested that whatever is responsible for the lateralization of language must have involved the process of keeping the temporal order of signals. They provide much evidence in the clinical as well as neurological data to show that the left hemisphere has indeed a much finer temporal resolution power than the right (Hammond, 1982) and that the cortical areas that control motor-sequential movements are also responsible for phoneme identification (Ojemann & Mateer, 1979). Once they were able to establish that difference in the temporal resolution power between the two hemispheres may be responsible for the laterality effects observed for language processing, they ran two experiments: first, to show that perceptual asymmetries in tachistoscopic recognition of words can also be related to such a temporally based mechanism, and second, to examine the properties of such temporal processing.

In the first experiment, right-handed subjects were asked to view a sequence of three briefly presented letters via a tachistoscope. Their task was to integrate three letters to form an English word. The critical aspect of the experimental procedure is the presentation location of each letter. Take the word *cat* for example. The three letters *C, A,* and *T* were presented in that temporal order. However, the first letter, *C,* was presented in the center of the RVF (or LVF), the second letter, *A,* was presented $\frac{1}{4}$ inch above the location where the first letter had just been shown, and the third letter, *T,* was presented $\frac{1}{4}$ inch below the location of the first letter. Only a single letter was shown on the screen at a time. If subjects correctly integrated the temporal sequence, then they should report the word *cat.* However, if they failed to code the temporal sequence, then there should be a high probability that they would report the word *act* instead because what was still available in their icon should be a string of letters arranged vertically as *A*, *C*, and *T*. This procedure not only forced the subjects to pay strict attention to temporal order but also avoided confounding because either alternative can be a word. A significant RVF superiority was observed.

In the second experiment, the procedure was identical to the first except that letters were replaced by three different-colored dots randomly chosen from five different-colored dots. It was found that there was no laterality difference during the first block of 60 trials in which right-handed subjects attempted to identify the sequential order of three colored dots. However, during the second block of another 60 trials, after subjects become more or less familiar with the range of possible pattern permutation, a RVF advantage was again observed. According to Tzeng and Wang (1984), results of the second experiment are important for three reasons. First, they indicate that results from the first experiment with letters were not due to the claim that the left hemisphere knows more words than the right hemisphere (Kimura, 1961; Zaidel, 1976). Rather, these data suggest that the reason for the observed left-hemisphere superiority in word recognition lies in its greater ability at tracking the sequences of segments, regardless of whether they are audible or visual. Second, the results of the color-dot experiment, taken together with the observation of severe deficit in manual and oral sequential movements among left-hemisphere lesion patients, indicate that the temporally based left-hemisphere timing mechanism is amodal as well as prelinguistic in nature. Third, the fact that the left hemisphere gains some advantage only after subjects become familiar with these stimulus patterns suggests that such a sequential coding is beneficial only when input stimuli become unitized. It is this third property of temporal processing that was employed by Tzeng and Wang (1984) to account for some anomalous findings in perceptual asymmetry studies. Let us examine these in more detail.

CHANGES OF REA MAGNITUDE IN SPEECH PERCEPTION

With a dichotic-listening procedure, it has been found that the largest REA is produced when stop consonants /b,p,d,t,g,k/ are presented in pairs, while liquids /l,r/ produce a less strong REA and steady-state vowels (such as /æ/ and /ɛ/) produce no such effect. Schwartz and Tallal (1980) noticed that these stimuli not only belong to different phonetic classes, but also differ in the rate of change of acoustic cues that characterize their spectra (Liberman, 1982). Indeed, in a dichotic-listening experiment with normal right-handed subjects, they were able to demonstrate that altering the temporal component of the acoustic spectra within a phonetic class results in significant changes in the magnitude of the REA. This demonstration is, of course, consistent with Tzeng and Wang's (1984) contention that the superiority of the left hemisphere for linguistic processing reflects left-hemispheric competence in processing rapidly changing acoustic features by binding together phonetic segments so that at rapid transmission rates, the temporal order and segmentation for speech are preserved.

EXPERT EFFECTS

It has been shown that trained musicians show a left-hemisphere superiority in the recognition of melodies, while musically inexperienced listeners show a right-hemisphere advantage (Bever & Chiarello, 1974; Gordon, 1978; Shanon, 1980). Similar patterns of hemispheric laterality differences have also been demonstrated in skilled and novice Morse code operators (Papcun, Krashen, Tarbeek, Remington, & Harshman, 1974). It would be absurd to suggest that the left hemisphere is prodigious at learning complicated musical compositions or Morse code communication; however, other interpretations are available. For instance, it has been argued that melody perception is a gestalt phenomenon for naïve listeners, while for musicians the melody is perceived as an articulatory set of component elements (Bever, 1980). But this interpretation is vague and also cannot handle data from studies in which a right-hemisphere superiority has been demonstrated with musicians as subjects (Bartholomeus, 1974; Kimura, 1967). Based upon results from their second experiment mentioned above, Tzeng and Wang (1984) advance an entirely different interpretation.

They argue that calibration of timing in order to discover the sequential order of the input signals would be useful, as well as meaningful, only if the sequence can find an entry in the preexisting storage (i.e., a lexicon). Since the segments in the lexical unit are arranged in sequence, a timing mechanism that facilitates the detection of signal order is essential for locating the correct entry. In other words, if there is not a preexisting lexicon, then detecting the signal order is useless. Thus, the difference between experts and novices is that the former have at their disposal a wealth of already unitized lexical units (for music or for Morse code patterns) whose recognition requires the ability to code the signals in correct sequence, while the latter has not. A direct implication of such a theoretical position is that not all sequentially presented items result in left-hemisphere advantage; a lexicon-like system of various stimulus patterns has to be established before any cerebral asymmetry can be demonstrated.

LEARNING EFFECTS AND THE FREQUENCY EFFECT

In addition to the expert effect, the above interpretation is ready to handle the so-called learning effect, as well as the frequency effect, within an experimental session in most perceptual asymmetry experiments. One example of such learning effects is the demonstration of a shift in superiority from the right hemisphere initially to the left hemisphere during the course of the experiment, even though the stimulus materials and the task requirements remain the same. The shift has been observed for both auditory and visual stimuli (Bradshaw & Gates, 1978; Gordon & Carmon, 1976; Kallman & Corballis, 1975; Miller & Butler, 1980; Perl & Haggard, 1975). In all these studies, the shift in the hemispheric superiority reflects the dropout of the perceptual factor and the novelty effect (hence, initial right-hemisphere advantage) once the stimulus patterns have been learned (i.e., item information becomes secondary) and the increasing involvement of the left-hemisphere timing mechanism to detect the order information (which now becomes the primary task) among segments embedded in the stimulus patterns.

The frequency effect is the phenomenon in perceptual asymmetry studies in which the laterality effects are enhanced when a small number of stimuli are used very frequently during a single experiment as compared with the use of different stimuli on each trial. Hardyck, Tzeng, and Wang (1978) suggest that this occurs because a small, well-learned stimulus set allows a comparison-to-memory and that the hemispheres somehow differ more in terms of such comparisons. Such a frequency effect (as expressed by the ratio of experimental stimuli to trials) was also confirmed by a direct test by Hellige (1980). To account for these effects, Tzeng and Wang (1984) again point to the fact that in the act of perceiving, timing is important only when there is already a preexisting lexicon (for natural language or for a set of artificial stimulus patterns) such that detecting order information enables the perceiver to access the correct lexical entry more efficiently and more rapidly. This account is very close to Goldberg and Costa's (1981) interpretation of the observed practice effects. Their model rests on the assumption that the left hemisphere can better handle any class of stimuli that can be fitted into a routine descriptive system. Tzeng and Wang's temporal coding account gives a further rationale of why this should be the case.

Although Bradshaw and Nettleton's (1983) extensive review ends on a pessimistic note, we still believe that Tzeng and Wang's model has sufficient flexibility to enable it to account for individual differences and for the effects of development and experience (such as the expert effect) and practice (such as the learning and the frequency effect), which have been shown to be associated with right-to-left hemisphere shifts.

SUMMARY AND CONCLUSION

Research on how language is served by the brain presents one of the supreme challenges to scientists at every level. In fact, what can be more thrilling than the true meaning of such research: At every step of the intellectual pursuit, what we are doing involves processes of "language probing language and of brain studying brain" (Tzeng & Wang, 1984, p. R910). It has been more than a hundred years since Broca's attempt to relate left-hemispheric damage to disturbances of language. Volumes of books and journal articles have been written to characterize various aphasic and dyslexic patterns, and a great deal of effort has been devoted to relating different syndromes to different portions of the cerebral hemispheres. During the last 30 years or so, with the advent of new techniques such as electroencephalography, blood-flow studies, and especially the newer methods of computerized axial tomography, we have learned a great deal about the brain and we know more about the anatomy and physiology of its many interrelated structures. However, we are still much at a loss about the relationship between measurable features of neurological organization in normal people and psychological function in ordinary behavior. Now, under the new surge of information-processing research, we have been trying to relate models developed for speech processing, word recognition, syntactic parsing, and sentence comprehension to theories of hemispheric specializations derived from clinical and neurological data. One of the basic stumbling blocks in this endeavor has been that there is too much variance generated from perceptual asymmetries even in right-handed male subjects as compared to the clinical population as a whole. Of course, such variance can no longer be treated as statistical error, and it needs to be seriously accommodated in any theory of brain and language. Such a concern has led many neuropsychologists to take a serious look at the issue of individual differences (e.g., Bradshaw & Nettleton, 1983; Hardyck, 1983; Hellige & Wong, 1983; Levy, 1983; Segalowitz & Bryden, 1983).

In this chapter, we have reviewed different positions on how individual differences in perceptual asymmetries should be approached. They represent different theoretical positions at different levels of conceptualization. At the anatomical level, there is an impressive degree of individual variation in the structure of the planum temporale, a presumably neurolinguistically critical area (see Witelson, 1980, for review). Also, there is the possibility that some individuals may even have a reversed dominance of ipsilateral over contralateral input under dichotic-listening situations (Teng, 1981). At the neurological level, individual differences in characterized and habitual arousal asymmetries in the two hemispheres may account for part of the variance in perceptual asymmetries (Levy, 1983). At the psychological level, mental-state variations and momentary attentional shifts may also contribute to individual differences in perceptual task performance. It is highly probable that the observed attention-activation influence is simply the consequence of variations in the resource compositions drawn from the two hemispheres (Friedman & Polson, 1981), though we do need to know more about how to define operationally the concept of resource compositions if we hope to have a better understanding of individual differences in perceptual asymmetries and of how they relate to hemispheric asymmetries.

Finally, Tzeng and Wang (1984) provide still another way of looking at many of the anomalous effects observed in the perceptual asymmetry studies. According to their temporal coding view, the expert effect (a subject variable), the familiarity effect (a stimulus variable), the practice or learning effect (a process variable), and the frequency and the complexity effect (a task variable), once regarded as methodological anomalies, are in fact the logical consequences of a left-hemispheric timing mechanism for detecting order information.

Of course, these approaches are by no means the only ways to account for the individual differences in perceptual asymmetry tasks. Traditional psychometric methods and some newly developed statistical procedures such as LISREL have not yet been applied to uncover the underlying factors, or *latent variables,* that cannot be easily detected by ordinary experimental procedures. Furthermore, one has to be puzzled by the usually small samples run in most hemispheric and perceptual asymmetries studies. Though we understand that the small number of subjects in a clinical setting is not by any investigator's choice, the small sample size is certainly less than desirable in running experiments with normal subjects, especially when every experimenter is aware of the apparent capriciousness of the perceptual asymmetry phenomena (see Friedman & Polson, 1981; Hardyck, 1983, on their frustrating attempts to summarize findings in visual perceptual lateralization). It is important for experimenters to avoid believing in the law of small numbers (Tversky & Kahneman, 1971) and to increase the sample size of their experimental subjects.

Individual differences in perceptual and cognitive activities have haunted experimental psychologists for years. Now the discrepancy between clinical and normal data with respect to the question of hemispheric asymmetries has once again forced researchers to pay attention to this problem. In order to make progress in understanding the neuropsychological relationship, it will no doubt be necessary to determine just how much variance in perceptual asymmetry data should be attributed to hemispheric asymmetries and how much to nonhemispheric factors at various levels of psychological functions. We are glad to see that more and more researchers are coming to appreciate this issue. Friedman and Polson (1981) urge investigators to use populations that show the largest and most consistent hemisphere differences, to use within-subjects designs whenever possible, and to pay very close attention to the types of task used and so forth in order to get rid of the nuisance variance. This is a typical experimental psychologist's approach to reducing error variance in an experiment. We urge that, rather than trying to get rid of the variance, investigators should face the issue of individual differences and make serious attempts to account for the resulting variance. Such awareness will definitely make our theories more sophisticated and our methodologies better refined. Then and only then can we begin to hope for a unified theory of neurocognitive science.

REFERENCES

Arndt, S., & Berger, D. E. Cognitive mode and asymmetry in cerebral functioning. *Cortex,* 1978, *14,* 78–86.

Bakan, P. Hypnotizability, laterality of eye movements and functional brain asymmetry. *Perceptual and Motor Skills,* 1969, *28,* 927–932.

Bartholomeus, B. Effects of task requirements on ear superiority for sung speech. *Cortex,* 1974, *10,* 215–223.

Bellugi, U., Poizner, H., & Klima, E. S. Brain organization for language: Clues from sign aphasia. In D. Kimura (Ed.), *Human Neurobiology, Special Issue on Language,* in press.

Berlin, C. I. Hemispheric asymmetry in auditory tasks. In S. Harnard, R. W. Doty, L. Goldstein, J. Jaynes, & G. Krauthamer (Eds.), *Lateralization in the nervous system.* New York: Academic Press, 1977.

Bever, T. G. Broca and Lashley were right: Cerebral dominance is an accident of growth. In D. Caplan (Ed.), *Biological studies of mental processes.* Cambridge, MA: MIT Press, 1980.

Bever, T. G., & Chiarello, R. J. Cerebral dominance in musicians and non-musicians. *Science,* 1974, *185,* 537–539.

Blumstein, S., Goodglass, H., & Tartter, V. The reliability of ear advantage in dichotic listening. *Brain and Language,* 1975, *2,* 226–236.

Bradshaw, J. L., & Gates, E. A. Visual field differences in verbal tasks: Effects of task familiarity and sex of subject. *Brain and Language,* 1978, *5,* 166–187.

Bradshaw, J. L., & Nettleton, N. C. *Human cerebral asymmetry.* Englewood Cliffs, NJ: Prentice-Hall, 1983.

Broca, P. Remarques sur le siège de la faculté du langage articulé suivies d'une observation d'aphemie. Bulletin de la Société Anatomique de Paris, 1861, *6,* 330–357.

Bruder, G. E., & Yozawitz, A. Central auditory processing and laterality in psychiatric patients. In J. Gruzelier & P. Flor-Henry (Eds.), *Hemisphere asymmetries of function and psychopathology.* Amsterdam: Elsevier, 1979.

Bryden, M. P. *Laterality: Functional asymmetry in the intact brain.* New York: Academic Press, 1982.

Chen, S. H., Hung, C. C., & Chen, R. C. *A study of cerebral speech dominance in right-handed Chinese.* Paper presented in the Sixth Asian and Oceanian Congress of Neurology. Taipei, Taiwan, November 13–17, 1983.

Dabbs, J. M., Jr., & Choo, G. Left–right carotid blood flow predicts specialized mental ability. *Neuropsychologia,* 1980, *18,* 711–713.

Damasio, A. The nature of aphasia: Signs and syndromes. In M. T. Sarno (Ed.), *Acquired aphasia.* New York: Academic Press, 1981.

Damasio, A. R., Lima, A., & Damasio, H. Nervous function after right hemispherectomy. *Neurology,* 1975, *25,* 89–93.

Damasio, H. Cerebral localization of the aphasias. In M. T. Sarno (Ed.), *Acquired aphasia.* New York: Academic Press, 1981.

Dax, M. Lésions de la moitié de l'encéphale coïncidant avec l'oubli des signes de la pensée. *Gazette Hebdomadaire de Médecine et de Chirurgie,* 1836, *32,* 259–269. (As printed in 1865.)

Descartes, R. Les Passions de l'âme, Amsterdam, 1650. In E. S. Haldahe and G. R. T. Ross (Trans.), *The philosophical works of Descartes.* Cambridge, England: University Press, 1931.

Ehrlichman, H., & Weinberger, A. Lateral eye movements and hemispheric asymmetry: A critical review. *Psychological Bulletin,* 1978, *85,* 1080–1101.

Friedman, A., & Polson, M. C. The hemispheres as independent resource systems: Limited capacity processing and cerebral specialization. *Journal of Experimental Psychology: Human Perception and Preformance,* 1981, *7,* 1031–1058.

Friedman, A., Polson, M. C., Dafoe, C. G., & Gaskill, S. Dividing attention within and between hemispheres: Testing a multiple resource approach to limited-capacity information processing. *Journal of Experimental Psychology: Human Perception and Performance,* 1982, *8,* 625–650.

Gall, F. J. Sur les fonctions du cerveau et sur celles de chacune de ses parties (Vols. 4, 6). Paris: Baillière, 1825.

Gazzaniga, M. S. Right hemisphere language following brain bisection: A 20-year perspective. *American Psychologist,* 1983, *38,* 525–537.

Gazzaniga, M. S., Bogen, J. E., & Sperry, R. W. Some functional effects of sectioning the cerebral commissures in man. *Proceedings of the National Academy of Sciences,* 1962, *48,* 1765–1769.

Geffen, G., Bradshaw, J. L., & Nettleton, N. C. Hemispheric asymmetry: Verbal and spatial coding of visual stimuli. *Journal of Experimental Psychology,* 1972, *95,* 25–31.

Geschwind, N. Disconnexion syndromes in animals and man. *Brain,* 1965, *88,* 237–294.

Geschwind, N., & Levitsky, W. Human brain: Left–right asymmetries in temporal speech region. *Science,* 1968, *161,* 186–187.

Glick, S. D., Jerussi, T. P., & Zimmerberg, B. Behavioral and neuropharmacological correlates of nigrostriatal asymmetry in rats. S. Harnad, R. W. Doty, L. Goldstein, J. Jaynes, & G. Krauthamer (Eds.), *Lateralization in the nervous system.* New York: Academic Press, 1977.

Goldberg, E., & Costa, L. Hemisphere differences in the acquisition of the descriptive systems. *Brain and Language,* 1981, *14,* 144–173.

Goodglass, H., & Calderon, M. Parallel processing of verbal and musical stimuli in right and left hemispheres. *Neuropsychologia,* 1977, *15,* 397–407.

Gopher, D., Brickner, M., & Navon, D. Different difficulty manipulations interact differently with task emphasis: Evidence for multiple resources. *Journal of Experimental Psychology: Human Perception and Performance,* 1982, *8,* 146–157.

Gordon, H. W. Hemispheric asymmetry for dichotically presented chords in musicians and non-musicians. *Acta Psychologica,* 1978, *42,* 383–395.

Gordon, H. W., & Carmon, A. Transfer of dominance in speed of verbal response to visually presented stimuli from right to left hemisphere. *Perceptual and Motor Skills,* 1976, *42,* 1091–1100.

Gur, R. C., & Gur, R. E. Handedness and individual differences in hemispheric activation. In J. Herron (Ed.), *Neuropsychology of left-handedness.* New York: Academic Press, 1980.

Gur, R. E., Gur, R. C., & Harris, L. J. Cerebral activation, as measured by subjects' lateral eye movements, is influenced by experimenter location. *Neuropsychologia,* 1975, *13,* 35–44.

Hammond, G. Hemispheric differences in temporal resolution. *Brain and Cognition,* 1982, *1,* 95–118.

Hardyck, C. Seeing each other's points of view: Visual perceptual lateralization. In J. B. Hellige (Ed.), *Human cerebral asymmetry: Method, theory, and application.* New York: Praeger, 1983.

Hardyck, C., Tzeng, O. J. L., & Wang, W. S-Y. Cerebral lateralization of function and bilingual decision processes: Is thinking lateralized? *Brain and Language,* 1978, *5,* 56–71.

Hécaen, H., & Albert, M. L. *Human neuropsychology.* New York: Wiley, 1978.

Heilman, K. M., & Watson, R. T. Mechanisms underlying the unilateral neglect syndrome. In E. A. Weinstein & R. P. Friedland (Eds.), *Hemi-inattention and hemisphere specialization: Vol. 18. Advances in neurology.* New York: Raven, 1977.

Hellige, J. B. Visual laterality patterns for pure- versus mixed-list presentation. *Journal of Experimental Psychology: Human Perception and Performance,* 1978, *4,* 121–131.

Hellige, J. B. Effects of perceptual quality and visual field of probe stimulus presentation on memory search for letters. *Journal of Experimental Psychology: Human Perception and Performance,* 1980, *6,* 639–751.

Hellige, J. B., & Cox, P. J. Effects of concurrent verbal memory on recognition of stimuli from the left and right visual fields. *Journal of Experimental Psychology: Human Perception and Performance,* 1976, *2,* 210–221.

Hellige, J. B., Cox, P. J., & Litvak, L. Information processing in the cerebral hemispheres: Selective hemispheric activation and capacity limitations. *Journal of Experimental Psychology: General,* 1979, *108,* 251–279.

Hellige, J. B., & Wong, T. M. Hemisphere-specific interference in dichotic listening: Task variables and individual differences. *Journal of Experimental Psychology: General,* 1983, *112,* 218–239.

Hockett, C. F. The origin of Speech. *Scientific American,* 1960, *203,* 88–96.

Huang, C. Y. *Varieties of deep dyslexia in Chinese orthography.* Paper presented in the sixth Asian and Oceanian Congress of Neurology. Taipei, Taiwan, November 13–17, 1983.

Hung, D. L., & Tzeng, O. J. L. Orthographic variations and visual information processing. *Psychological Bulletin,* 1981, *90,* 377–414.

Iversen, S. D. Brain dopamine systems and behavior. In L. L. Iversen, S. D. Iversen, & S. H. Snyder (Eds.), *Drugs, neurotransmitters, and behavior: Vol. 8. Handbook of psychopharmacology.* New York: Plenum Press, 1977.

Kahnaman, D. *Attention and effort.* Englewood Cliffs, New Jersey: Prentice-Hall, 1973.

Kallman, H. J. Can expectancy explain reaction time ear asymmetries? *Neuropsychologia,* 1978, *16,* 225–228.

Kallman, H. J., & Corballis, M. C. Ear asymmetry in reaction time to musical sounds. *Perception and Psychophysics,* 1975, *17,* 368–370.

Kantowitz, B. H., Knight, J. L. On experimenter-limited processes. *Psychological Review,* 1976, *83,* 502–507.

Kimura, D. Cerebral dominance and the perception of verbal stimuli. *Canadian Journal of Psychology,* 1961, *15,* 166–171.

Kimura, D. Dual functional asymmetry of the brain in visual perception. *Neuropsychologia,* 1966, *4,* 275–285.

Kimura, D. Functional asymmetry of the brain in dichotic listening. *Cortex,* 1967, *3,* 163–178.

Kinsbourne, M. Eye and head turning indicates cerebral lateralization. *Science,* 1972, *176,* 539–541.

Kinsbourne, M. The cerebral basis of lateral asymmetries in attention. *Acta Psychologia,* 1970, *33,* 193–201.

Kocel, K., Galin, D., Ornstein, R., & Merrin, E. Lateral eye movements and cognitive mode. *Psychonomic Science,* 1972, *17,* 223–224.

Levy, J. Psychobiological implications of bilateral asymmetry. In S. J. Dimond and J. G. Beaumont (Eds.), *Hemisphere function in the human brain.* London: Paul Elek, 1974.

Levy, J. Individual differences in cerebral hemisphere asymmetry: Theoretical issues and experimental considerations. In J. B. Hellige (Ed.), *Cerebral hemisphere asymmetry: Method, theory, and application.* New York: Praeger, 1983.

Levy, J., & Reid, M. Variations in cerebral organization as a function of handedness, hand posture in writing, and sex. *Journal of Experimental Psychology: General,* 1978, *107,* 119–144.

Levy, J., Heller, W., Banich, M., & Burton, L. Are variations among right-handed individuals in perceptual asymmetries caused by characteristic arousal differences between hemispheres? *Journal of Experimental Psychology: Human Perception and Performance,* 1983, *9,* 329–359.

Ley, R. G. Emotion and the right hemisphere. Unpublished Ph.D. dissertation. University of Waterloo, 1980.

Liberman, A. M. On finding that speech is special. *American Psychologist,* 1982, *37,* 148–167.

Miller, L. K., & Butler, D. The effect of set size on hemifield asymmetries in letter recognition. *Brain and Language,* 1980, *9,* 307–314.

Mishkin, M., & Forgays, G. D. Word recognition as a function of retrieval locus. *Journal of Experimental Psychology,* 1952, *43,* 43–48.

Morais, J., & Landercy, M. Listening to speech while retaining music: What happens to the right-ear advantage? *Brain and Language,* 1977, *4,* 295–308.

Naville, H., & Bellugi, U. Patterns of cerebral specialization in congenitally deaf adults: A preliminary report. In F. Siple (Ed.), *Understanding language through sign language research.* New York: Academic Press, 1978.

Navon, D., & Gopher, D. On the economy of the human-processing system. *Psychological Review,* 1979, *86,* 214–255.

Norman, D. A., & Bobrow, D. G. On data-limited and resource-limited processes. *Cognitive Psychology,* 1975, *7,* 44–64.

Ojemann, G., & Mateer, C. Human language cortex: Localization of memory, syntax, and sequential motor-phoneme identification systems. *Science,* 1979, *205,* 1401–1403.

Ojemann, G. A., & Whitaker, H. A. Language localization and variability. *Brain and Language,* 1978, *6,* 239–260.

Oltman, P. K., Ehrlichman, H., & Cox, P. W. Field dependence and laterality in the perception of faces. *Perceptual and Motor Skills,* 1977, *45,* 255–260.

Papcun, G., Krashen, S., Terbeek, D., Remington, R., & Harshman, R. Is the left hemisphere specialized for speech, language and/or something else? *Journal of the Acoustical Society of America,* 1974, *55,* 319–327.

Perl, N., & Haggard, M. Practice and strategy in a measure of cerebral dominance. *Neuropsychologia,* 1975, *13,* 347–352.

Porter, R. J., & Hughes, L. F. Dichotic listening to CVs: Method, interpretation, and application. In J. B. Hellige (Ed.), *Cerebral hemisphere asymmetry: Method, theory and application.* New York: Praeger, 1983.

Posner, M. I., & Snyder, C. R. R. Attention and cognitive control. In R. L. Solso (Ed.), *Information processing and cognition.* Hillsdale, NJ: Erlbaum, 1975.

Rosenzweig, M. R. Responsiveness of brain size to individual experience: Behavioral and evolutionary implications. In M. E. Hahn, C. Jensen, and B. C. Dudek (Eds.), *Development and evolution of brain size: Behavioral implications.* New York: Academic Press, 1979.

Schwartz, J., & Tallal, P. Rate of acoustic change may underlie hemispheric specialization for speech perception. *Science,* 1980, *207,* 1380–1381.

Searleman, A. A review of right hemisphere linguistic capabilities. *Psychological Bulletin,* 1977, *84,* 503–528.

Segalowitz, S. J., & Bryden, M. P. Individual differences in hemispheric representation of language. In S. J. Segalowitz (Ed.), *Language function and brain organization.* New York: Academic Press, 1983.

Shanon, B. Lateralization effects in musical decision tasks. *Neuropsychologia,* 1980, *18,* 21–31.

Shiffrin, R. M., & Schneider, W. Controlled and automatic human information processing: II. Perceptual learning, automatic attending and a general theory. *Psychological Review,* 1977, *84,* 127–190.

Smokler, I. A., & Shevron, I. Cerebral lateralization and personality style. *Archives of General Psychiatry,* 1979, *36,* 949–954.

Spellacy, F., & Blumstein, S. The influence of language set on ear preference in phoneme recognition. *Cortex,* 1970, *6,* 430–439.

Teng, E. L. Dichotic ear difference is a poor index for the functional asymmetry between the cerebral hemispheres. *Neuropsychologia,* 1981, *19,* 235–240.

Trevarthen, C. Brain bisymmetry and the role of the corpus callosum in behavior and conscious experience. In J. Cernacek & F. Podivinsky (Eds.), *Cerebral hemisphere relations.* Bratislava, Czechslovakia: Slovak Academy of Science, 1972.

Tversky, A., & Kahneman, D. Belief in the law of small numbers. *Psychological Bulletin,* 1971, *76,* 105–110.

Tzeng, O. J. L., & Hung, D. L. Higher cortical functions in reading Chinese characters. Paper presented in the sixth Asian and Oceanian Congress of Neurology, Taipei, Taiwan, November 13–17, 1983.

Tzeng, O. J. L., & Wang, W. S-Y. The first two R's. *American Scientist,* 1983, *71,* 238–243.

Tzeng, O. J. L., & Wang, W. S-Y. In search of a common neurocognitive mechanism for language and movement. *American Journal of Physiology,* 1984, *246,* R904–R911.

Vaid, J. Bilingualism and brain lateralization. In S. Segalowitz (Ed.), *Language function and brain organization.* New York: Academic Press, 1982.

Wada, J. A., Clarke, R., & Hamm, A. Cerebral hemispheric asymmetry in humans. *Archives of Neurology,* 1975, *32,* 239–246.

Wernicke, K. *Der aphasische symptomkomplex.* Breslau: Cohn and Weigert, 1874.

Witelson, S. F. Neuroanatomical asymmetry in left-handers: A review and implications for functional asymmetry. In J. Herron (Ed.), *Neuropsychology of left-handedness.* New York: Academic Press, 1980.

Witelson, S. F., & Pallie, W. Left hemisphere specialization for language in the newborn: Neuroanatomical evidence of asymmetry. *Brain,* 1973, *96,* 641–646.

Zaidel, E. Auditory vocabulary of the right hemisphere following brain bisection of hemidecortication. *Cortex,* 1976, *12,* 191–216.

Zaidel, E. *The split brain as a model for functional recovery from language deficits.* Paper presented in the annual meeting of the Claremont Conference on Applied Cognitive psychology, April 1983.

Zoccolotti, P., Passafiume, D., & Pizzamiglio, L. Hemispheric superiorities on a unilateral tactile test: Relationship to cognitive dimensions. *Perceptual and Motor Skills,* 1979, *49,* 735–742.

Zurif, E. B. Language mechanisms: A neuropsychological perspective. *American Scientists,* 1980, *68,* 305–311.

6

Mnemonic Vocabulary Instruction: What's Fact, What's Fiction*

Joel R. Levin and Michael Pressley

INTRODUCTION

In this chapter we discuss recent developments in the area of vocabulary learning. Although some of our discussion deals with vocabulary learning in general, the emphasis is on the acquisition of native-language English vocabulary. The chapter begins with a consideration of tried-and-true, and of old and new, techniques for acquiring vocabulary. Distinctions are made among processes and strategies referred to as either *automatic, rehearsal,*

*The work represented here was funded by a grant to the first author from the National Institute of Education through the Wisconsin Center for Education Research and by a grant to the second author from the Natural Sciences and Engineering Council of Canada. The first author's work was facilitated by a Romnes Faculty Fellowship awarded by the Graduate School of the University of Wisconsin. We are grateful to our colleagues and critics who contributed to the issues that we respond to here.

145

semantic, transsensory, or *mnemonic.* We then respond to a number of issues (essentially, critical questions) that have been raised in relation to the mnemonic-strategy approach with which we are associated. In our responses, we attempt to separate out subjective impressions and other mysticism (fiction) from empirical data that are firmly in hand (fact). In the two final issues considered, we respond to various aspects of mnemonic vocabulary instruction that relate to differences among students.

VOCABULARY-LEARNING
PROCESSES AND STRATEGIES

It is a truism that from birth onward, human beings expand their spoken and written language by acquiring the meanings of new words. Two global questions about vocabulary acquisition follow. The first is, How is it accomplished? This question has been dealt with principally by researchers in the area of language development (e.g., Anglin, 1977; Clark & Clark, 1977; Nelson, Rescorla, Gruendel, & Benedict, 1978). Although we are not concerned here with issues of such naturalistic or *automatic* vocabulary-acquisition processes, we do note that the available data suggest that vocabulary development is a long, slow process. This slowness in the development of vocabulary prompts the second question, How can vocabulary acquisition be accomplished most efficiently? This question is the major focus of the present chapter. Because readers of this volume are probably familiar with documented examples of individual differences in language learning (e.g., the rate differences among Adam, Eve, and Sarah in R. Brown, 1973), it may come as a surprise that researchers have only infrequently studied individual differences in the vocabulary-learning domain. Although we touch on studies directly relevant to differential psychology, more often our comments about individual differences represent what *ought* to be studied. For example, information-processing differences associated with different learners using different vocabulary-learning strategies is one topic alluded to throughout the chapter. We hope that our comments will stimulate other researchers to consider the many potential individual-differences dimensions of vocabulary learning that could be studied profitably.

Before reviewing the various strategies that have been proposed to promote efficient vocabulary acquisition, an additional preliminary comment is in order. The term *strategy* has been applied somewhat differently by researchers interested in naturalistic vocabulary acquisition and by those interested in facilitating vocabulary instruction. Psycholinguists often use the term to refer to any process involved in language. For example, when children respond with actions instead of words, they are referred to as using an *action strategy* (see Shatz, 1978; and especially Clark & Clark, 1977). In contrast, in the cognitive–developmental and educational–psychological literatures, strategy usually implies intention on the part of the learner in pursuit of a cognitive goal. For example, a *memory strategy* is a course of action, or plan, that is deliberately undertaken for the purpose of remembering (e.g., A. L. Brown, 1978; Flavell, 1970; Meacham, 1972; Pressley, Heisel, McCormick, & Nakamura, 1982). Throughout this chapter, our use of the term strategy is consistent with this second sense. Whether or not any of the strategies mentioned is in fact an *effective* vocabulary-learning strategy is considered later.

FOUR VOCABULARY-LEARNING STRATEGIES

REHEARSAL STRATEGIES

DEFINITION

Our definition of *rehearsal* is restricted to a learner's repeated rote processing of an item (in this context, a vocabulary item and its meaning). That this qualifies as an ecologically valid—and intentionally applied—vocabulary-learning strategy is well documented in the annals of pedagogy. Although this mode of learning is typified by Ichabod Crane–like schoolmasters and parochial students reciting catechism, it also represents a principal strategy among the spontaneous study techniques reported by contemporary learners. Thus, in a variety of associative-learning situations, learners report using rote rehearsal as a common study strategy (e.g., Pressley, 1982; Pressley & Levin, 1983). Whether or not all learners apply rehearsal spontaneously in a vocabulary-learning context has yet to be investigated, although rehearsal failures in other tasks by retarded (A. L. Brown, 1974) and learning-disabled children (Torgesen, 1982) suggest that rehearsal may not be a universal associative-learning strategy. Research on the vocabulary learning of educationally handicapped students would be particularly revealing in this regard.

EXAMPLE

Throughout the chapter, we will draw from a list of vocabulary words that were presented to fourth- and fifth-grade students in a study by Levin, Johnson, Pittelman, Hayes, Levin, Shriberg, and Toms-Bronowski (1984). Three new words the students had to learn were *angler* (a person who likes to go fishing), *equestrian* (a person who rides horses), and *ornithologist* (a person who studies birds). An example of a rehearsal strategy in this context is easy to describe. As each new vocabulary item is presented, the learner simply repeats the word, together with its meaning, over and over, either aloud or silently. Thus, to apply a rehearsal strategy a student would say: "*Angler* means 'a person who likes to go fishing'. *Angler* means 'a person who likes to go fishing'. *Angler* means 'a person who likes to go fishing'. *Angler* . . .' "

SEMANTIC STRATEGIES

DEFINITION

Semantic strategies involve relating unfamiliar terms to familiar concepts and experiences. Thus, new material is connected to one's prior knowledge; in vocabulary learning, prior knowledge includes both world knowledge and word knowledge. *World knowledge* refers to the store of information that one has accumulated about previously encountered concepts and events. *Word knowledge* refers to one's stored information about linguistic properties of words (i.e., a word's orthographic, phonological, and lexical properties) that contribute to comprehension.

Semantic activities encompass both the previously discussed automatic processes (where a child nondeliberately acquires a vocabulary word by simply hearing it) and strategies that are applied intentionally to teach or learn new words. Automatic semantic processing of words occurs when children encounter new vocabulary words in books, movies, the media, or the conversations of parents and friends. Based on learning-theory principles, it is reasonable to assume that with multiple exposures to new vocabulary words, children will come to acquire the words and their meanings—even without applying any conscious effort to remember them. That is, children could be expected to learn the words on the basis of automatic processes rather than through the deployment of deliberate strategies.

In contrast, semantic strategies involve deliberately deployed meaningful activities with, and analyses of, new vocabulary items. For instance, teachers commonly provide sentence examples when introducing new vocabulary items in order to make the new terms concrete and meaningful. More elaborate semantic strategies consist of examining the defining attributes of new words in relation to other known words and concepts, interpreting new vocabulary words in terms of familiar experiences, and utilizing available contextual clues within a sentence or a paragraph to infer the meanings of new words (e.g., Gipe, 1979; Levin et al., 1984; Margosein, Pascarella, & Pflaum, 1982; Sternberg, Powell, & Kaye, 1983). Although not researched specifically in the area of vocabulary learning, semantic strategies are applied neither automatically nor equally effectively by all children (e.g., Ceci, 1982). Investigation of the individual-differences dimensions contributing to differential application of semantic strategies should be a high priority in the future.

EXAMPLES

Two examples from the Levin et al. (1984) study are presented here. One semantic strategy, referred to as *semantic mapping,* consists of students learning the meanings of new words by constructing "maps" of the superordinate, subordinate, and coordinate relationships between the new words and vocabulary with which the students were already familiar. Thus, *angler, equestrian,* and *ornithologist* are all mapped as members of the superordinate category *sports and hobbies* and as belonging to the set of people in this category (along with the familiar terms *stamp collector* and *gardener*). A second semantic strategy, *contextual analysis,* requires students to search for contextual clues within short paragraphs in order to infer and confirm the meanings of new words. Thus, for *angler,* the following paragraph is presented: "The *angler* carried a lot of things down to the stream. He carried a net and a tackle box, as well as a fishing pole. He hoped to catch a lot of fish that afternoon" (p. 3). The experimenter pointed out the specific fishing- and fisherman-related words within the paragraph, for example, *fishing pole* and *he* (to signify that an angler is a person), that could furnish clues for deducing the meaning of *angler.*

TRANSSENSORY STRATEGIES

DEFINITION

Transsensory strategies are based on the assumption that learning a new vocabulary—and more generally, learning a new language—requires experiencing that vocabulary through multiple sensory channels. In particular, vocabulary should not be processed at an analytic cognitive level, but rather should be experienced more holistically (primarily through affective and motoric experiences). This is the philosophy that pervades the so-called immersion approach to second-language learning, the highly publicized drama-based method developed by Roussas at Dartmouth University, and the Total Physical Response method of Asher (e.g., 1981). Total involvement at the macroscopic level of language communication is the key to these transsensory strategies. If such involvement occurs, word meanings and subtleties of meanings presumably follow. This approach generates enthusiasm because of the resounding success of real-world immersion programs (Grosjean, 1982; McLaughlin, 1978). Strong support exists for the position that immersion in the midst of a second-language culture facilitates second-language learning for both children and adults. The examples offered here are attempts to approximate immersion in the classroom.

EXAMPLES

For *angler,* Roussas and his students might play the roles of fishermen, complete with props and costumes. Similar events would occur in Asher's classes, with students performing fishing-related actions (e.g., baiting a hook, casting a line, pulling in a fish) in response to the instructor's verbal requests. Initially, the students' actions are carefully guided by the instructor so that they are made without error; eventually, through repetition and practice, the students perform the appropriate actions independently in response to the instructor's specific requests.

MNEMONIC STRATEGIES

DEFINITION

The vocabulary-learning strategy that is most clearly identified with the present authors—Atkinson's (1975) *keyword method*—is one born out of the psychological literature on learning, memory, and mnemonics. A mnemonic device is a set of systematic procedures that can improve one's memory. For free recall of a word list, a mnemonic device may be as simple as the first-letter mnemonic (Morris & Cook, 1978), where the first letter of each list item is combined into a single memorable whole. Thus, for example, it pays to be SMART (Semantic, Mnemonic, Automatic, Rehearsal, and Transsensory) when attempting to remember the various vocabulary-learning processes and strategies being discussed here. In learning the definitions of new vocabulary words, alternative mnemonic devices have been devised (e.g., Atkinson, 1975; Paivio & Desrochers, 1979). Effective associative mnemonic devices have three properties in common, which Levin (1983) mnemonically refers to as the "three *R*'s": they require a *R*ecoding of the functional stimulus into a more familiar nominal stimulus, followed by a *R*elating of the recoded nominal stimulus to the to-be-associated response; and they furnish a direct route for *R*etrieving the desired response from the functional stimulus (see also Bellezza, 1981).

At the outset, we note that there exist important information-processing differences associated with different learners' use of mnemonic strategies, some of which have already been investigated and others that have yet to be. For example, young children often have difficulty executing the relating component of associative-learning strategies on their own, particularly when the relationship is to be constructed as an internal visual image (e.g., Levin, 1976; Pressley & Levin, 1978). Also, young children's retrieval of mnemonic mediators is far from automatic (e.g., Pressley & Levin, 1980; Pressley & Mac Fayden, 1983). Although we have conducted some research on how such limitations affect children's use of mnemonic strategies, our basic approach is to design mnemonic interventions that circumvent students' information-processing limitations.

EXAMPLE

Levin et al. (1984) included a keyword method strategy condition in their vocabulary-learning study. For each new vocabulary word, students were presented a keyword, which is simply a familiar concrete word that resembles part of the unfamiliar vocabulary word. For example, the keyword for *angler* was *angel*. The keyword *angel* was then depicted as interacting with the meaning of *angler* in the line drawing given as Figure 6.1. With these two components in place, a direct retrieval path from the vocabulary word through the keyword back to the meaning was created. In particular, the vocabulary word *angler* elicits the keyword *angel,* which in turn elicits the picture of an angel fishing (with the latter conveying the essential meaning of *angler*). It can be readily seen that the keyword method encompasses Levin's (1983) three associative mnemonic *R*'s.

ANGLER (ANGEL) a person who likes to go fishing

FIGURE 6.1 Keyword illustration for the vocabulary item *angler* (from Levin et al., 1984).

MNEMONIC VOCABULARY INSTRUCTION: CRITICAL ISSUES

Having described a variety of strategies for vocabulary learning, we now consider several issues in that domain that are of concern to both educators and researchers. As indicated previously, the present authors have been investigating characteristics of mnemonic strategies over the past several years. What we present here is intended as an information update of discussions that have appeared in our earlier writings (Levin, 1981; Levin & Pressley, 1983; Pressley, Levin, & Delaney, 1982) based on new data available. The data provided, and our interpretations of them, constitute the basis for addressing the specific issues that have been raised.

THE MOST EFFECTIVE STRATEGY ISSUE

The question most frequently asked by educators is, Which vocabulary-learning strategy is best? Unfortunately, the question worded in this way does not have an answer. In the first place, some of the strategies mentioned in the previous section have not been studied in relation to other strategies. Secondly, and of critical importance, the question as it is stated elicits the return question, Best for what? That is, progress in answering the original question requires attention to more precise subquestions: Which vocabulary-learning strategy is best for helping students *remember the meanings* of new words? Which is best for enabling students to *infer the meanings* of new words in context? Which is best for facilitating *language comprehension and communication?* Which is best for developing skill in *spelling?* Which is best for *motivating students* to learn new vocabulary? and so on.

Surprisingly, many researchers have overlooked this multiple-objectives aspect of vocabulary-learning strategies. Even some who apparently are aware of the importance of multiple objectives do not take the issue into account when contrasting strategies of different kinds (e.g., Sternberg et al., 1983). In particular, Sternberg and his associates have failed to recognize that the theoretical strength of mnemonic strategies resides in the *memory* side of vocabulary acquisition, whereas the theoretical strength of semantic strategies resides in the *comprehension* side (see Levin, 1982; and also Jenkins & Dixon, 1983). Thus, comprehension-directed processes and strategies might well be expected to facilitate subjects' performance on vocabulary-inference tasks, such as those described by Sternberg et al. and van Daalen-Kapteijns and Elshout-Mohr (1981); that is, students who are adept at deploying effective semantic strategies should be better able to infer the meanings of undefined new words on the basis of either internal cues (e.g., familiar root words) or external cues (e.g., surrounding context). This individual-differences hypothesis is currently receiving research attention by Sternberg and his colleagues. A similar relationship would not be expected, however, between semantic-strategy deployment and memory for the definitions of newly learned vocabulary items, inasmuch as semantic strategies provide no direct means of strengthening the associative links between vocabulary items and their definitions. In contrast, it is on just such definition-memory tasks that mnemonic strategies would be expected to exhibit their primary impact, inasmuch as the mnemonic links provide a direct route from the vocabulary items to their definitions (see Pressley, Levin, Kuiper, Bryant, & Michener, 1982). Additional data supporting the relative ineffectiveness of semantic contextual strategies with respect to definition memory are found in the recent studies of Shaughnessy (1982) and McDaniel and Pressley (1984).

REMEMBERING THE MEANINGS OF NEW WORDS

In our earlier review of the mnemonic keyword as a vocabulary-learning strategy (Pressley, Levin, and Delaney, 1982), we arrived at the following conclusion:

> The evidence is overwhelming that use of the keyword method, as applied to recall of vocabulary definitions, greatly facilitates performance. This is based on the positive outcomes obtained using varying materials, namely, abstract and concrete words taken from different grammatical form classes . . . using subjects of varying ages and abilities, namely, 3-year-olds to adults, including good and poor vocabulary learners as well as native and foreign English speakers . . . [and] with *respect not just to subjects allowed to learn vocabulary meanings however they wish, but also to subjects who are instructed in alternative strategies.* . . . In short, keyword method effects are pervasive and of impressive magnitude. (Pressley, Levin, & Delaney, 1982, pp. 70–71; italics added)

The evidence reviewed in that article is difficult to refute: With respect to definition memory, no strategies investigated to date (principally, strategies based on either rehearsal or semantic processes) have rivaled the mnemonic keyword method in either their consistency or potency. Included for consideration here is the Levin et al. (1984) study, one that was not available at the time of the Pressley, Levin, and Delaney (1982) review. In two populations of elementary school children (higher and lower achieving), students who were taught new English vocabulary words via the keyword method remembered substantially more definitions than did students who employed either a contextual analysis or a semantic mapping strategy, which produced comparable levels of performance. One aspect of this study that deserves emphasis is that the contextual–analysis strategy used by Levin et al. was considerably more extensive than previously devised contextual strategies (e.g., Gipe, 1979; Levin, McCormick, Miller, Berry, & Pressley, 1982; Pressley, Levin, & Miller, 1982), conforming in its essential aspects to what Sternberg et al. (1983) argue constitutes an optimal contextual strategy: providing explicit tuition in using internal and external context cues to infer meanings. Despite this "new, improved" version of a contextual strategy, it proved inferior to the keyword method with respect to definition recall, just as other semantic strategies have (Levin et al., 1982; Pressley, Levin, Kuiper, Bryant, & Michener, 1982; Pressley, Levin, & Miller, 1982).

FACILITATING OTHER VOCABULARY-LEARNING OBJECTIVES

At present, there is an insufficient research base to provide conclusive answers to questions pertaining to differences among strategies on other vocabulary-learning measures (see Pressley, Levin, & Delaney, 1982, for data that are available). For example, in the case of remembering the new vocabulary words in response to their definitions (backward recall), we are aware of the conditions under which mnemonic strategies will and will not be facilitative (Pressley & Levin, 1981). In addition, some preliminary evidence bearing on measures of vocabulary comprehension will be discussed shortly. However, controlled empirical comparisons of different strategy variations on, for example, a Sternberg et al. (1983) vocabulary-inference task or on an Asher (1981) action-performance task have not yet appeared in the literature. Neither is it known how various strategies would fare with respect to students learning to differentiate the meaning nuances of conceptually similar vocabulary items (Lesgold, 1983). Comparative effectiveness speculations are therefore truly speculations, for as Levin and Pressley (1983) show, even the most intuitively appealing hypotheses are frequently disconfirmed when subjected to empirical test.

THE ITEM RESTRICTIVENESS ISSUE

Can mnemonic vocabulary-learning strategies be applied successfully to only a very restricted set of items? Pressley, Levin, and Delaney (1982) conclude that positive keyword effects have been obtained with a wide variety of vocabulary items, including concrete nouns with simple definitions, such as *lamia*-"devil" (McGivern & Levin, 1983); nouns with more complex definitions, such as *gaskin*-"part of the hind leg of a horse" (Pressley, Levin, Kuiper, Bryant, & Michener, 1982); abstract nouns and verbs, such as *surplus*-"having some left over, having more than was needed" and *persuade*-"when you talk someone into doing something" (Levin et al., 1982); and other parts of speech, such as the adjective *exorbitant*-"more than it should be" (Levin et al., 1984). In each of these mentioned studies, keyword-instructed students recalled significantly more definitions than did either no-strategy control subjects or subjects instructed to use various semantic strategies. In summary, then, definition-recall benefits associated with mnemonic strategies are not restricted to concrete nouns with simple definitions.

The item-restrictiveness issue would also be valid, however, if the keyword method were effective only when investigators handpicked particular items to be included in a vocabulary list. For example, Is it critical that only vocabulary items with obvious, concrete keywords be included? Based on the empirical data available, the answer to this question is clearly, no. In Experiment 1 of the Levin et al. (1982) study, an educator who wanted to challenge the keyword method selected items that had difficult-to-discover keywords and that represented complex concepts. In Experiment 2 of that study, items were randomly selected from the materials used in a previous vocabulary-learning study in which semantic and control strategies had been compared (Gipe, 1979). And in the Levin et al. (1984) study, items were selected primarily on the basis of their being hospitable to the semantic-mapping classification strategy.

In all of these experiments, the investigators had to work within the constraints of the selected items when deriving plausible keywords and interactions. Although in many cases reasonably good keywords could be derived (e.g., *angel* for *angler; camera* for *camaraderie*), in many other cases they could not (e.g., *exercise* for *exorbitant; orchestra* for *equestrian*); the same is true of the keyword/meaning interactions created. The important thing to remember in this discussion is that, even though there were individual item differences associated with the use of specific strategies, averaged across items the keyword method produced considerably higher levels of recall in each experiment. (It should be mentioned that the keyword method has also been applied successfully to other curricular content, such as learning the states and capitals and the order of U.S. presidents; Levin, 1981. In situations such as these, where an a priori item set is clearly defined, a researcher must "make do" with whatever items are in that set.) Because of such findings, the item-restrictiveness issue does not appear to be warranted; but even if it were valid with respect to use of the keyword method, alternative mnemonic strategies could be devised (e.g., first-letter mnemonics) to deal with the selected items (see Pressley, Levin, & Delaney, 1982, p. 84).

The preceding discussion follows from the results of research based on elementary and junior high school students who were *provided* keywords and keyword illustrations for all items. It might be hypothesized that item characteristics (in particular, keyword obviousness) would play a more prominent role with keyword-instructed adult subjects who are required to generate their own keywords and interactive images. Particularly in a *sophisticated* adult population (e.g., a select college population), it might be expected that when vocabulary items are not associated with obvious keywords, keyword-instructed subjects would perform less effectively than would subjects left to their own devices. Assuming that under such circumstances, the generation of keywords would be a long, tedious (and, in some cases, unsuccessful) process, sophisticated adult learners given no-strategy control instructions might spontaneously apply their own efficient vocabulary-learning strategies within the same time frame. This hypothesis is consistent with a large volume of research documenting that adults are spontaneously strategic in associative-learning tasks, and much more so than children (e.g., Pressley, 1982). However, before firm general conclusions bearing on this hypothesis can be reached in a vocabulary-learning context, the relevant research needs to be conducted.

THE MEMORY VERSUS COMPREHENSION ISSUE

Thus far, the data considered have been based on students' memory for the definitions of vocabulary items. That is, following one or more trials of studying vocabulary words and their definitions, the student is required to recall the definition of each vocabulary word as it is presented. It is on such measures of definition memory that the mnemonic keyword method has proven to be particularly beneficial. But what about other vocabulary-learning outcomes? In particular, how would mnemonic-strategy subjects perform on measures that are thought to require more than pure associative-memory processes? The issue here is whether mnemonic strategies produce a lower level of understanding, or comprehension, of the vocabulary word than that achieved via automatic processes or semantic strategies.

Before responding to this issue, we must make a few preliminary remarks. Although *memory* can be easily operationalized, exactly what constitutes *comprehension* is not clear. There has been much debate in the language-development and reading literatures about what it means to comprehend something. Not surprisingly, therefore, there is little consensus about how comprehension should be assessed. What are appropriate comprehension tasks? Should they include problem-solving or conceptual components? Should they be designed to exclude memory factors? Questions such as these continue to plague psychologists. Nonetheless, various tasks have been accepted as tapping comprehension of vocabulary items more than does simple definition recall. These tasks include requiring subjects to make decisions regarding the proper use or appropriateness of vocabulary items in context (i.e., in sentences or paragraphs). In other comprehension tasks students must construct plausible sentences using the vocabulary items or supply missing sentence parts in a cloze format. We do not claim that such tasks measure comprehension optimally; neither do we claim that they measure comprehension to the exclusion of memory (see also Levin, Dretzke, Pressley, & McGivern, in press). Rather, we rely on these tasks both because they are commonly included by investigators studying comprehension and because they have some face validity as measures of comprehension.

In several recent studies in which a variety of measures were utilized, students' comprehension did not suffer from mnemonic vocabulary instruction (Aurentz, 1982; Levin et al., in press; Levin et al., 1984; McDaniel & Pressley, 1984; Pressley, Levin, & Miller, 1981a). In fact, in each study cited, there was at least one reliable indicator that mnemonic-strategy instruction *facilitated* students' comprehension. For example, in the Pressley, Levin, and Miller study, keyword learners statistically outperformed no-strategy control subjects on tests of sentence judgments (Experiment 1 and 2), sentence completion (Experiment 3), and sentence construction (Experiment 4). Similar significant effects were obtained in the other studies listed, even when the keyword method was compared with semantic strategies. The mean comprehension performance of mnemonically taught students was never even slightly lower than the mean of semantic or no-strategy control groups. Research in progress continues to address this fascinating memory-versus-comprehension issue; and, obviously, the role of individual differences with respect to strategy use and comprehension deserves special consideration.

THE ATTENTIONAL ISSUE

What are the underlying psychological mechanisms responsible for the effectiveness of mnemonic vocabulary-learning strategies? Based on the examples provided thus far, one might conclude that the explanation for the success of mnemonic strategies is primarily attentional; in particular, that the provision of novel illustrations heightens students' attention, which in turn improves their learning. According to this explanation, differences between mnemonic and nonmnemonic strategies need not be described in terms of theories of *learning* per se. Rather, because illustrations are provided with mnemonic strategies but not with alternative techniques, differences in performance can be accounted for as byproducts of *motivation and attention*.

However, this is a "pseudo-issue" (Higbee, 1978; Levin & Pressley, 1983) for several reasons. First, the effectiveness of mnemonic strategies does not depend on the use of illustrations. Unlike the adaptation we have frequently used with children (see Figure 6.1), the original keyword method of vocabulary learning (Atkinson, 1975) was based on subjects generating their own internal visual images. Moreover, verbal (i.e., nonpictorial) versions of the keyword method are equally effective (e.g., Pressley, Levin, & Miller, 1981b). Our personal attraction to the pictorial-illustration version of the method follows from a desire to reduce the information-processing load associated with visual imagery generation—a load that is known to be excessive for certain kinds of learners (e.g., young children and educationally handicapped students).

Although mnemonic successes based on nonpictorial variations serve to counter an exclusive pictorial-attention account of mnemonic strategy effects, it could still be argued that the crucial component of such strategies is an attentional one. That is, mnemonic strategies capture students' attention more effectively than do alternative strategies. The most compelling evidence against this argument comes from the Levin et al. (1982) study, where a nonmnemonic-picture condition was included. In that condition, students were shown contextual illustrations that resembled those shown to keyword subjects in all but one respect. The one ingredient that was missing was the mnemonic (keyword) link, which, according to the three associative-mnemonic R's (Levin, 1983), is critical. For example, a nonmnemonic picture version of Figure 6.1 would include characters who were not angels (with the dialogue modified accordingly). Compared to students in a mnemonic-picture condition, those in the nonmnemonic-picture condition remembered far few vocabulary definitions. In fact, the level of performance of nonmnemonic-picture subjects was virtually identical to that of students in a no-strategy control condition (see also Pressley, 1977; Pressley & Levin, 1978; and Pressley, Samuel, Hershey, Bishop, & Dickinson, 1981).

It should also be emphasized that the degree of attention and involvement required of semantic-strategy users typically is at least as great as that required of mnemonic-strategy users (Levin et al., 1982; Levin et al., 1984; Pressley, Levin, Kuiper, Bryant, & Michener, 1982; Pressley et al., 1981b). This is especially apparent in the Levin et al. (1984) study, where students in the contextual analysis and semantic mapping treatments were actively involved in experimenter-directed activities throughout the treatment, including responding to questions and providing their own examples and instances (see also Pressley, Levin, Kuiper, Bryant, & Michener, 1982, Experiment 3). One would be hard pressed to argue that such semantic-processing activities were not as attention-demanding as were the activities required of mnemonic subjects. An especially strong argument against the position that reduced definition recall in semantic-strategy conditions is due to reduced attention in those conditions is the finding that certain aspects of vocabulary learning are better in semantic than in mnemonic conditions. Consistent with Morris, Bransford, and Franks' (1977) notion of "*transfer appropriate processing,"* Pressley, Levin, Kuiper, Bryant, and Michener (1982) found that students' nonassociative memory of foreign vocabulary meanings per se (i.e., memory without the requirement of having to recall specific vocabulary/meaning associations) was better in two semantic conditions than in a mnemonic-keyword condition. In that same series of experiments, Pressley et al. showed that students' associative memory of vocabulary items and their meanings was much greater in the mnemonic than in either semantic or control conditions.

For all of these reasons, it is not apparent to the present authors how a simple attentional explanation of mnemonic effects can satisfactorily account for the existing data.

THE LONG-TERM RETENTION ISSUE

RETENTION OF THE CONTENT

The issue of whether or not mnemonic-strategy effects are durable (i.e., whether they persist over time) is of extreme practical importance. Thus, it is one thing for the keyword method to produce performance benefits on tests administered immediately following learning, but it is quite another to find that similar benefits are produced on retention tests administered the next month, the next week, or even the next day. Such longer-term effects are clearly necessary to convince educators of the value of a particular method or strategy.

To date, little research has been conducted on the durability of mnemonic-strategy effects in the vocabulary-learning domain. In two studies that examined the issue, however, one detected significant long-term (1-week delay) mnemonic effects (Levin et al., 1984) and one did not (Aurentz, 1982). Recent research in other educational domains has indicated that mnemonic effects do persist beyond the immediate testing situation (e.g., Levin, Shriberg, Miller, McCormick, & Levin, 1980; McCormick & Levin, 1984; Peters & Levin, 1984; Shriberg, 1982). Thus, we are cautiously optimistic regarding the prognosis for producing enduring effects in the area of mnemonic vocabulary instruction.

RETENTION OF THE STRATEGY

We have just considered the issue of retention of the content initially learned. A related issue concerns retention of the strategy itself, as subsequently applied both to the same class of materials (maintenance) and to somewhat different ones (transfer). Thus, the issue is whether or not a mnemonic strategy is so highly specific to the task and items to which it was originally applied that it will not be maintained in, or transferred to, other similar situations. Both Pressley and Dennis-Rounds (1980) and O'Sullivan and Pressley (1984) found that adolescent and adult subjects can transfer the keyword method to untrained domains (see also Jones & Hall, 1982), although much more explicit instruction about when the strategy can and should be used is required with children than is necessary with adults (O'Sullivan & Pressley, 1984; Pressley, Levin, & Ghatala, 1984). In addition, Levin et al. (1980) suggest that the complexity of the instructed mnemonic strategy should be considered with regard to the issue of strategy retention. Although further research is required to determine the limits and limiting variables associated with mnemonic-strategy retention, the available data suggest that explicit instruction in one domain can produce a generalizable cognitive skill.

THE MNEMONIC DEPENDENCE ISSUE

The final issue to be considered in this section is one originally raised by Higbee (1978) with respect to the retention of mnemonically learned content. According to Higbee, critics of mnemonic techniques often argue that information learned mnemonically can never be remembered as an independent entity because it is linked forever to the originally applied "artificial" mnemonic device. For example, Are the mnemonically taught students of the Levin et al. (1984) study so dependent on the vocabulary-learning mnemonics they were shown that even when those children are "old and gray" they will continue to associate fishermen with angels? Though intuitively appealing, this mnemonic-dependence issue has not been investigated directly.

Certain empirical data in hand suggest that the issue may be overstated, however. In the first place, if the information to be retrieved were so closely tied to the invented mnemonics, then there would be far more instances of retrieval confusions than have appeared in the literature. That is, the level of recall of mnemonic subjects would be adversely affected because the information they recalled would be more evenly split between fact (the target information) and fiction (the invented mnemonics). The documented impressive recall levels of mnemonic-strategy users suggest that nothing approaching this kind of mnemonic confusion exists. Secondly, even though successful mnemonic subjects do indeed initially go through the systematic retrieval process that includes the originally invented mediators, there is no reason to believe that they must do so indefinitely. In studies measuring subjects' response latencies, dramatic increases have been found in the retrieval speed of mnemonically taught subjects following repeated testing on the same items (e.g., Corbett, 1977; Levin, Dretzke, McCormick, Scruggs, McGivern, & Mastropieri, 1983). Thus, with practice, either such subjects become not as dependent on the original mnemonics or the mnemonic retrieval process becomes more automatized. Questions related to mnemonic-strategy use and speed of information processing and retrieval are likely to provide a fertile area of investigation for individual-differences researchers.

Finally, it should be noted that even if it does turn out that the retrieval of mnemonic-strategy users is forever connected to the invented mnemonics, that connection is not necessarily bad. One can imagine, for example, mnemonic dependence being far less consequential in the case of recalling the meanings of individual vocabulary items than in the case of conversational fluency. Once again, specific instructional objectives need to be taken into account before specific instructional strategies are either praised or condemned.

MNEMONIC VOCABULARY STRATEGIES
AND INDIVIDUAL-DIFFERENCES ISSUES

As far as the present volume is concerned, issues related to individual differences in the mnemonic vocabulary-learning domain are especially pertinent. As we indicated earlier, although research on mnemonic strategies and individual differences is not abundant, the work that does exist points to reliable individual differences associated with mnemonic-strategy use. What is most striking from an educator's perspective, however, is that the aptitude-by-treatment interactions that have materialized have been *ordinal* rather than *disordinal* in nature (Cronbach & Snow, 1977). That is, there is no evidence to suggest that mnemonic strategies are better suited to certain kinds of students and that alternative strategies are better suited to other kinds of students. Rather, and consistent with the findings in other learning-strategy domains (see Levin, 1976), the interactions produced here reveal that students of *all* kinds can benefit from mnemonic vocabulary-learning strategies, but to different degrees. The *can* in the preceding sentence is critical, however, and bears clarification. Even though (1) conclusions about the effectiveness of mnemonic strategies are basically generalizable across students (rather than restricted to certain kinds of students), what will be seen is that (2) different *variations* of a mnemonic strategy often need to be devised to suit the needs of different kinds of students. Let us consider these two issues in turn.

MNEMONIC STRATEGIES
AND COGNITIVE ABILITY DIFFERENCES

A statement often made about specially designed instructional techniques is that even though they may be helpful to, or even necessary for, the poorer learners, they will not benefit the better learners. As the argument goes, poorer learners do not spontaneously apply effective learning strategies and, thus, need all the help they can get. Maximally structured learning materials (e.g., experimenter-provided pictures) and strategies (e.g., very explicit instructions and retrieval prompts) should therefore be both beneficial and welcomed for such students (Pressley, 1983). In contrast, better learners presumably use their own effective learning strategies. Consequently, any aids or suggestions provided to them would not be expected to be beneficial. Even worse, the alternative techniques provided might differ so fundamentally from the better learners' own preferred strategies that the alternative techniques would be disruptive to the point of producing a negative effect on performance.

Although the empirical evidence relating to this concern is somewhat equivocal, it clearly does not support the extreme ("negative effect for better learners") version of the argument. In the first place, some of the mnemonic strategies investigated to date have been either sufficiently complex or sufficiently difficult to execute in the study time allotted that only subjects of higher ability were able to execute the strategy effectively (e.g., Griffith & Actkinson, 1978; Levin et al., 1983). Moreover, in none of the research reported in the literature have subjects of higher ability suffered from the application of mnemonic strategies, and in most cases they have benefitted as much as or more than subjects of lesser ability. For example, in a sample of military personnel, Griffith (1981) found that the keyword method of foreign-vocabulary learning was equally effective for subjects at different levels of general technical aptitude. In the Levin et al. (1984) native-vocabulary study with elementary school children, two schools were selected to represent very different achievement levels: one in which the mean scores were considerably above the national norms and the other in which the mean achievement scores were somewhat below the national norms. Students from both populations remembered more vocabulary definitions following keyword method instruction than they did following instruction in either of two semantic strategies (semantic mapping and contextual analysis). Similarly, in a foreign-vocabulary study with adults, Pressley, Levin, Nakamura, Hope, Bispo, and Toye (1980) found that both very skilled and less skilled vocabulary learners benefitted from use of the keyword method. Inasmuch as only a large main effect of instructed strategy (keyword method versus no-strategy control) was produced—with no interaction between instructed strategy and learner type (skilled versus less skilled)—it was concluded that both types of learners benefitted substantially and equally from mnemonic-strategy instruction.

The one piece of evidence to contraindicate the detection of positive mnemonic effects with better learners comes from a native-vocabulary study by McDaniel and Pressley (1984, Experiment 1). In that study, based on a very select college population, students were provided either keyword or no-strategy control instructions. It was found that although students with lower verbal aptitude scores (Scholastic Aptitude Test [SAT] scores less than 560) benefitted from use of the keyword method, higher-ability students (SAT scores greater than 560) did not. (At the same time, it should be noted that the performance of the higher-ability students did not *suffer* from using the keyword method.)

The foreign-vocabulary results of Pressley et al. (1980) appear to be at odds with the native-vocabulary results of McDaniel and Pressley (1984). However, it is important to mention that the participants in the former study were from a less selective state university, whereas the subjects in the latter study were enrolled in a selective private institution. Thus, there was probably a considerable difference in the level of ability represented in the two studies. In particular, the better students in the Pressley et al. study may have been more comparable to the poorer students in the McDaniel and Pressley study. Thus, a hypothesis arising from this and other related research with adults (see Pressley, Levin, & Delaney, 1982) is that for the very best (i.e., most sophisticated) adult learners in the population, use of the keyword method will not improve their vocabulary learning beyond the level attained via use of their own preferred strategies.

In addition to including samples of extremely able adult learners in order to assess the validity of this hypothesis, future studies should examine more direct measures of subjects' *processing* (e.g., subjects' differential attention to different items, response latencies, and postexperimental reported strategies) than has been done in most mnemonic strategy investigations to date. These more direct process measures are critical for evaluating the hypothesis that when positive keyword effects are not produced with high-ability subjects, it is because subjects in the control condition are spontaneously employing effective strategies. The hypothesis follows from previous observations of moderate correlations between subjects' reports of effective strategy deployment and their level of associative recall (e.g., Levin et al., 1983; Pressley, Levin, Digdon, Bryant, & Ray, 1983; Pressley, Levin, Kuiper, Bryant, & Michener, 1982).

Other evidence documenting the generalizability of mnemonic strategy effects across subject populations is reviewed by Pressley, Levin, and

Delaney (1982). In their review, a number of individual-differences dimensions, such as verbal versus spatial ability (Delaney, 1978), vocabulary knowledge (McGivern & Levin, 1983), creativity (Mullis, 1976), and chronological age (Pressley & Levin, 1978), are considered. Students varying on each of these dimensions were able to benefit from some form of mnemonic strategy instruction. Studies by Mastropieri, Scruggs, and Levin (in press-a, in press-b) and Berry (1985), which included learning-disabled students can be added to the list of generalizable mnemonic successes. Mastropieri et al. (in press-a) also found that mnemonic instruction was extremely effective for educable mentally retarded junior high school students. After reviewing the individual-differences data, Pressley, Levin, and Delaney conclude that positive mnemonic effects have been obtained with "subjects of varying ages and abilities, namely, 3-year-olds to adults, including good and poor vocabulary learners as well as native and foreign English speakers (p. 70)." The most recent data, based on educationally handicapped students, clearly support this conclusion.

MNEMONIC STRATEGIES AND METACOGNITIVE
ABILITY DIFFERENCES

Before concluding this section, let us mention yet another individual-differences dimension that probably affects the efficacy of mnemonic-strategy instruction. As discussed earlier in this chapter, there is evidence that at least some learners maintain and transfer mnemonic strategies. Borkowski and Pressley (1983) hypothesize that wide-ranging metamemorial knowledge about a strategy is a major prerequisite for such maintenance and transfer. Thus, subjects who understand the utility of a trained strategy, how the strategy can be modified, and the strategy's range of potential application should be more likely than those without such knowledge to continue to use the strategy in other situations.

In support of this position, there is a substantial body of literature documenting correlational linkages between children's metamemory and strategy maintenance and transfer (see Pressley, Borkowski, & O'Sullivan, 1985; and Borkowski & Pressley, 1983; for an overview). Notably, transfer of simple elaborative strategies has been shown to depend on the metacognitive state of the learner (Kendall, Borkowski, & Cavanaugh, 1980; Kurtz, Reid, Borkowski, & Cavanaugh, 1982), although no study correlating metacognitive awareness and use of the keyword method has yet been reported. Given the broad base of evidence supporting the relationship between subjects' metacognitions and strategy transfer, it is reasonable to assume that whether children acquire a general cognitive skill as a result of keyword instruction depends on their strategy metacognitions. On the other hand, O'Sullivan and Pressley (1984) demonstrated with fifth and sixth graders that by providing supplementary metacognitive information concerning the efficacy of the keyword method during instruction, it was possible to increase children's transfer of that strategy. Indeed, it was possible through such an intervention to increase transfer to its theoretical maximum, as defined by the level of performance observed under explicit strategy instruction in the transfer domain (see Pressley & Dennis-Rounds, 1980). Thus, although individual differences in strategic knowledge may affect strategy maintenance and transfer in children, high levels of each are to be expected following instruction that presumably fills in the metacognitive gaps for learners who would otherwise be deficient.

Finally, we have already indicated in regard to general cognitive ability levels that it is the poorer students who are likely to profit most from mnemonic-strategy instruction. That argument pertains specifically to the initial learning context in which strategy instructions or materials are provided. A completely complementary argument can be made with respect to strategy retention, however, for it is in just such different situations that the better students would be expected to summon up previously learned strategies and reapply them. As with the other hypotheses put forth in the present section, this one, too, awaits empirical test.

THE STRATEGY VARIATIONS ISSUE

O'Sullivan and Pressley's (1984) demonstration that some learners require metacognitive-enriched strategy instruction in order to transfer a mnemonic strategy successfully brings us back to the second point mentioned in the introduction to this section, namely, that different strategy variations may need to be devised for different kinds of students. Thus, we do not claim that exactly the same mnemonic strategy, or the same kind of mnemonic-strategy instruction, will be maximally effective—or effective at all—for all students. In fact, the existing data suggest that different variations of mnemonic strategies should be developed for different learners. By *variations,* we refer both to modifications (often simplifications) of an existing mnemonic strategy and to alternative mnemonic strategies, although, as will become apparent, the distinction between these two types of variations is not always clear-cut.

Pressley, Levin, and Delaney (1982) claim that the keyword method of vocabulary learning has proven beneficial for subjects ranging from three-year-olds to adults. However, the specific operationalizations of the keyword method that are needed to ensure success are quite different with subjects at the two age extremes. Adults can employ the relating component of the method in exactly the way prescribed by Atkinson (1975), that is, by generating their own internal interactive images. In contrast, young children require presentation of actual illustrations of the keywords and definitions in order for the method to be effective (e.g., Pressley & Levin, 1978; Pressley, Samuel, Hershey, Bishop, & Dickinson, 1981). More concrete support is also required for subjects at the lower levels of other ability dimensions (Berry, 1985; McGivern & Levin, 1983). Thus, we conclude that for certain kinds of students, mnemonic strategies will be effective only if explicit concretizations of the three R components are provided in order to circumvent the information-processing demands associated with self-generation of mnemonic images.

In a related vein, Delaney (1978) administered both the original imagery version and a verbal variation of the keyword method to college students who differed in spatial and verbal abilities. Consistent with the two individual-differences issues discussed here, Delaney found that (1) students of all abilities benefitted from the imagery version of the strategy (i.e., mnemonic facilitation generalized across ability levels), but (2) only subjects with higher verbal ability benefitted from the verbal keyword-strategy variation. And in a mnemonic prose-learning context, Shriberg (1982) noted the tendency of a similar interaction to emerge—in this case, one between students' reading achievement level and the type of mnemonic representation of the factual information to be remembered (see Levin, 1982, for a more detailed description of the study). Specifically, only students of higher reading ability benefitted from phonetic-based mnemonic representations, whereas all students profitted from semantic-based mnemonic representations. If replicable, such mnemonic-strategy variation-by-ability interactions could be exploited to maximize students' learning in the important educational domains of vocabulary development and reading comprehension.

To summarize, with respect to facilitating students' memory for vocabulary definitions, mnemonic strategy effects appear to be more general than restricted. Although interactions between strategies and student characteristics have emerged, these ordinal interactions are of the form that mnemonic vocabulary-learning strategies are *at least as effective* as alternative strategies for all types of students, with the magnitude of the mnemonic advantage varying reliably with students' level of aptitude, skill, or achievement. In addition, interactions between mnemonic-strategy variations and student characteristics have been reported, with the implication that mnemonic techniques should be adapted to different types of students. Finally, it should be noted that research on mnemonic strategies and individual differences has been sparse. Given the brief history of research on mnemonic vocabulary-learning strategies (Atkinson, 1975), however, we expect more educationally relevant aptitude-by-treatment interactions to be uncovered in the future.

CONCLUDING REMARKS

Various educators and researchers have begun to suggest that mnemonic vocabulary-learning strategies are being "oversold" relative to more naturalistic semantic strategies (e.g., Sternberg et al., 1983). However, based on the available empirical data, the present authors are convinced that exactly the opposite is true; that is, it is the semantic strategies that have been oversold. For example, in a widely cited work on vocabulary instruction, Johnson and Pearson (1978) recommend that to learn the meanings of new words, students should engage in a number of semantic-processing activities, such as semantic mapping, semantic feature analysis, and contextual analysis. The specific techniques recommended by Johnson and Pearson are commonly advocated by curriculum theorists (e.g., Dale, O'Rourke, & Bamman, 1971; Harris & Smith, 1976; Spache & Spache, 1977), and teachers are known to be using these techniques in their classrooms (e.g., Addy, 1941; Petty, Herold, & Stoll, 1968); see also Ahlfors (1979). Despite the current popularity of semantic approaches, however, we have not seen a single empirical study in which subjects instructed in a semantic strategy have outperformed subjects instructed in a mnemonic strategy on any educationally valued vocabulary-learning measures. In fact, and as has been reiterated throughout this chapter, on measures of definition recall (and, in some cases, vocabulary comprehension), it is the subjects instructed in a mnemonic strategy who clearly outperform subjects instructed in a semantic strategy. Moreover, mnemonic techniques are sufficiently powerful to overcome any potential negative effects associated with sources of individual differences; this is something that should be of particular interest to readers of this volume.

Traditions die hard. So do educators' intuitions about what constitute "good" techniques. Even sophisticated learners do not always behave in the most rational or efficient manner. For instance, Pressley et al. (1984) described the mnemonic keyword method and an ineffective rehearsal strategy to a group of college students in a vocabulary-learning context. The students were then instructed to choose the method that would permit them to remember the most vocabulary items following a period of study. When these students made their choices in the absence of an opportunity to try the two methods, they were about equally divided in their selection of the keyword method and the rehearsal strategy. However, when the students made their strategy selections following brief experience with each on a practice list (where half the items were studied via the keyword method and half via rote rehearsal), the preponderance of students selected the keyword method. Pressley et al. were further able to establish that it was not until the test on the practice items that students came to realize that the keyword method was a good deal more effective than rote rehearsal. Similar strategy-selection shifts were found by Pressley et al. in their experiments with children, but these occurred only after the researchers provided more explicit feedback concerning the children's relative performance under the two strategies. Pressley, Ross, Levin, and Ghatala (in press) found this to be true with respect to children's choices between mnemonic (keyword) and semantic (naturalistic-context) vocabulary-learning strategies. Data such as these support the adage, "People do not always know what is good for them."

Of course, one cannot blame the educational community for being reluctant to base a change in practices on psychological analyses of the learning process, given the long history of psychologists suggesting instructional innovations that have failed (see Mann, 1979). It is entirely appropriate for the educational community to demand stringent criteria of proof before widespread acceptance and dissemination of any new technique is justified. In order for mnemonic vocabulary instruction to claim a seat of respectability in the classroom, several related events need to occur. First, researchers must continue to accumulate data documenting the effectiveness of mnemonic techniques under controlled conditions. Second, effectiveness must be demonstrated with respect to a variety of vocabulary-learning objectives, not just verbatim recall of definitions. At the same time, however, it must be recognized that mnemonic techniques are unlikely to be a panacea for facilitating *all* desired vocabulary-learning objectives—just as any other technique is unlikely to be a panacea either. Third, the benefits of mnemonic techniques must prove to be durable enough to withstand the test of time. Educators, parents, and politicians will not be impressed if the positive effects that are "here today" are "gone tomorrow." Fourth, mnemonic successes in the laboratory must be translated into similar successes in the classroom. Fifth, such successes must be highly publicized in the media. Sixth, mnemonic techniques must find their way into the textbooks and teaching materials of commercial publishers. And finally, mnemonic techniques must overcome the negative connotations associated with them: that they are "tricks," that they are "crutches," that they inhibit comprehension, and so on (see Higbee, 1978). Even if the first six events do occur, it is the final one that will be the persisting nemesis of mnemonic techniques in the classroom. Why? Because, as history has consistently shown us with respect to most avenues of change, it takes far more than fact to combat the fiction of firmly entrenched personal philosophies.

REFERENCES

Addy, M. L. Development of a meaning vocabulary in the intermediate grades. *Elementary English Review,* 1941, *18,* 22–26.

Ahlfors, G. *Learning word meanings: A comparison of three instructional procedures.* Unpublished doctoral dissertation, University of Minnesota, 1979.

Anglin, J. M. *Word, object, and conceptual development.* New York: Norton, 1977.

Asher, J. J. The total physical response (TPR): Theory and practice. *Annals of the New York Academy of Science,* 1981, *379,* 324–331.

Atkinson, R. C. Mnemotechnics in second-language learning. *American Psychologist,* 1975, *30,* 821–828.

Aurentz, J. *Self-instruction and the keyword method: Effects upon vocabulary usage.* Unpublished manuscript, Florida State University, 1982.

Bellezza, F. S. Mnemonic devices: Classification, characteristics, and criteria. *Review of Educational Research,* 1981, *51,* 247–275.

Berry, J. K. Doctoral research in progress. University of Wisconsin, 1985.

Borkowski, J. G., & Pressley, M. *Children's metamemory: Cognitive interventions and prior knowledge states.* Unpublished manuscript, University of Notre Dame, 1983.

Brown, A. L. The role of strategic behavior in retardate memory. In N. R. Ellis (Ed.), *International review of research in mental retardation.* New York: Academic Press, 1974.

Brown, A. L. Knowing when, where, and how to remember: A problem of metacognition. In R. Glaser (Ed.), *Advances in instructional psychology,* Hillsdale, N.J.: Erlbaum, 1978.

Brown, R. *A first language: The early stages.* Cambridge, MA: Harvard University Press, 1973.

Ceci, S. J. Extracting meaning from stimuli: Automatic and purposive processing of the language-based learning disabled. *Topics in Learning and Learning Disabilities,* 1982, *2,* 46–53.

Clark, H. H., & Clark, E. V. *Psychology and language: An introduction to psycholinguistics.* New York: Harcourt, Brace, Jovanovich, 1977.

Corbett, A. T. Retrieval dynamics for rote and visual image mnemonics. *Journal of Verbal Learning and Verbal Behavior,* 1977, *16,* 233–246.

Cronbach, L. J., & Snow, R. E. *Aptitudes and instructional methods.* New York: Irvington, 1977.

Dale, E., O'Rourke, J., & Bamman, H. A. *Techniques of teaching vocabulary.* Palo Alto, CA: Field, 1971.

Delaney, H. D. Interaction of individual differences with visual and verbal elaboration instructions. *Journal of Educational Psychology,* 1978, *70,* 306–318.

Flavell, J. H. Developmental studies of mediated memory. In H. W. Reese & L. P. Lipsett (Eds.), *Advances in child development and behavior* (Vol. 5). New York: Academic Press, 1970.

Gipe, J. Investigating techniques for teaching word meanings. *Reading Research Quarterly,* 1979, *14,* 624–644.

Griffith, D. An evaluation of the key-word technique for the acquisition of Korean vocabulary by military personnel. *Bulletin of the Psychonomic Society,* 1981, *17,* 12–14.

Griffith, D., & Actkinson, T. R. Mental aptitude and mnemonic enhancement. *Bulletin of the Psychonomic Society,* 1978, *12,* 347–348.

Grosjean, J. *Life with two languages.* Cambridge, MA: Harvard University Press, 1982.

Harris, L. A., & Smith, C. B. *Reading instruction: Diagnostic teaching in the classroom.* New York: Holt, Rinehart, & Winston, 1976.

Higbee, K. L. Some pseudo-limitations of mnemonics. In M. M. Gruneberg, P. E. Morris, & R. N. Sykes (Eds.), *Practical aspects of memory.* New York: Academic Press, 1978.

Jenkins, J. R., & Dixon, R. Vocabulary learning. *Contemporary Educational Psychology,* 1983, *8,* 237–260.

Johnson, D. D., & Pearson, P. D. *Teaching reading vocabulary.* New York: Holt & Co., 1978.

Jones, B. F., & Hall, J. W. School applications of the mnemonic keyword method as a study strategy by eighth graders. *Journal of Educational Psychology,* 1982, *74,* 230–237.

Kendall, C. R., Borkowski, J. G., & Cavanaugh, J. C. Maintenance and generalization of an interrogative strategy by EMR children. *Intelligence,* 1980, *4,* 255–270.

Kurtz, B. E., Reid, M. K., Borkowski, J. G., & Cavanaugh, J. C. On the reliability and validity of children's metamemory. *Bulletin of the Psychonomic Society,* 1982, *19,* 137–140.

Lesgold, A. M. Discussant's comments for *Applied imagery research in the 1980s: Traditional themes and new approaches.* Symposium presented at the annual meeting of the American Educational Research Association, Montreal, April 1983.

Levin, J. R. What have we learned about maximizing what children learn? In J. R. Levin & V. L. Allen (Eds.), *Cognitive learning in children: Theories and strategies.* New York: Academic Press, 1976.

Levin, J. R. The mnemonic '80s: Keywords in the classroom. *Educational Psychologist,* 1981, *16,* 65–82.

Levin, J. R. Pictures as prose-learning devices. In A. Flammer & W. Kintsch (Eds.), *Discourse processing.* Amsterdam: North-Holland, 1982.

Levin, J. R. Pictorial strategies for school learning: Practical illustrations. In M. Pressley & J. R. Levin (Eds.), *Cognitive strategy research: Educational applications.* New York: Springer-Verlag, 1983.

Levin, J. R., Dretzke, B. J., McCormick, C. B., Scruggs, T. E., McGivern, J. E., & Mastropieri, M. A. Learning via mnemonic pictures: Analysis of the presidential process. *Educational Communication and Technology Journal,* 1983, *31,* 161–173.

Levin, J. R., Dretzke, B. J., Pressley, M., & McGivern, J. E. In search of the keyword method/vocabulary comprehension link. *Contemporary Educational Psychology,* in press.

Levin, J. R., Johnson, D. D., Pittelman, S. D., Hayes, B. L., Levin, K. M., Shriberg, L. K., & Toms-Bronowski, S. A comparison of semantic- and mnemonic-based vocabulary-learning strategies. *Reading Psychology,* 1984, *5,* 1–15.

Levin, J. R., McCormick, C. B., Miller, G. E., Berry, J. K., & Pressley, M. Mnemonic versus nonmnemonic vocabulary-learning strategies for children. *American Educational Research Journal,* 1982, *19,* 121–136.

Levin, J. R., & Pressley, M. Understanding mnemonic imagery effects: A dozen "obvious" outcomes. In M. L. Fleming & D. W. Hutton (Eds.), *Mental imagery and learning.* Englewood Cliffs, N.J.: Educational Technology Publications, 1983.

Levin, J. R., Shriberg, L. K., Miller, G. E., McCormick, C. B., & Levin, B. B. The keyword method in the classroom: How to remember the states and their capitals. *Elementary School Journal,* 1980, *80,* 185–191.

Mann, L. *On the trail of process.* New York: Grune & Stratton, 1979.

Margosein, C. M., Pascarella, E. T., & Pflaum, S. W. Effects of semantic mapping instruction on vocabulary and comprehension of junior high school students. *Journal of Early Adolescence,* 1982, *2,* 185–194.

Mastropieri, M. A., Scruggs, T. E., & Levin, J. R. Direct instruction vs. mnemonic instruction: Relative benefits for exceptional learners. *Journal of Special Education,* in press. (a)

Mastropieri, M. A., Scruggs, T. E., & Levin, J. R. Mnemonic strategy instruction with learning-disabled adolescents. *Journal of Learning Disabilities,* in press. (b)

McCormick, C. B., & Levin, J. R. A comparison of different prose-learning variations of the mnemonic keyword method. *American Educational Research Journal,* 1984, *21,* 379–398.

McDaniel, M. A., & Pressley, M. Putting the keyword method in context. *Journal of Educational Psychology,* 1984, *76,* 598–609.

McLaughlin, B. *Second-language acquisition in childhood*. Hillsdale: NJ: Erlbaum, 1978.

McGivern, J. E., & Levin, J. R. The keyword method and children's vocabulary learning: An interaction with vocabulary knowledge. *Contemporary Educational Psychology*, 1983, *8*, 46–54.

Meacham, J. A. The development of memory abilities in the individual and in society. *Human Development*, 1972, *15*, 205–228.

Morris, C. D., Bransford, J. D., & Franks, J. J. Levels of processing versus transfer appropriate processing. *Journal of Verbal Learning and Verbal Behavior*, 1977, *16*, 519–533.

Morris, P. E., & Cook, N. When do first letter mnemonics aid recall? *British Journal of Educational Psychology*, 1978, *48*, 22–28.

Mullis, L. L. *Second-language vocabulary learning: An interaction of the keyword method, mediation, and level of divergent thinking*. Unpublished doctoral dissertation, Mississippi State University, 1976.

Nelson, K., Rescorla, L., Gruendel, J., & Benedict, H. Early lexicons: What do they mean? *Child Development*, 1978, *49*, 960–968.

O'Sullivan, J. T., & Pressley, M. Completeness of instruction and strategy transfer. *Journal of Experimental Child Psychology*, 1984, *38*, 275–288.

Paivio, A., & Desrochers, A. Effects of an imagery mnemonic on second language recall and comprehension. *Canadian Journal of Psychology*, 1979, *33*, 17–28.

Peters, E. E., & Levin, J. R. *Effects of a mnemonic imagery strategy on good and poor readers' prose recall*. Paper presented at the annual meeting of the American Educational Research Association, New Orleans, April 1984.

Petty, W. T., Herold, C. P., & Stoll, E. *The state of the knowledge about the teaching of vocabulary*. Champaign, IL: National Council of Teachers of English, 1968.

Pressley, M. Children's use of the keyword method to learn simple Spanish vocabulary words. *Journal of Educational Psychology*, 1977, *69*, 465–472.

Pressley, M. Elaboration and memory development. *Child Development*, 1982, *53*, 296–309.

Pressley, M. Making meaningful materials easier to learn: Lessons from cognitive strategy research. In M. Pressley & J. R. Levin (Eds.), *Cognitive strategy research: Educational applications*. New York: Springer-Verlag, 1983.

Pressley, M., Borkowski, J. G., & O'Sullivan, J. T. Children's metamemory and the teaching of memory strategies. In D.-L. Forrest-Pressley, G. E. MacKinnon, & T. G. Waller (Eds.), *Metacognition, cognition, and human performance* (Vol. 1). Orlando: Academic Press, 1985.

Pressley, M., & Dennis-Rounds, J. Transfer of a mnemonic keyword strategy at two age levels. *Journal of Educational Psychology*, 1980, *72*, 575–582.

Pressley, M., Heisel, B. E., McCormick, C. B., & Nakamura, G. V. Memory strategy instruction with children. In C. J. Brainerd & M. Pressley (Eds.), *Verbal processes in children: Progress in cognitive development research*. New York: Academic Press, 1982.

Pressley, M., & Levin, J. R. Developmental constraints associated with children's use of the keyword method of foreign language vocabulary learning. *Journal of Experimental Child Psychology*, 1978, *26*, 359–372.

Pressley, M., & Levin, J. R. The development of mental imagery retrieval. *Child Development*, 1980, *51*, 558–560.

Pressley, M., & Levin, J. R. The keyword method and recall of vocabulary words from definitions. *Journal of Experimental Psychology: Human Learning and Memory*, 1981, *7*, 72–76.

Pressley, M., & Levin, J. R. (Eds.), *Cognitive strategy research: Psychological foundations*. New York: Springer-Verlag, 1983.

Pressley, M., Levin, J. R., & Delaney, H. D. The mnemonic keyword method. *Review of Educational Research*, 1982, *52*, 61–91.

Pressley, M., Levin, J. R., Digdon, N., Bryant, S. L., & Ray, K. Does method of item presentation affect keyword method effectiveness? *Journal of Educational Psychology,* 1983, *75,* 686–691.

Pressley, M., Levin, J. R., & Ghatala, E. S. Memory-strategy monitoring in adults and children. *Journal of Verbal Learning and Verbal Behavior,* 1984, *23,* 270–288.

Pressley, M., Levin, J. R., Kuiper, N. A., Bryant, S. L., & Michener, S. Mnemonic versus non-mnemonic vocabulary-learning strategies: Additional comparisons. *Journal of Educational Psychology,* 1982, *74,* 693–707.

Pressley, M., Levin, J. R., & Miller, G. E. How does the keyword method affect vocabulary comprehension and usage? *Reading Research Quarterly,* 1981, *16,* 213–226. (a)

Pressley, M., Levin, J. R., & Miller, G. E. The keyword method and children's learning of foreign vocabulary with abstract meanings. *Canadian Journal of Psychology,* 1981, *34,* 283–287. (b)

Pressley, M., Levin, J. R., & Miller, G. E. The keyword method compared to alternative vocabulary-learning strategies. *Contemporary Educational Psychology,* 1982, *7,* 50–60.

Pressley, M., Levin, J. R., Nakamura, G. V., Hope, D. J., Bispo, J. G., & Toye, A. R. The keyword method of foreign vocabulary learning: An investigation of its generalizability. *Journal of Applied Psychology,* 1980, *65,* 635–642.

Pressley, M., & Mac Fayden, J. Mnemonic mediator retrieval at testing by preschool and kindergarten children. *Child Development,* 1983, *54,* 474–479.

Pressley, M., Ross, K. A., Levin, J. R., & Ghatala, E. S. The role of strategy utility knowledge in children's strategy decision making. *Journal of Experimental Child Psychology,* in press.

Pressley, M., Samuel, J., Hershey, M. M., Bishop, S. L., & Dickinson, D. Use of a mnemonic technique to teach young children foreign language vocabulary. *Contemporary Educational Psychology,* 1981, *6,* 110–116.

Shatz, M. On the development of communicative understanding: An early strategy for interpreting and responding to messages. *Cognitive Psychology,* 1978, *10,* 271–301.

Shaughnessy, J. J. Personal Communication, September 1982.

Shriberg, L. K. *Comparison of two mnemonic encoding strategies on children's recognition and recall of abstract prose information.* Unpublished doctoral dissertation, University of Wisconsin, 1982.

Spache, G. D., & Spache, E. B. *Reading in the elementary school.* Boston: Allyn & Bacon, 1977.

Sternberg, R. J., Powell, J. S., & Kaye, D. B. Teaching vocabulary-building skills: A contextual approach. In A. C. Wilkinson (Ed.), *Classroom computers and cognitive science.* New York: Academic Press, 1983.

Torgesen, J. K. The learning disabled child as an inactive learner. *Topics in Learning and Learning Disabilities,* 1982, *2,* 45–52.

van Daalen-Kapteijns, M. M., & Elshout-Mohr, M. The acquisition of word meanings as a cognitive learning process. *Journal of Verbal Learning and Verbal Behavior,* 1981, *20,* 386–399.

7

Assaying, Isolating, and Accommodating Individual Differences in Learning a Complex Skill

Dennis E. Egan and Louis M. Gomez

INTRODUCTION

Using Individual Differences to Discover
What Makes a Cognitive Skill Difficult

Our main goal in this chapter is to demonstrate how analyses of individual differences can lead to understanding complex cognitive skills. As a case study, we analyze individual differences in the difficulty of learning computer text editing. We first show that the amount of difficulty people experience as they learn a particular text-editing system strongly correlates with certain characteristics of the learners. Using component task analyses, we then attempt to isolate where these characteristics exert their effects. The task analyses suggest how individual differences in learning difficulty depend on the design of the text-editing system. When we observed people learning a system having a different design, the set of characteristics correlating with learning difficulty changed in predictable ways. Taken together, our studies suggest how the design of computer editing systems and the training of text-editing skills might accommodate a wide range of learners.

While the substantive results we present are narrowly constrained to one particular cognitive skill, the methods of analysis are quite general. Other complex skills (e.g., those involving human–computer interaction, decision making, or troubleshooting) might be understood in terms of the mental capacities or other characteristics that correlate with the difficulty of learning the skills. Task analyses of such skills may show that the effects of some learner characteristics are concentrated in particular component operations. Skilled performance might be improved and patterns of correlation altered by changing specific components or by supporting them with training. The analysis of individual differences may be a useful general approach to problems of system design and training for complex skills.

Assaying, Isolating, and Accommodating
Individual Differences

THE APPROACH

Our approach employs three steps: assaying, isolating, and accommodating individual differences. This approach derives its power from the information contained in individual differences in the difficulty of learning a complex skill. In general, individual differences in measures of learning difficulty reflect the capabilities required for skill acquisition and skilled performance.

ASSAYING INDIVIDUAL DIFFERENCES

The first step of our approach is to take a complex, poorly understood task and try to discover the important sources of individual differences in learning the task. In the present studies we did this by developing reasonable measures of task performance and examining correlations between these measures and certain learner characteristics. To gain some understanding in this step, the learner characteristics should be simpler and better understood than the performance being analyzed. While we do not yet have a "periodic table" of well known learner characteristics, we do have useful methods, tasks, and data to aid in this assay. The initial assay should account for individual differences in the performance of the complex task in terms of a small number of simple learner characteristics.

ISOLATING INDIVIDUAL DIFFERENCES

The next step of the method is to isolate the effects of learner characteristics in particular task components. We attempted to do this in the present studies by analyzing performance on text-editing component operations that we simulated with paper and pencil tasks. In general, measures such as overall time or errors for a complex task like text editing are composites that combine the time or errors of task components (see Egan, 1978). To know how to change a complex task to accommodate individual differences, one or more components of the task causing those differences must be isolated. This step should produce a task decomposition showing how the individual differences that are found important in overall performance exert their effects in certain component processes.

ACCOMMODATING INDIVIDUAL DIFFERENCES

The final step of our approach addresses individual differences in complex performance by removing or changing specific task components. This step was carried out in the present studies by comparing one form of text editing (line editing) with a modified form (display editing) in which a particular component process was greatly simplified. One general way of accommodating individual differences in a complex skill is to redesign the tools used in performing the skill so as to minimize the difficulty of particular task components. Providing different processing strategies or performance aids are other ways to accommodate individual differences.

PROPOSED APPROACH VERSUS CONVENTIONAL USE
OF INDIVIDUAL DIFFERENCES

The present approach of using individual differences to understand and to do something about the difficulty of learning a skill can be distinguished from the conventional use of job-related individual differences. Historically, the purpose of analyzing individual differences has been to predict who would perform well in a given job. The method amounted to an actuarial process in which a host of learner characteristics were assessed and were used to predict subsequent criteria such as grades in a training course, records of advancement, or supervisors' ratings. Equations were developed to relate the most predictive learner characteristics to future job success. If the measures of the characteristics were reliable and valid predictors of the criteria, the equations could be used to select people for the job.

The approach we propose differs from this conventional approach in its goal and methods. First, the goal of the proposed approach is to find a way to enable a wide range of people to acquire a complex skill that may be part of a job. We seek better ways to accommodate people by system design and training rather than better ways to select people for a given job. The description of people who have more or less difficulty learning a complex skill is an important first step in our approach. However, it is only a step, which serves to focus further efforts at system design and training.

The methods of the proposed and conventional approaches also differ. In the conventional approach, a predictor variable can be absolutely opaque and still be considered very useful if it accounts for unique variance in a criterion measure. Understanding why a particular variable is related to job success is not important, and inexpensive composite measures (e.g., quick-scoring intelligence tests) are often used as predictors in conventional work. In contrast, the approach we propose values simpler variables that assess specific cognitive capacities: Ideally, the difficulty of learning a complex skill can be predicted by a small set of characteristics that are well understood. This goal may not be achieved in every practical situation, but it should be regarded as the optimal outcome of the assay of individual differences.

The reason for emphasizing simpler variables is that they can be linked more easily than composites to manipulations that might influence their importance. Knowing that more intelligent people learn a skill faster does not suggest how to change conditions to make learning easier. Knowing that learning a skill correlates with a rather specific capability (e.g., a specific memorial, spatial, or verbal aptitude, or a specific kind of experience) may suggest how to improve the situation. Much the same point has been made regarding aptitude variables in instructional studies of Aptitude × Treatment interactions (Bracht, 1970; Cronbach & Snow, 1977; Glaser, 1980).

COGNITIVE CORRELATES AND COMPONENTS

Our approach borrows heavily from two recent experimental approaches to understanding cognitive differences. Experiments 1, 2, and 4 in the following discussion involve a method similar in some respects to the method of *cognitive correlates* (see Hunt, Frost, & Lunneborg, 1973). The goal of that method is to explain individual differences in a complex ability (e.g., verbal ability) by relating them to differences in simpler, theoretically based information-processing measures (e.g., the time to make a physical or name match of alphabetic characters). In the approach we propose, the same kinds of techniques are used, but the goal is to understand a particular skill rather than a general ability.

The third experiment reported here uses a method akin to *componential analysis* (Sternberg, 1977), another technique recently developed to study cognitive differences. That technique breaks down test-like tasks (e.g., analogical reasoning) into a series of component mental operations (e.g., encoding, inference, mapping, application, and response). While we use component task analyses, the components we derive for computer text editing are more macroscopic and task specific than the kind of components identified for reasoning and other aptitude-test–like tasks. In general, the experiments reported here focus on text editing as a particular cognitive skill and are aimed at finding out what the correlates of that skill are and how they might be altered.

COMPUTER TEXT EDITING AS A CASE STUDY

THE IMPORTANCE OF THIS SKILL

We chose to apply our approach to computer text editing because it makes a good case study. Computer text editing is first and foremost an important skill. Many people's introduction to computers begins as they learn to deal with a computer text editor to create and change files of typewritten material. Computer text editing is, therefore, a gateway to many jobs and services involving the computer. Programmers use text editors to write and modify their programs. Secretaries use text editors to prepare memos, correspondence, and documents. Clerks use text editors to process bills, inventories, and records of sales. Librarians use text editors to store and retrieve catalog entries. In the future, many executives may use text editors to write messages on computer mail systems or to annotate memoranda. Some form of text editing also may be required for many home information systems.

SELECTIVE REVIEW OF RESEARCH ON TEXT EDITING

Because of its growing importance, text editing has been the subject of a number of recent human-factors studies. One set of studies has focused on the efficiency with which people who are highly skilled at text editing can perform routine editing tasks (see Embly & Nagy, 1981, for a review). Card, Moran, and Newell (1980b) developed the Keystroke-Level Model that accounts for editing time in terms of the sum of time taken for individual mental and physical operations required by the task. The same authors (1980a) proposed a more-macroscopic GOMS (Goals, Operators, Methods, Selection) model for describing the editing strategies that experts use. Roberts (1980; see also Roberts & Moran, 1983) and Allen and Scerbo (1983) have used the Keystroke-Level Model with varying success to predict the efficiency of different editing systems for a variety of tasks.

A second set of studies analyzed linguistic aspects of the difficulty of learning computer text editing (see Black & Sebrechts, 1981, for a review). Black and Moran (1982), as well as Barnard, Hammond, MacLean, and Morton (1982), show that more-discriminating command names are easier to learn than fairly general names for the same operations. However, Landauer, Galotti, and Hartwell (1980) found that about the same amount of difficulty is involved in learning a minimal editor whether command names are a commonly used set, a set carefully selected to be natural, or a randomly selected set. In a study by Gomez, Egan, and Bowers (in press) randomly selected names were more difficult to recall after a week than were commonly used names. However, the effects of different names on actual editing performance was very small and was confined to the initial time taken to read the instructional manual. In addition to these studies of command names, other studies have investigated such linguistic factors as command arguments and the syntax of names and arguments.

In a third set of studies, first-time users of computers "think out loud" as they read a self-instructional manual and attempt text-editing exercises—a situation similar to the one we explore in the following sections of this chapter. Bott (1979) used verbal protocols obtained in this situation to define the semantic knowledge people bring to bear as they learn computer text editing. Bott found that certain knowledge structures often were activated inappropriately and that learners tried to assimilate new concepts to these structures. This process led to such basic problems as misinterpreting that a command was something a person gives a computer, rather than vice versa. Lewis and Mack (1982) found similar evidence. For example, their subjects often generalized from their prior experiences with typewriters and concluded that certain editing operations would or would not work. The activity of their subjects also was extremely difficult to control because subjects failed to read or follow directions, often got into tangled problems, or did not realize what they had done or why.

DIFFERENCES AMONG PEOPLE
LEARNING COMPUTER TEXT EDITING

Not only is computer text editing an important skill, but it is also one that is likely to produce large individual differences in learning difficulty. Consider the heterogeneity of the group of people who try to learn this skill: The group includes people in all the occupations mentioned earlier (clerks, executives, homemakers, librarians, programmers, secretaries, etc.). The characteristic aptitudes, education, and backgrounds of the people in these occupations tends to differ widely; and a sample of learners across these occupations is likely to show much more variability in learning a skill than, say, a sample drawn from any single occupation, educational level, or age group.

Indeed, as we began our pilot studies, we were not disappointed by the range of learning difficulty reported for learning text editing. Teachers of a word-processing course noted that some of their students seemed to have little difficulty and mastered the basics of text editing rather quickly, while other students struggled, resisted, and ultimately dropped out of the course. In the experiments reported here and others we have done, the variability in difficulty due to different subjects has been many times greater than that due to experimental factors we have manipulated in text-editor design and instruction.

POSSIBILITIES FOR ACCOMMODATING INDIVIDUAL DIFFERENCES

Perhaps the most intriguing aspect of using computer text editing as a case study is the possibility for accommodating individual differences in this skill. Exactly what a learner must sense and how a learner must respond can be changed by fairly simple alterations to the human–computer interface of a text-editing system. This flexibility of design may make it possible to accommodate the characteristics of different individuals or groups by tailoring the tools they use.

If the actual design of a system cannot be changed, important individual differences still might be accommodated by training or performance aids. We have ample evidence from other cognitive skills that procedures can be taught for coping with human limitations, and performance supports can be developed to reduce cognitive demands; for example, waiters in restaurants use mnemonic strategies or paper and pencil to reduce the cognitive demands of their jobs. People can be taught to execute very efficient problem-solving strategies that might not occur to them spontaneously (Egan, 1983). The capacities that limit reasoning performance depend on the reasoning strategy people adopt (MacLeod, Hunt, & Matthews, 1978; Sternberg & Weil, 1980). These facts suggest that we might be able to train specific procedures or provide performance aids to reduce the cognitive demands made on people trying to learn a complex skill like text editing.

SUMMARY

In this chapter, we present an approach to understanding complex cognitive skills. The approach is to assay, isolate, and accommodate individual differences in the difficulty of learning the skill. Whereas individual differences have been used previously to predict the performance of a given skill, our approach attempts to use individual differences to understand and ultimately change the requirements of a skill. The approach borrows from methods embodied in recent research on cognitive correlates, cognitive components, and Aptitude × Treatment interactions. We use computer text editing as a case study because of its growing importance, its potential for producing large individual differences in learning difficulty, and the intriguing possibilities for accommodating individual differences in this skill.

EXPERIMENT 1: ASSAYING INDIVIDUAL DIFFERENCES IN THE DIFFICULTY OF LEARNING COMPUTER TEXT EDITING

Two Preliminary Studies

INTERVIEWS

We first investigated potential correlates of text editing difficulty that were suggested in individual interviews of a teacher and four students from a course on computer text editing. The students were secretaries or clerks who had volunteered for the course. Two of the students had performed extremely well in the course, two had performed poorly. The students and teacher were asked how potentially successful and unsuccessful students might be distinguished before the course began. They were also asked what kind of preparation students should have for the course, what they found difficult in the course, and a number of other similar questions.

Several potential correlates of the difficulty of learning text editing emerged in the interviews. The characteristics most often cited as distinguishing successful and unsuccessful learners were affective ones. Successful learners were described as "confident" in their approach toward computers, "willing to try things on their own," and "motivated." Unsuccessful learners were described as lacking these qualities. People's attitudes toward and experience with machines and mechanical devices were also suggested as potential predictors of success. Several of the subjects cited learners' age as a possible correlate of success since older students seemed to have more difficulty than younger ones in the course. "Step-by-step logical thinking" was also noted by some subjects as a characteristic of successful students. Some subjects mentioned that a good memory was required to deal with the different editing commands. Regarding preparation for the course, the only particular requisite skill noted in the interviews was touch typing.

A questionnaire was constructed to assess potentially important learner characteristics suggested by the interviews. In addition to asking for subjects' age and typing speed, sections of the questionnaire were designed to assess specific candidate variables. One section assessed subjects' attitudes towards computers. In this section, subjects rated how well they agreed or disagreed with statements like, "I am afraid of computers," "When a computer is introduced to a job, people lose control over their work," and "I would really enjoy learning how to use a computer." A second section assessed subjects' experience with and desire to use computer-like devices (automated bank tellers, programmable timers, etc.) and mechanical devices (kitchen appliances, garage door openers, etc.). A third section asked subjects to write detailed step-by-step directions telling a child how to execute a complicated procedure. This question attempted to measure systematic thinking abilty; but it took a long time to complete and proved difficult to score, so it was not used in the main study. The final section assessed knowledge of special terms used in computer text editing. This section was included because of reported difficulty in remembering text-editing commands and because of the findings of the research reviewed earlier concerning the effects of naming and semantic knowledge. Each of these sections in the questionnaire was comprised of 7–12 specific questions.

VERBAL PROTOCOLS

In a second preliminary study, six adult female subjects completed the questionnaire and then gave verbal protocols as they worked through a tutorial on computer text editing. This study led to modifying the questionnaire and training materials for use in the first main experiment. It also suggested some useful measures of subjects' actual text-editing performance.

METHOD

LEARNER CHARACTERISTICS ASSESSED

The learner characteristics assessed in the main study were those measured by the questionnaire and three standard psychometric tests. The tests were selected as reliable measures of distinct characteristics that might be important in learning computer text editing. The Controlled Associations Test (Ekstrom, French, & Harman, 1976) measures the fluency with which subjects can generate semantic associations. This test was selected because associational fluency might be important in verbal processes such as understanding and remembering the names of text-editing commands. The Building Memory Test (Ekstrom, French, & Harman, 1976) measures the ability to remember the spatial arrangement of objects. This test was selected because spatial memory might be important in such processes as visualizing changes made to a text, finding the locations of changes, and matching spatial patterns of text. Finally, the Nelson–Denny Reading Test (1973) was used to measure subjects' reading skill. The total score on this test is a composite of vocabulary and reading comprehension subscores. We expected that reading skill would be important because the text-editor tutorial involved comprehending written instructions.

SUBJECTS

Thirty-three adult women participated in the study. All subjects knew how to touch-type but had little or no experience working with computers. Subjects ranged from 28 to 62 years of age ($\overline{X} = 44.7$) and typically were homemakers from the Murray Hill, New Jersey, area. In all of our studies, subjects sampled in this way have mean scores beyond the fifteenth grade level on the reading test and approximately one standard deviation above the mean of published norms (Ekstrom, French, & Harman, 1976) for military enlisted personnel on standard aptitude tests, such as the Controlled Associations and Building Memory Tests.

TEXT-EDITOR TUTORIAL

Subjects were given a tutorial consisting of an instructional manual and an interactive program that presented exercises to be completed after each section of the manual. The manual introduced six text-editing operations: adding lines of text, removing lines of text, inserting characters within a line, removing characters within a line, replacing lines of text, and exchanging one character string for another within a line. These operations involved using three text-editing commands in different ways. There were six sections to the manual, each describing how to perform an operation. After reading a section, subjects performed an exercise practicing the operation they had just learned.

Exercises were presented by the interactive program that was a preprocessor to the UNIX™ editor, *Ed* (see Landauer, Galotti, & Hartwell, 1980, for a complete description of the preprocessor). When a subject was ready to start an exercise, she typed "START N" where *N* was the number of the exercise. The program then read a file containing the text to be edited for that exercise. The program stored every keystroke made by the subject and recorded the elapsed time whenever the subject pressed the return key. The exercises were performed on a Texas Instruments 700 terminal running at 300 baud (bits per second), and connected to a VAX 11/780 with a UNIX time-sharing system.

The three *Ed* commands the subjects learned were *append,* used to add text following a specified line, *delete,* used to remove lines of text, and *substitute,* used to exchange one string of characters for another within a line of text. The ordinary form of each command required a line number followed by the first letter of the command (see Figure 7.1). The text editor that

	EXAMPLE OF "APPEND"	EXAMPLE OF "DELETE"	EXAMPLE OF "SUBSTITUTE"
ORIGINAL TEXT DISPLAY	JACK AND JILL WENT UP THE HILL TO FETCH A PAIL JACK FELL DOWN	LITTLE MISS MUFFET SAT ON A TUFFET EATING HER CURDS AND WHEY EATING HER CURDS AND WHEY ALONG CAME A SPIDER	MARY HAD A LITTLE LAMB WHOSE FLEECE WAS WHITE AS RAIN AND EVERYWHERE THAT MARY WENT THE LAMB WAS SURE TO GO
COMMAND	3a < RETURN > OF WATER < RETURN > • < RETURN >	3d < RETURN >	2s/RAIN/SNOW/ < RETURN >
MODIFIED TEXT DISPLAY	JACK AND JILL WENT UP THE HILL TO FETCH A PAIL OF WATER JACK FELL DOWN	LITTLE MISS MUFFET SAT ON A TUFFET EATING HER CURDS AND WHEY ALONG CAME A SPIDER	MARY HAD A LITTLE LAMB WHOSE FLEECE WAS WHITE AS SNOW AND EVERYWHERE THAT MARY WENT THE LAMB WAS SURE TO GO.

FIGURE 7.1   Examples of commands learned in the text-editor tutorial.

subjects learned was a subset of the actual *Ed* editor. This experimental version of *Ed* printed all the text in the edit buffer at the terminal after each command to provide immediate feedback of the results of each operation. In all other respects, the editor that our subjects learned was similar to many other line-oriented text editors.

GENERAL PROCEDURE

The study was run in two parts on different days. In the first part, the psychometric tests and questionnaires were administered in a group testing situation. In the second part, subjects returned 1 to 4 days after the testing to work through the text-editor tutorial. Generally, two subjects participated at a time. They were isolated from each other, but were allowed to ask the experimenter for help if, after attempting an exercise, they could not figure out how to proceed.

RESULTS

PERFORMANCE MEASURES

Given a fairly complete record of the subjects' interactions with the terminal, we selected three primary measures to characterize the difficulty of learning computer text editing. The first measure was reading time, the total amount of time a subject spent between finishing an exercise and starting the next. This measure was obtained simply by subtracting the time when subjects completed the last operation on exercise $N - 1$ from the time when subjects entered "START N" and then summing these times for all exercises.

The second measure was execution time per successful change. This is a productivity measure equalling the total amount of time a subject spent working the six exercises divided by the number of required text changes that the subject ultimately accomplished.

The final performance measure we used was first-try errors. This measure was defined as the number of times a subject made an error on her first attempt to start an exercise or make a change required by the exercise divided by the total possible number of such first attempts. We chose to analyze first-try errors rather than some other measure of error, because first-try errors were made when all subjects were in a common situation. After a first-try error, additional errors tended to occur in idiosyncratic situations and proved very difficult to score.

Table 7.1 gives the means, standard deviations, and ranges of the three measures. The large ranges of the performance measures (e.g., 0–62% for first-try errors) substantiates the claim that individual differences in this task are sizable. Reading time and first-try errors were essentially uncorrelated ($r = .09$). Execution time per successful change correlated significantly with reading time ($r = .45$, $p < .01$) suggesting that part of the execution time may be spent rereading the manual. Execution time per successful change correlated even more strongly with first-try errors ($r = .70$, $p < .01$) suggesting that the amount of time it takes a person to accomplish an editing change depends strongly on whether first attempts at interacting with the system are correct.

SELECTION OF LEARNER CHARACTERISTICS

A small set of learner characteristics, the Building Memory Test score, the Nelson–Denny Reading Test score, and age, were selected for further analysis. Each of these characteristics correlated particularly strongly ($p < .001$) with reading time, execution time per successful change, or first-try errors (see Table 7.2). Moreover, with one exception these were the only

TABLE 7.1

Means, Standard Deviations, and Ranges of the Performance Measures

Measure	$\overline{X}$	SD	Range
Reading time (min)	11.6	3.9	5.4–25.7
Execution time per successful change (min)	3.1	1.4	1.2–6.5
First-try errors (%)	28.1	15.6	0.0–62.5

TABLE 7.2
Correlations between Learner Characteristics and Performance Measures

Measure	Spatial memory test	Reading test	Age
Reading time	− .41*	− .66***	.11
Execution time per successful change	− .58***	− .41*	.57***
First-try errors	− .49**	− .21	.50**

*$p < .05$. **$p < .01$. ***$p < .001$.

predictors that correlated reliably with any of the three criterion measures. None of the correlations between the three criterion measures and the Controlled Associations Test, Estimated Typing Speed, or the attitude scale approached significance (all r's had $p > .10$). One measure of the frequency of using mechanical devices had a marginally significant correlation with execution time per successful change, but this correlation was in the unexpected direction—higher frequency of use tended to be associated with greater text-editing difficulty. The only other reliable correlation was that between the score on the special vocabulary test and execution time per successful change ($r = -.36, p < .05$). People who did not know the meaning of command names (e.g., *append*) and other terms (e.g., *buffer*) used in the instructional manual tended to have more difficulty than those who could accurately define such terms before the experiment began.

The three predictor variables on which we focus capture rather distinct characteristics of the learners in our studies. In this experiment, for example, the Building Memory Test score correlated reliably but not extremely highly with the Nelson–Denny Reading Test score ($r = .36, p < .05$), and did not correlate reliably with age ($r = -.16, p > .10$). The Nelson–Denny Reading Test score was uncorrelated with age ($r = .00$). Similar patterns were found in each of the subsequent studies.

MULTIPLE REGRESSION MODELS

For each of the performance measures, a simultaneous multiple regression equation was obtained giving the best-fitting linear prediction based on reading skill, spatial memory, and age (see Table 7.3). Each regression equation accounted for a sizable portion of the variance in the corresponding performance measure.

The pattern of regression coefficients in Table 7.3 has a fairly straightforward interpretation. On one hand, reading skill appears to predict those aspects of learning difficulty that directly involve reading, namely, reading time and execution time per successful change (which presumably includes some time to reread the manual). On the other hand, spatial memory

TABLE 7.3
Standardized Coefficients from Multiple Regression Equations

Measure	Spatial memory test	Age	Reading test	R^2
Reading time	−.18	.09	−.60***	.475**
Execution time per successful change	−.41**	.50***	−.26*	.627***
First-try errors	−.39**	.44**	−.08	.426**

$*p < .05.$ $**p < .01.$ $***p < .001.$

and age appear to be strongly related to the part of learning that involves interacting with the computer. These two variables are the only ones contributing reliably to the prediction of first-try errors, and they join reading skill in making significant contributions to the variance in execution time per successful change.

DISCUSSION

Two results of this attempt to assay individual differences in the learning of text editing encouraged us. The huge variability in subjects' difficulty of learning text editing apparently is systematic, and a large part of it can be captured by a small number of distinct characteristics.

Neither of these results need have been true. The difficulty experienced by people in their first encounter with a computer might have proved totally idiosyncratic or random. This study demonstrates, however, that people's performance the first time they interact with a computer text editor can be predicted to some extent. Furthermore, not all characteristics of people were equally important in predicting performance. The majority of characteristics we assessed (including typing speed, verbal aptitude, several aspects of previous experience, and attitudes towards computers) did not correlate with any of the three criteria we chose. Instead, time spent in reading was predicted primarily by a reading test, but time spent and errors made interacting with the computer were predicted by spatial memory and age.

EXPERIMENT 2:
A REPLICATION AND EXTENSION

OBJECTIVES AND METHOD

Given the large number of potential predictor variables in the first study, we were concerned that some of our correlational results may have capitalized on chance. The main reason for the second experiment was simply to see if our first assay of individual differences could be reproduced. Rather than strictly replicating the conditions of the first study, we used different texts for the exercises, different terminals (video terminals instead of printing terminals), and a different baud rate (1200 instead of 300 baud) for this study. Since execution times in the first study were on the order of minutes, we felt that the specific terminals and baud rate used were not limiting factors of text-editing performance. Consequently, the results of our first study should be robust with respect to these factors, which are found to vary in everyday text-editing situations.

This experiment also was designed to investigate the learning that took place as subjects worked through the tutorial. Our first study did not allow for a precise assessment of learning, because the actual commands that subjects used changed with each exercise. The correlational results we found also could have been due mainly to the novelty of people's first interaction with a computer. Predictors of text-editing difficulty might change as learning progresses. For example, a characteristic, such as typing speed, that apparently is not important early in practice may become more important later.

To get a better assessment of learning and the correlates of performance after some practice, we had subjects work through the same tutorial on two occasions separated by a week. We chose to look at retention over a week's time because some courses on computer skills meet approximately once a week. One week also seemed to be a reasonable estimate of the interval between successive uses of a computer system by "casual users"—people who occasionally use a computer system for a specific purpose but never expect to become experts.

This study also asked whether the age and spatial-memory measures found to predict learning difficulty might actually be standing for something else. Subjects' age, for example, might actually be important because age tends to be correlated with other characteristics such as the amount of education a person has, the recency of education, or perhaps attitudes towards computers. A measure of spatial memory might be correlated with the difficulty of learning text editing because memory in general is important or, perhaps, because the Building Memory test involves strategies akin to reasoning. We did not have data on these covariates of age and spatial memory in the first study.

For these reasons, we assessed several potential predictors of text-editing skill in addition to age, spatial memory, and reading skill. Subjects indicated how many years of education they had completed, gave the date of the last classroom course they had taken, and completed an extensive questionnaire about their attitudes towards computers. Subjects also took a test of associative memory (the Object–Number Test) and a test of logical reasoning (The Diagramming Relations Test; see Ekstrom, French, & Harman, 1976) in addition to the spatial-memory and reading tests used previously. These additional measures allowed us to ask whether age and spatial memory make unique contributions to the prediction of learning difficulty.

The general procedure in this study was similar to the previous one. Subjects ($N = 41$) completed the tests and questionnaire (asking for education, age, typing speed, and attitudinal data) in one session, then returned within several days to work through the text-editor tutorial for the first time (Day 1). Exactly 1 week later, subjects worked through the same tutorial for a second time (Day 2). The experiment also included a factor manipulating the names of text-editing commands between subjects (see Gomez, Egan, & Bowers, in press), but the results of this manipulation were small and restricted to the reading time measure. The data presented here have been collapsed across the naming factor after first standardizing the dependent variables within each condition.

RESULTS AND DISCUSSION

LEARNING

Table 7.4 leaves little doubt that subjects learned from their first interaction with a computer and remembered enough to improve their performance a week later. All three performance measures show an improvement of 30–40% for Day 2 compared to Day 1. Despite this overall improvement, all three measures also continue to show a sizable range of individual performance on Day 2. For example, some subjects on Day 2 still made an error half the time they first tried a problem, but other subjects made a first-try error on only 3% of their attempts.

Correlations among the three criterion measures for Day 1 and Day 2 are given in Table 7.5. The correlation between Day 1 and Day 2 observations for a given measure is an estimate of the measure's reliability. Reliabilities where .67 for reading time, .68 for first-try error and .86 for execution time per successful change. Just as in Experiment 1, execution time per successful change correlated strongly with the number of first-try errors subjects made. However, the pattern of correlations involving reading time in this experiment was quite different from that found in the first study (see below).

PREDICTORS OF TEXT-EDITING DIFFICULTY

Spatial memory and age again were the best predictors of text-editing difficulty. Each of these measures correlated significantly with first-try errors and execution time per successful change on both Day 1 and Day 2. We used forward stepwise multiple regression to investigate which variables made reliable and unique contributions to predicting performance. Candidates for the regression models included all the variables (logical reasoning,

TABLE 7.4

Comparison of Performance Measures on Day 1 and Day 2[a]

Measure	$\overline{X}$	SD	Range
Reading time (min)			
Day 1	10.4	2.8	4.7–17.7
Day 2	6.8	2.4	2.1–10.9
Execution time per successful change (min)			
Day 1	2.2	1.0	0.8–5.8
Day 2	1.5	0.9	0.6–4.4
First-try errors (%)			
Day 1	26.4	13.3	2.8–66.7
Day 2	17.8	11.1	2.8–50.0

[a] For each measure, the mean for Day 1 is significantly larger than the mean for Day 2 ($p < .001$).

associative memory, estimated typing speed, and years since last class, in addition to spatial memory, age, and reading skill) that correlated significantly with either first-try errors or execution time per successful change on either day. The variable that accounted for the most variance in performance entered the regression equation first. Additional variables entered if they accounted for at least marginally significant ($p > .10$) additional variance in performance.

Results (see Table 7.6) for Day 1 indicated that age and spatial memory were the only variables to enter the equation for each performance measure. For Day 2, subjects' estimated typing speed as well as spatial memory and age accounted for significant and unique variance in performance. A backward stepwise regression procedure, in which all candidate variables are entered at first and then removed one by one if they do not make a significant contribution, produced the same final equations.

TABLE 7.5

Correlations among Criterion Measures[a]

Measure	Measure				
	2	3	4	5	6
1. Day 1 reading time	−.31	−.46	.67	−.33	−.45
2. Day 1 execution time per successful change		.84	−.16	.86	.71
3. Day 1 first-try errors			−.22	.71	.68
4. Day 2 reading time				−.07	−.20
5. Day 2 execution time per successful change					.86
6. Day 2 first-try errors					

[a] For $N = 41$, $r \geq .31$ ($p < .05$) and $r \geq .40$ ($p < .01$).

TABLE 7.6
Standardized Coefficients from Multiple Regression Equations[a]

Measure	Spatial memory test	Age	Estimated typing speed	R^2
Execution time per successful change				
Day 1	$-.32$*	.39**	—	.352***
Day 2	$-.41$**	.37**	$-.36$**	.521***
First-try errors				
Day 1	$-.28$	.30	—	.235**
Day 2	$-.38$*	.32*	$-.23$	.380***

*$p < .05$. **$p < .01$. ***$p < .001$. For coefficients with no asterisk, $.10 > p > .05$.

Whereas the results for first-try errors and execution time per successful change were very similar to those found in the first study, results for reading time differed across the studies in the following ways:

1. Reading time on Day 1 in this study was significantly shorter ($p < .02$) than reading time for the identical text in the previous study.
2. Reading time on Day 1 of this study also was not strongly associated with reading skill as it had been previously. The correlation between reading time and the Nelson–Denny Reading Test score was $r = .18$ ($p > .10$) compared to $r = -.66$ ($p < .001$) in Experiment 1. These correlations across experiments differ reliably ($z = 4.03, p < .001$).
3. Subjects who spent more time reading on Day 1 in this study made fewer first-try errors ($r = -.46, p < .01$) and had faster execution times ($r = -.31, p < .05$). Precisely the opposite pattern was found in the previous experiment.

What factor in the second study caused people to reduce the amount of time spent reading and altered the relationships among reading time, reading skill, and other performance measures? One possibility is that the terminals and baud rates used in the studies affected the amount of time people chose to spend reading before attempting an exercise. The faster, quieter, video terminals in Experiment 2 may have imposed a smaller penalty for making errors compared to the slower, noisier terminals in Experiment 1. This explanation is consistent with a study (Grossberg, Wiesen, & Yntema, 1976) showing that people spend more time thinking before entering commands on a system when the system's response time is slow. The change of terminals and baud rate in the second study improved the system's response time over that in Experiment 1. Subjects in the second study may have been induced to attempt to use new text editing commands without first taking enough time to understand how to use them correctly.

ANALYSIS OF TEXT-EDITING ERRORS

This study provided an opportunity to classify first-try errors and examine the correlates of various error types. Error analysis proved possible in this study because the exercises required subjects to make a large number of editing changes and because each subject worked through the exercises twice. We had more errors to work with in this study than in any other we have done.

A preliminary analysis suggested that first-try errors fall into seven categories—typographical, pattern, omission, line number, multiple, comprehension, and direction-following errors—which are defined in Table 7.7. For present purposes, comprehension and direction-following errors are ignored because subjects averaged less than one of each of these errors across the two days of practice. Figure 7.2 shows the mean number of first-try errors in each category for Day 1 and Day 2.

Correlations between subjects' characteristics and the total number of errors they made in each category begin to suggest more precisely how spatial memory and age affect performance (see Table 7.8). Spatial memory test scores, on one hand, most strongly predict the frequency of pattern errors in which subjects fail to produce the correct sequence of characters and symbols for a command ($r = -.41, p < .01$). On the other hand, age predicts the frequency of omission errors ($r = .31, p < .05$) in which elements of a command are missing. Age as well as spatial memory predict multiple errors in which a command is wrong on two or more grounds ($r = .52, p < .01$ and $r = .33, p < .05$, respectively).

Ideally, we should be able to report the conditions under which various types of errors were made. Knowing when a particular kind of error is likely might be important in training text-editing skill. Unfortunately, there were

TABLE 7.7
Definition of Error Categories

Error classification	Definition
Typographical	A typographical error.
Pattern	The order or spacing of command elements is wrong.
Omission	One or more elements of a command are missing.
Line number	The wrong line number is given for a command.
Multiple	A combination of two or more types of errors.
Comprehension	An inappropriate command is used.
Direction following	Subject attempts to make changes other than those required.

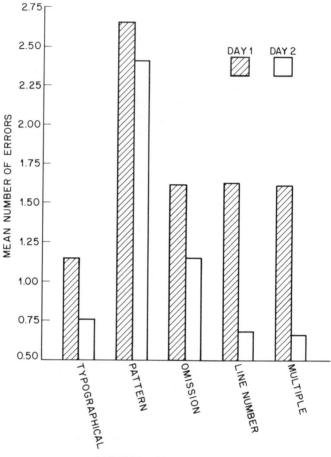

FIGURE 7.2 Mean number of various types of first-try errors made on Day 1 and Day 2.

simply too few first-try errors to construct a reliable error Type × Condition matrix. We can, however, note several observations about the conditions for making errors. First, pattern errors most often occurred in the substitute command when subjects failed to specify precisely the pattern of text to be matched or substituted. Second, omission errors often occurred in the append command when subjects forgot to leave the append mode (by inserting a dot on a line by itself) and in the substitute command when one or more of the pattern delimiters were omitted. These observations together with the correlations in Table 7.8 suggest that low spatial-memory subjects may have great difficulty with the substitute command and older subjects may have

TABLE 7.8
Correlations between Learner Characteristics and Types of Errors

Error classification	Spatial memory test	Age
Typographical	−.18	.28
Pattern	−.41**	.13
Omission	−.13	.31*
Line number	.07	.12
Multiple	−.33*	.52**
$N = 41$		

*$p < .05$. **$p < .01$.

difficulty with the append as well as the substitute command. Finally, Figure 7.2 shows that of all error types, pattern and omission errors persisted most strongly on Day 2. This finding is consistent with the regression analyses in Table 7.6 showing that spatial memory and age had somewhat stronger effects on performance for Day 2 than they did for Day 1.

EXPERIMENT 3: ISOLATING COMPONENTS OF TEXT–EDITING SKILL

DECOMPOSING THE EDITING TASK

The results so far show that individual differences in the difficulty of learning text editing are related to learners' age and spatial memory. This kind of information may by itself have some practical value. For example, these correlational patterns may enable teachers to anticipate the amount of difficulty various groups of students would encounter when learning to use a computer text editor. These results also suggest the likelihood of certain patterns of self-selection for jobs and patterns of preference for devices that require text-editing skill.

Understanding how to *accommodate* differences in learners' age and spatial memory requires studies that go beyond the fairly coarse-grained correlational results we have presented so far. To get some leverage on this problem, we attempted to break down the computer text-editing task into smaller components. Our specific goals in the following study were to identify which components of the text-editing task account for the most variance in actual text-editing difficulty and to find out which components are the most sensitive to subjects' age and spatial memory. This kind of information might pinpoint those aspects of text editing that could be made easier by software design, training, or performance supports.

PROPOSED COMPONENTS

We propose that a typical text-editing operation [1] can be decomposed into three general components (see Figure 7.3): FINDING, COUNTING, and GENERATING. FINDING is the process of locating the place at which a change needs to be made in the computer's version of a text. COUNTING is the process of obtaining the line number for an editing change. We chose this term because, in our experiments, subjects actually had to count lines on the computer's display in order to obtain the line number: They did not have aids such as context search or line-number indicators. GENERATING is the process of producing the correct sequence of symbols and patterns to accomplish the desired editing change. The most complicated such commands for the line editor we have studied are those involving string substitutions of the form: *s*/old text string/new text string/ (see Figure 7.1).

COMPONENT–TASK SIMULATIONS

The component processes were assessed by means of tasks that simulated specific parts of actual computer text editing. Each simulation was presented in paper and pencil form and included a large number of items requiring one, two, or all three component operations. Subjects completed as many of the items as they could within an overall time limit chosen so that few subjects could finish all the items for a task.

The FINDING component was assessed by means of the task illustrated in Figure 7.4. Subjects worked with two versions of the same text printed on opposite sides of a sheet of paper. One version was a text that had been processed by a text formatter to look like a draft of a manuscript. It had double spacing, standard margins, paragraph indenting, and was printed in a standard typewriter font. A number of editing changes were indicated on this text. On the other side of the sheet, the same text was printed to look like the display of the corresponding unformatted computer text file. It was single spaced, had 80-character lines, no paragraph indenting, and a type font typical of some computer displays. The task was to find an editing change indicated on the formatted side of the page and then circle the corresponding

---

[1] More precisely, we refer here and elsewhere to copyediting, or the process of changing a drafted document. The text editing that occurs while a person is composing may have somewhat different characteristics because it does not involve refering to two forms of the same text.

FINDING

COUNTING

GENERATING

FIGURE 7.3 Proposed component operations for text editing.

SIDE 1

The man looked out the window into the ~~rain~~ snow covered
street. It was difficult to see ~~Because~~ be the snow was coming
down heavily, so the man squinted as he moved his head from
side to side, ~~saærchng~~ Sea the length of the boulevard. Many
cars stopped at the curb in front of the building in which the man
stood. Some of the cars picked up passengers and others
dischargedthem, but none drew the man's attention.

   Many of the cars were sliding as they attempted to
climb the (very) small hill to the man's right. Few of the
cars had snow tires on, and the plow and salt trucks had not
yet come by. People were complaining about the road conditions
as they entered the building.

   A voice came over the ~~Loud~~ lou speaker from the ceiling
above the man's head informing everyone that the rest of the
night's ~~courses~~ classes were cancelled. Most off   in t   oyer
      re t   st   a

SIDE 2

The man looked out the window into the (ai) covered street. It was difficult
to see (B)cause the snow was coming down heavily, so the man squinted as he
moved his head from side to side, searching the length of the boulevard.
Many car (t) the curb in front of the building in which the man stood.
Some of the cars picked up passengers and others dischargedthem, but none
drew the man's attention.
Many of the cars were sliding as they attempted to climb the very small hill to
the man,s right. Few of the cars had snow tires on, and the plow and salt
trucks had not yet come by. People were complaining about road conditions
as they entered the building.
A voice came over the Loud speaker from the ceiling above the man's head
informing everyon that the rest of the night's courses were cancelled.
Most of those in   where the man stood sheeredbut the man paid no
atter   to the   ed ok   h indo
Ou'   t the   ar   p   orn.   l th   on
th

FIGURE 7.4 Example of materials used to assess FINDING.

location in the text on the other side. The score for the FINDING task was the number of items circled correctly in three minutes.

Materials for the COUNTING task are illustrated in Figure 7.5. Each item required subjects to find a target letter in a list of random letters arranged vertically, one to a line, and then count from the top of the list to obtain the line number of the target letter. The score for the COUNTING task was the number of items for which the subject wrote the correct line number next to the target letter in a 3-minute time period.

The GENERATING task (Figure 7.6) simulated the process of producing a correct string-substitution command. Subjects first were instructed

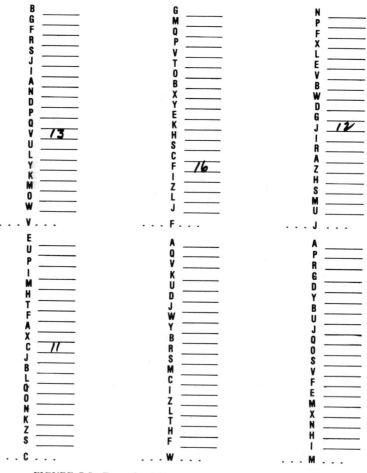

FIGURE 7.5 Example of material used to assess COUNTING.

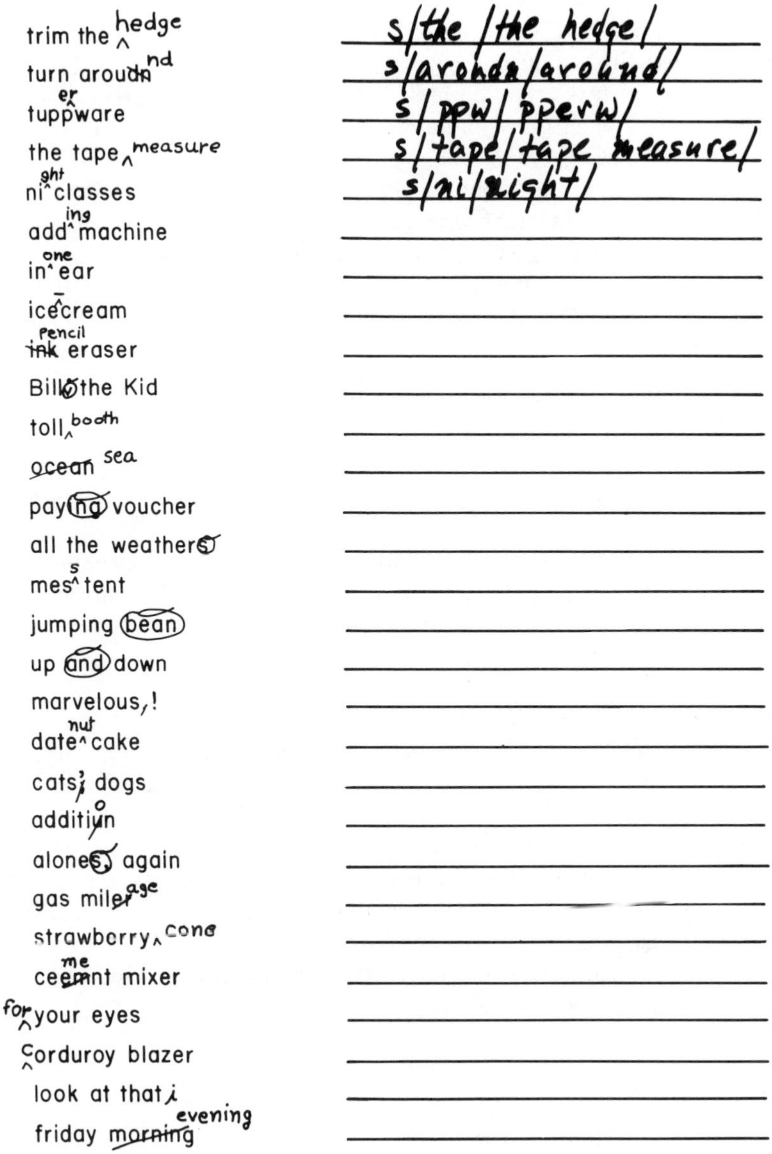

trim the $\wedge$ hedge   s/the /the hedge/

turn arou$\text{d}$n nd   s/arohda/around/

tupp$\wedge$ware (er)   s/ppw/pperw/

the tape $\wedge$ measure   s/tape/tape measure/

ni$\wedge$ classes (ght)   s/ni/night/

add$\wedge$ machine (ing)

in$\wedge$ ear (one)

ice cream

ink eraser (pencil)

Bill the Kid

toll$\wedge$ (booth)

ocean (sea)

pay(ing) voucher

all the weathers

mes$\wedge$ tent (s)

jumping (bean)

up (and) down

marvelous /!

date $\wedge$ cake (nut)

cats; dogs

additi(o)n

alone(s) again

gas mile(age)

strawberry $\wedge$ (cone)

ce(me)nt mixer

for$\wedge$ your eyes

Corduroy blazer

look at that;

friday morning (evening)

FIGURE 7.6 Example of materials used to assess GENERATING.

how to form these commands. Then they were given a large number of short phrases, and for each phrase a simple editing change was indicated. Subjects had to write out the correct string-substitution command for each phrase. The score on the GENERATING task was the number of such commands written correctly in 3 minutes.

In addition to tasks that simulated a single component process, other tasks were constructed that simulated two or three component processes. The FINDING + COUNTING task required subjects to locate an editing change and indicate its line number. The FINDING + GENERATING task required subjects to locate a change and write out the correct string-substitution command. The COUNTING + GENERATING task required subjects to give the line number and string-substitution command for one phrase in a list. The COMPLETE task, illustrated in Figure 7.7, required all three component processes and, therefore, should be the most accurate simulation of actual text editing.

METHOD

SUBJECTS

The subjects were 44 people who had participated in either Experiment 1 ($N = 19$) or 2 ($N = 25$) and who were available for this subsequent study. This study was run approximately three months after Experiment 2 and nine months after Experiment 1.

PROCEDURE

Subjects participated in one of three sessions. Each subject performed two 3-minute task simulations for the three single components, the three paired components, and the complete task. The first forms of all task simulations were presented, followed by a short break. The second forms of all simulations were then presented in an order opposite to that used for the first forms. Correlations between the two 3-minute parts for each task were corrected by the Spearman–Brown formula to yield estimates of the reliability of scores summed across the two parts. The estimated reliability of the task simulations ranged from .73 to .85.

RESULTS

HOW THE COMPONENTS RELATE
TO ACTUAL TEXT EDITING

To compare performance on the component tasks with actual text-editing performance, subjects' previously obtained text-editing data were standardized within each experiment, and the subsequent analyses were per-

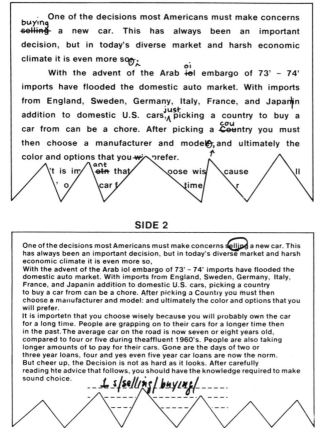

FIGURE 7.7   Example of COMPLETE task simulation.

formed on z-scores for first-try errors and execution time per successful change. The correlations between performance on the component tasks and these z-scores are shown in Table 7.9. The same correlations corrected for attenuation in the component and criterion measures are also shown.

Correlations between the component process scores and actual text-editing difficulty support three conclusions. First, the COMPLETE task is a reasonably good simulation of actual text editing. The correlation between COMPLETE task performance and actual first-try errors ($r = -.64$) approaches the reliability of the error data ($r = .68$). Second, however, the FINDING + GENERATING task correlates almost as strongly with actual text-editing difficulty as the COMPLETE task does. In predicting first-try errors, these two tasks have correlations significantly higher (all p's $< .05$) than any other component or component pair. For execution time per suc-

TABLE 7.9

Correlations between Component Tasks and Actual Text Editing[a]

Component	First-try errors		Execution time per successful change	
Finding	− .25	(− .35)	− .44**	(− .55)
Counting	− .27	(− .38)	− .35*	(− .43)
Generating	− .42**	(− .58)	− .61**	(− .74)
Finding + Counting	− .34*	(− .47)	− .50**	(− .62)
Finding + Generating	− .58**	(− .79)	− .68**	(− .83)
Counting + Generating	− .35*	(− .48)	− .58**	(− .68)
Complete Task	− .64**	(− .86)	− .68**	(− .82)

[a] Correlations in parentheses have been corrected for attenuation.
$*p < .05.$ $**p < .01$).

cessful change, these two tasks again have the highest correlations, but they are not in all cases significantly higher than correlations involving other components. Finally, among the three single components, GENERATING tended to produce the highest correlation with measures of actual text-editing difficulty.

HOW THE COMPONENTS RELATE
TO SPATIAL MEMORY AND AGE

Subjects' age and spatial memory test scores were used in multiple regression equations to predict each component task (see Table 7.10). Age had a significant regression coefficient in predicting every process involving the GENERATING component and only those processes. This result suggests that the extra difficulty older people experience in text editing may be tied to the process of generating complicated editing commands. Spatial memory

TABLE 7.10

Relationships among Component Tasks, Age, and Spatial Memory

Component	Regression coefficients	
	Age	Spatial memory
Finding	− .27	.35*
Counting	− .28	.27
Generating	− .31*	.44**
Finding + Counting	− .18	.37*
Finding + Generating	− .47**	.37*
Counting + Generating	− .32*	.50**
Complete Task	− .37**	.44**

$*p < .05.$ $**p < .01.$

had a significant regression coefficient for every process involving either FINDING or GENERATING. A person's spatial-memory capacity apparently is important in more than one component of text editing.

A Working Hypothesis

TENTATIVE NATURE OF THESE RESULTS

Figure 7.8 presents a working hypothesis based on these results. Our working hypothesis suggests that the effect of age is concentrated in the GENERATING process, while spatial memory influences both the FINDING and GENERATING processes. The term *working hypothesis* is used advisedly here because the data in Table 7.10 are not definitive. Consider, for example, the effect of age. Although the regression coefficients for age in tasks involving GENERATING are larger than coefficients involving other component processes, in most cases these differences are not statistically significant. The hypothesis depicted in Figure 7.8 is useful, however, because it suggests where to look for potentially corroborating or disconfirming evidence.

SOME CORROBORATING EVIDENCE

Further evidence consistent with the hypothesis in Figure 7.8 comes from performance on a rewriting task. The rewriting task was a precursor of the component task simulations, and subjects performed it as a warmup exercise just before they began the tutorial in the second study. The task required subjects to write out corrected versions of four paragraphs in longhand under severe time constraints. For two of the paragraphs, editing changes (insertions, deletions, and substitutions) were indicated by proof readers' marks penciled in red and superimposed on the text. For the other two paragraphs, the same kind of corrections were separated from the text in a

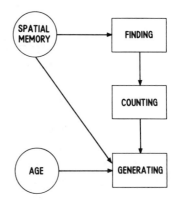

FIGURE 7.8 Working hypothesis relating age and spatial memory to text-editing component operations.

TABLE 7.11
Standardized Partial Regression Coefficients from Equations Predicting Rewriting Task

	Age	Spatial memory
Corrections superimposed on text	− .02	+ .32*
Corrections separated from text	− .08	+ .46**

$^*p < .05.$ $^{**}p < .01.$

list at the bottom of the page. These corrections were of the form "In the line beginning 'Mr. Jones drove his car,' change Mountain Ave. to Valley Rd."

Figure 7.8 predicts certain patterns of correlation among performance on the rewriting task, spatial memory and age. First, the FINDING component in the rewriting task should be difficult because subjects are writing in one place on a page but must find the text and corrections at another location. The FINDING difficulty should be compounded when the corrections are separated from the text and subjects must deal with information in three locations. Figure 7.8 suggests, then, that the rewriting task should correlate with subjects spatial-memory test scores, particularly when the corrections are separated from the text. On the other hand, the process used to generate the correct text—handwriting—is a highly practiced skill. On the basis of Figure 7.8, we would not expect a subject's age to be a strong predictor of rewriting task performance.

The data in Table 7.11 are consistent with these expectations. The number of changes subjects wrote correctly was strongly related to their spatial-memory test scores, particularly when the changes were separated from the text. On the other hand, rewriting task performance was not strongly related to subjects' age. This pattern of results is consistent with the idea that age and spatial memory exert their influence on distinct aspects of text editing. These results also suggest that the correlates of text editing can be altered in predictable ways by changes in the editing task.

EXPERIMENT 4: ACCOMMODATING INDIVIDUAL DIFFERENCES

THE DISPLAY EDITOR

In the final experiment, we explored the difficulty people experience in learning to use a display text editor. Display editors exemplify how different computer software can change the nature of the text editing task.

Although various display editors have somewhat different configurations, in general two features of display editors distinguish them from line editors. One feature is that changes are made to a text by positioning a cursor at the location of the change on the computer's text display and then making the change at that location. The second feature typical of most display editors is that operations are performed by using labeled function keys rather than a command language. This second feature is not essential to display editors. In fact, early display editors, and even some very powerful modern display editors, use a command language rather than function keys.

The display editor used in this study was a simplified version of the screen editor, *Ted* (Sharma & Gruchacz, 1982). *Ted* incorporates both of the features just described. Subjects make changes by positioning a cursor at the appropriate location and then typing additional text or deleting unwanted text.[2] Four step-keys labeled with arrows cause the cursor to move up, down, left, or right. Other labeled function keys are used to delete individual characters, delete lines of text, and start and restart exercises. All these special function keys were located on the top row of the keyboard.

HOW MIGHT THE CORRELATES OF DISPLAY EDITING AND LINE EDITING DIFFER?

A NAÏVE THEORY

If we set aside the results of the previous experiments, we might entertain a naive theory of how the nature of text-editing difficulty depends on whether people are learning to use a line editor or a display editor. The difference in the appearance and even the names suggest that a *display* editor might require less spatial processing in some general sense compared to a *line* editor. Such a theory might be founded on the idea that display editors might require less visualization than line editors or, perhaps, that working directly on a body of text should be less spatially demanding than working on a line removed from the location where a change is to be made.

A LESS NAÏVE THEORY

A theory that takes into account the working hypothesis in Figure 7.8 suggests that the GENERATING process may be an important difference between display and line editors. GENERATING text-editing commands using the display editor's function keys seems intuitively much simpler than GENERATING commands using the line editor's command language. The

---

[2] This editor could be described as operating in the input mode at all times. Other screen editors have a command mode similar to that of line editors in addition to the input mode.

display editor does not require symbolically coding location, remembering command labels, or producing complicated command syntax. A theory of text-editing difficulty based on Figure 7.8 would suggest that the correlation between age and learning difficulty ought to be less for display editors than for line editors.

The implications of Figure 7.8 for the correlation between spatial memory and display editing difficulty are not as clear. On one hand, the FINDING process remains essentially the same no matter which kind of editor is used, so spatial memory still should be important. Positioning a cursor in a display editor may be a more spatially demanding way of specifying location than the counting process in a line editor. On the other hand, to the extent that the GENERATING process is simpler with display editors, the spatial aptitude requirements due to that component may be reduced. On balance, the working hypothesis suggests that the effect of age should be reduced but the effect of spatial memory might be about as strong in display editing as in line editing.

METHOD

The procedure for this study was similar to that used in Experiment 2. Forty subjects first participated in a group testing session where they gave background information (age, typing speed, education) and took a number of standard tests. They later returned individually to work through a tutorial on using the display editor. The tutorial manual was written to be similar to the one used to introduce the line editor in Experiment 2. The same kinds of editing operations were covered in Exeriment 4 as in Experiment 2. Exercises and terminals were also identical across the two studies. Of course, the actual wording of the manuals in the two studies differed because of the different text-editing system the subjects learned.

Three additional standard tests were given besides the Building Memory Test and Nelson–Denny Reading Test used previously. The Diagramming Relations Test was given again to assess logical reasoning. The Two-Dimensional Space Test (1963) was given to assess spatial visualization. This test allowed us to check whether a different measure of spatial processing would predict performance as well as the spatial memory test. Subjects also took a test of simple manual dexterity (Tapping Speed; Parker & Fleischman, 1960). This test was included because positioning the cursor by using step keys requires a large number of keystrokes; this suggests that manual dexterity may be an important skill when using a display editor.

RESULTS

OVERALL PERFORMANCE
The display editor resulted in much faster execution times but about the same error rate (see Table 7.12) compared to the line editor learned by subjects in the previous studies (see Tables 7.1 and 7.4). The display editor might then be described as "more forgiving" because subjects could recover from their errors more quickly with it than they could with a line editor. Reading times for the manuals used to introduce the display editor and line editor were roughly comparable, but these times cannot be compared more precisely because of the differences in the instructional text.

PREDICTORS OF DISPLAY-EDITING DIFFICULTY
The learner characteristics predicting the difficulty of learning the display editor differed from those found to predict line-editor difficulty on the same problems. In general, the predictive power of age was greatly reduced for this display editor. By contrast, spatial memory was correlated with text-editing difficulty to about the same extent for both types of editors, and neither reasoning nor spatial visualization could account for the effect of spatial memory.

Two sets of analyses support the above conclusions. The first analysis used stepwise multiple regression (forward and backward procedures yielded the same final equations) to develop regression equations for the three main dependent variables. These results are summarized in Table 7.13. For the reading time equation, the Nelson–Denny Reading Test had a significant ($p < .05$) coefficient, while both the spatial visualization test and age had marginally significant coefficients ($.10 > p > .05$). Spatial memory ($p < .05$), reading ($p < .001$), and reasoning ($p < .01$) each accounted for significant and unique variance in execution time per successful change. Three variables also entered the prediction equation for first-try errors. Subjects

TABLE 7.12
Means, Standard Deviations, and Ranges of Performance Measures for Display Editor

Measure	$\overline{X}$	SD	Range
Reading time (min)	11.6	3.4	6.1–23.1
Execution time per successful change (min)	1.2	0.4	0.6–2.3
First-try errors (%)	29.5	13.5	9.4–62.5

TABLE 7.13
Standardized Coefficients from Multiple Regression Equations Predicting Display-Editor Performance

Measure	Spatial memory test	Age	Reading test	Estimated typing speed	Spatial visualization	Reasoning	R^2
Reading time	—	+.26	−.37*	—	−.26	—	.366**
Execution time per successful change	−.26*	—	−.50***	—	—	−.39**	.654**
First-try errors	−.29*	—	−.50***	+.36**	—	—	.472**

*$p < .05$. **$p < .01$. ***$p < .001$. All coefficients with no asterisk are marginally significant ($.10 > p > .05$).

TABLE 7.14

Coefficients for Spatial Memory and Age Predicting Performance on the Display Editor

Measure	Spatial memory test	Age	R^2
Execution time per successful change	−.37*	.31*	.277**
First-try errors	−.40*	−.15	.155*

*$p < .05$. **$p < .01$.

who scored higher on tests of spatial memory ($p < .05$) and reading ($p < .01$) made fewer errors. An unexpected result was that subjects' estimated typing speed was positively related ($p < .05$) to first-try errors: Faster typists made more errors on the screen editor. This relationship was due to negative transfer. The return key and space bar, which are often used for positioning the carriage on a typewriter, caused errors if subjects tried to use them to position the cursor.[3]

In a second set of analyses, spatial memory and age were forced into regression equations predicting first-try errors and execution time per successful change. The regression coefficients are given in Table 7.14. These data can be compared with the corresponding coefficients for performance in Experiment 2 (see Table 7.6) where subjects worked the same exercises

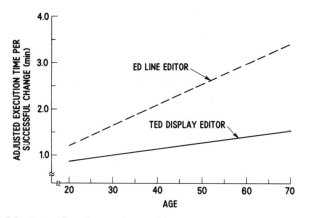

FIGURE 7.9 Interaction of age and text-editing systems for execution time per successful change.

---

[3] Because the screen editor operated in the input mode, pressing the space bar introduced additional spaces in the text and pressing the return key introduced a new line.

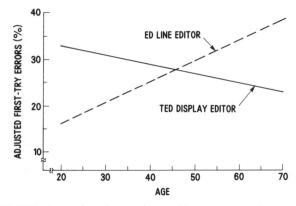

FIGURE 7.10   Interaction of age and text-editing systems for first-try errors.

with the line editor. The comparison shows that the effect of age is reduced when people learned the display editor rather than the line editor, but the effect of spatial memory remained approximately the same.

We tested whether the regression slopes for spatial memory and those for age are reliably different for the display-editor and line-editor data. To do this, we coded the data from Day 1 of Experiment 2 and of the present experiment using dummy variables to represent the type of Editor, the Editor × Age, and the Editor × Spatial Memory interactions. The complete model including all dummy variables was then tested, and variables failing to make a significant contribution to the variance were eliminated using the backward stepwise procedure. Results showed that the Editor × Age interaction accounted for significant variance in the final models for execution time per successful change ($p < .001$; see Figure 7.9), and for first-try errors ($p < .01$; see Figure 7.10). The Editor × Spatial Memory interaction did not approach significance for either dependent variable.

GENERAL DISCUSSION

A MORE DETAILED ANALYSIS OF TEXT EDITING

The flow chart in Figure 7.11 represents an attempt to flesh out the working hypothesis in Figure 7.8. This more detailed hypothesis accounts for the results of the display-editor study and the analysis of editing errors in the second study (Table 7.8). Here, the original FINDING process is broken into

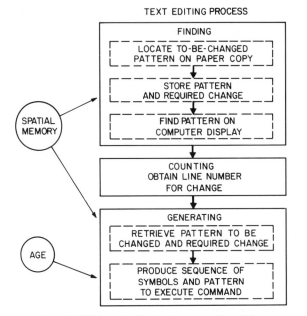

FIGURE 7.11 More detailed hypothesis relating age and spatial memory to text-editing component operations.

three steps: locating a pattern to be changed, storing the pattern and change, and finding the pattern on the computer display. The original GEN-ERATING process is further analyzed into two steps. In one of these steps, the original and changed text patterns are retrieved; in the other, elements of the editing command are produced.

This hypothesis suggests more precisely what role spatial memory plays in text editing. In this account, spatial memory is involved in FINDING because the pattern to be changed must be remembered and found in a different version of the same text. This process may require comparing the stored spatial pattern against many other patterns in the display until a correct match is found. While subjects rarely make overt errors in this process, they differ greatly in processing speed as assessed in the FINDING component task. Subjects who score higher on the spatial memory test may have more efficient ways of storing and matching spatial patterns. In further research we will explore whether measures of perceptual speed indicate the efficiency of FINDING as well as or better than measures of spatial memory do.

Spatial memory also comes into play at the time when a command, especially the substitute command, is generated. In GENERATING a substitute command, both the pattern to be matched and the changed pattern must be retrieved. These two patterns may interfere with each other because they often partially overlap. The delay between the time the patterns are stored and retrieved is another factor that could tax spatial memory. Pattern interference and output delays presumably account for the large number of pattern errors made by subjects scoring low on spatial memory, especially when the substitute command is used. Spatial memory also may be involved in GENERATING other commands. For example, learners may rely on spatial memory to remember the proper sequence of the command elements.

According to the hypothesis in Figure 7.11, age exerts its effect on the production of the correct sequence of symbols and patterns required to generate text-editing commands. Several bits of evidence are consistent with this idea. (1) In the components study, age made a significant contribution to every task involving the GENERATING component and only those tasks. (2) Subjects' age did not predict performance in the rewriting task where corrections were generated using a simple, overlearned process (handwriting). (3) The influence of age on actual text-editing difficulty was smaller in the display-editor data compared to the line-editor data. Since the FINDING process for both the line editor and display editor were essentially the same, and COUNTING was not a strong correlate of actual text-editing performance, the GENERATING process is implicated as the main difference in the two editing systems. Using labeled function keys to generate corrections for a text may not be as age-sensitive a process as using a command language to accomplish the same task.

The fact that age had a larger effect for the editor that produced the longer execution times is consistent with a large number of studies linking the effect of age to task complexity (see Cirella, Poon, & Williams, 1980). In those studies, conditions of tasks (e.g., choice reaction time) varied in complexity (e.g., number of alternatives). When data are normalized and compared across those studies, the size of the Age × Complexity interaction can be approximated by a linear function of the size of the Complexity effect (see Cirella, Poon, & Williams, 1980, Figure 24–1). If the data in Figure 7.9 are normalized appropriately, they produce a point that falls close to the Cirella, Poon, & Williams function. This is true despite the fact that the function was estimated using tasks that had response times of less than 5 seconds—far shorter than the 1 minute or more our subjects typically spent executing editing changes. This result does not explain the effect of age, but it does suggest a kinship between the kind of performance slowing, due to age, in such tasks as choice reaction time, memory scanning, card sorting, and the present task of text editing.

INTERFACE DESIGNS

One general implication of these results is that some people have difficulty learning to use a computer text editor because of their spatial-memory limitations. Since spatial memory seems to be implicated in both the FINDING and GENERATING components, this capacity may be important in other complex skills that involve similar processes. Any kind of performance that requires comparing different sources of visual input or storing and retrieving visual patterns in the face of interference and output delays is likely to be correlated with spatial-memory test scores.

There may be ways to design computer interfaces to reduce demands on spatial memory. Certain text-editing performance aids already have been designed to support the FINDING process. Context search, a function in which the computer does the pattern matching to find the location of a correction, may offload human spatial memory. Various ways of highlighting corrections (e.g., reverse video) or the location of the cursor also may have beneficial effects. Another approach to reducing the spatial demands of text editing might be to develop an intelligent verbal editor that entirely does away with a visual finding process by recognizing spoken corrections and matching them to the correct location in the text.

GENERATING commands is a process required by many human–computer interfaces. The model in Figure 7.11 suggests that some ways of sequencing the elements of a complex command may be less spatially demanding than others. If remembering a spatial pattern proves to be a difficult part of generating a command, then the command syntax could require that the spatial pattern be produced first in order to reduce memory failures due to delays and interference. In fact, the present experiments suggest a possible advantage to having line numbers come last in the substitute command sequence. A FINDING → GENERATING → COUNTING sequence may be less sensitive to spatial-memory limitations than the standard FINDING → COUNTING → GENERATING sequence. By having GENERATING immediately follow FINDING, the delay and intervening activity between storing and retrieving spatial patterns would be reduced.

System designs also may determine whether performance is more or less sensitive to users' age (see Figure 7.9). Our best guess is that the differential complexity of the command-generation process accounts for the differential effect of age in the text-editing systems we studied. Without further experiments, we cannot specify exactly why one sort of command-generation process is more complex than the other. However, the fact that our results fit with results of many diverse Age × Complexity studies suggests that fairly gross measures of a system's complexity will predict how sensitive the system is to learners' age. For example, ranking systems by their predicted editing time based on a task analysis like the Keystroke Level Model (Card, Moran, & Newell, 1980b) might roughly correspond to the ranking of the age effect in the various systems. In general, if one system consistently produces longer performance times than another to accomplish the same task, that system is also likely to be the more complex system and hence, the more age-sensitive system.

TRAINING TEXT-EDITING SKILL

Our studies demonstrate that people with poor spatial memory, older people, and poor readers experience difficulty learning the particular computer-based skill we examined. Without changing the design of the text-editing system, could different training procedures make learning less dependent upon spatial memory, age, and reading skill?

Training in processing strategies may help people with poor spatial memory cope with computer text editing. For example, the process shown in Table 7.15 has two features that may make it less spatially demanding than the one in Figure 7.11, which we think learners develop spontaneously. First, this new processing strategy calls for the learner to complete the COUNT-ING component before trying to remember patterns of characters. Second, it calls for going back to the original paper copy of the text to obtain the old string of characters and then the new string in separate steps. These two features may reduce interference and output delays and lead to fewer pattern errors than the mode of processing illustrated in Figure 7.11. Just as Aptitude × Strategy interactions are found in laboratory reasoning tasks (MacLeod, Hunt, & Mathews, 1978; Sternberg & Weil, 1980), the correlates of text-editing difficulty may depend on the processing strategy people are trained to use.

To make learning less age-sensitive, a complex procedure such as the string substitution command could be avoided, at least initially. In its place, subjects could be taught how to exchange one entire line of text for another either by combining the *delete* and *append* functions they have learned already or by learning a simple *change line* command. Commands that operate on entire lines tend to be easier to generate than character-string substitutions. The overall complexity of a text-editing system may be reduced if such commands are used initially to perform substitutions. Specialized substitution commands could be taught later in the instructional sequence so that subjects have the option of using them or not.

At first blush, the idea of retyping an entire line of text just to change a small string of characters within the line might seem terribly inefficient. However, this sort of inefficiency must be weighed against the problems of learning a complex system. For those older people who are skilled typists,

TABLE 7.15
An Alternative Text-Editing Strategy that May Reduce Demands on Spatial Memory

1. Get the line number for a change.
2. Type the line number followed by "s/".
3. Look at the paper copy of the text and get the exact string of characters to be changed.
4. Type in the characters to be changed followed by a "/".
5. Look at the paper copy of the text and get the exact string of new characters.
6. Type in the new characters followed by a "/".
7. Press the return key.

additional typing may pose much less of a burden than additional complexity early in learning.

Differences in students' reading skill cause pervasive problems in text-based instruction of any kind. One way to revise training to try to reduce the impact of reading skill would substitute nonverbal material (e.g., drawings, worked text-editing examples, tabular performance aids) for much of the narrative text. Another approach would explore the result in the second study where subjects generally spent less time reading and where reading skill was not strongly related to any of the performance measures including reading time. Since the amount of time a person spends reading an instructional text is determined by a personal criterion, there may be ways to influence reading time by manipulating variables that affect the criterion. Pacing reading, providing feedback, or adjusting the penalty for making errors may be effective ways to induce people to spend the optimal amount of time reading.

A CRITICAL REVIEW OF OUR APPROACH

SUMMARY OF THE APPROACH

The present studies have demonstrated a novel approach to problems of system design and training for complex skills. The approach puts to use the information contained in individual differences in the difficulty of learning a complex skill: It assays individual differences, isolates their effects in component processes, and then changes those processes to accommodate different people. In principle, this approach could be applied to many different complex skills. We conclude the chapter with a discussion of the potential pitfalls and promise of this approach.

THE PROBLEM OF A FAULTY ASSAY

Accounting for individual differences in a complex skill may go wrong in at least two ways. In one case, the characteristics identified as important can be misleading because they are actually only correlates of the truly effective characteristics. The only solution to this problem is to try other plausible candidate variables in much the same way that various controls are used in more traditional experimental work. This was part of the rationale for our second study in which we examined correlates of spatial memory (reasoning and associative memory) and correlates of age (educational indices and attitudes) to see which variables did the best job of accounting for variance in text-editing difficulty.

Another case of a faulty assay is one where the wrong kind of variable, perhaps one that is too complex or poorly understood, is used to account for individual differences. The problem is that little useful information may be gained from the assay. Here, foresight in selecting candidate variables is called for. The researcher should always ask the question, "Suppose variable *x* were to predict performance. What more would I know, and how could I use that information to accommodate individual differences?" This forward-looking emphasis is inherent in an approach that is not content with predicting who can perform a given complex skill.

PROBLEMS OF ISOLATING TASK COMPONENTS

At present, task analysis is still largely an art and not a single well-specified procedure. For this reason, an approach involving task analysis is susceptible to problems of uniqueness and validity that may cause difficulty in isolating exactly where important learner characteristics exert their effects. Any particular analysis of a complex task is not likely to be the uniquely correct way of decomposing the task. Various task decompositions may differ in the boundaries of component processes and in the level of detail at which processes are specified. The validity of the measures of component task performance also may be questionable: Components may behave differently in isolation than they do when executed together, or perhaps, the tasks used to assess components are not accurate simulations of actual parts of the complex task.

We have two criteria to apply to task analyses to deal with these potential problems. The first criterion is empirical validity. We assessed the validity of our task analysis in the third experiment (see Table 7.9), where performance on the task components was correlated with actual text-editing difficulty. This kind of analysis can confirm that performance on the component tasks is related to the original performance on the complex task. The second criterion we can apply is usefulness. While task analyses generally are not unique, they may or may not be useful. A useful task analysis identifies component processes that are responsible for individual differences in the complex task and that can be changed, removed, or supported. Again, the thrust to understand individual differences so that they can be accommodated may improve the chances of producing a useful analysis.

DIFFICULTIES IN ACCOMMODATING INDIVIDUAL DIFFERENCES

Once individual differences have been assayed and isolated, there is still no guarantee that experimental manipulations that are intended to address individual differences will work. The step of accommodating individual differences not only tests the analyses that precede it, but it also tests the theory of how an experimental manipulation, be it a new design, different training, or some other performance support, will change the original task. We may know, for example, that spatial aptitude is a strong correlate of a particular aspect of performance. How to deal with that is still a major question. On one hand, one could support performance with simple diagrams graphically portraying relationships that people low in spatial aptitude may have difficulty imagining. On the other hand, one could try to do away with any kind of pictorial material or spatial references. Even with extensive prior analyses, the design or training remedies for a complex skill are not always obvious.

The more optimistic view of this problem is that attempts to accommodate individual differences after assaying and isolating them almost certainly stand a better chance of succeeding than attempts undertaken without this prior analysis. A raft of discouraging Aptitude × Treatment interaction studies (see Cronbach & Snow, 1977) attests to the difficulty of trying to tailor instruction to individual differences without first understanding what kind of differences are important and why. Without the kind of assay and task analysis we did in the present studies, picking the important learner characteristics or understanding why one form of editing produced better results than the other would have been pure guesswork (see the section, "Interface Designs"). Our experience has shown that our own guesses are not very accurate.

THE PROMISE OF THIS APPROACH

Certain domains seem particularly promising for assaying, isolating, and accommodating individual differences. We think that the approach will be most useful in those situations where a large number of people from different backgrounds wish to learn a new complex skill for which there are good possibilities for accommodating individual differences. Our case study of computer text editing fits this description precisely. Many other new skills involving the use of computers or computer-like devices have characteristics that make them good candidates for this approach. The number of different people who can accomplish such tasks as troubleshooting, maintenance, assembly, and decision making may also increase if the right kind of changes are made to those tasks.

These studies have demonstrated a set of methods that may free us from the conventional mentality of selecting the "right" person for a given job. We have shown that individual differences in learning a complex task can be sorted out, that the components of the task causing some people great difficulty can be isolated, and that task components can be changed to accommodate a greater range of people. Instead of finding the right person for a given job, we may be able to focus on developing the right conditions (tool designs, training, performance aids) to enable a given person to accomplish a desired objective.

REFERENCES

Allen, R. B., & Scerbo, M. W. Details of command-language keystrokes. *ACM Transactions on Office Information Systems,* 1983, *1,* 159–178.
Barnard, P., Hammond, N., MacLean, A., & Morton, J. Learning and remembering interactive commands. *Proceedings of Human Factors in Computer Systems.* Gaithersburg, MD, March 15–17, 1982.
Black, J. B., & Moran, T. P. Learning and remembering command names. *Proceedings of Human Factors in Computer Systems.* Gaithersburg, MD, March 15–17, 1982.
Black, J. B., & Sebrechts, M. M. Facilitating human–computer communication. *Applied Psycholinguistics,* 1981, *2,* 149–177.
Bott, R. A. *A study of complex learning: Theory and methodologies.* Unpublished doctoral dissertation, University of California, San Diego, March 1979.
Bracht, G. H. Experimental factors related to aptitude-treatment interactions. *Review of Educational Research,* 1970, *40,* 627–645.
Card, S. K., Moran, T. P., & Newell, A. Computer text-editing: An information processing analysis of a routine cognitive skill. *Cognitive Psychology,* 1980, *12,* 32–74. (a)
Card, S. K., Moran, T. P., & Newell, A. The keystroke-level model for user performance time with interactive systems. *Communications of the ACM,* 1980, *23,* 396–410.(b)
Cirella, J., Poon, L. W., & Williams, D. M. Age and the complexity hypothesis. In L. W. Poon (Ed.), *Aging in the 1980s.* Washington, DC: American Psychological Association, 1980.
Cronbach, L. J., & Snow, R. E. *Aptitudes and instructional methods.* New York: John Wiley & Sons, 1977.
Egan, D. E. Characterizing spatial ability: different mental processes reflected in accuracy and latency scores (Report No. 1250), Pensacola, Florida: Naval Aerospace Medical Research Laboratory, 1978.
Egan, D. E. Retrospective reports reveal differences in people's reasoning. *Bell System Technical Journal,* 1983, *62,* 1675–1697.
Ekstrom, R. B., French, J. W., & Harman, H. H. *Manual for kit of factor-referenced cognitive tests.* Princeton, NJ: Educational Testing Service, August 1976.
Embly, D. W., & Nagy, G. Behavioral aspects of text editors. *Computing Surveys,* 1981, *13,* 33–70.
Glaser, R. General discussion: Relationships between aptitude, learning, and instruction. In R. E. Snow, P. Federico, & W. E. Montague (Eds.), *Aptitude, learning, and instruction volume 2: Cognitive process analyses of learning and problem solving.* Hillsdale, N.J.: Lawrence Erlbaum Associates, 1980.
Gomez, L. M., Egan, D. E., & Bowers, C. H. Learning to use a text editor: Some learner characteristics that predict success. *Human Computer Interaction,* in press.

Grossberg, M., Wiesen, R. A., & Yntema, D. B. An experiment on problem solving with delayed computer responses. *IEEE Transactions on Systems, Man, and Cybernetics,* 1976, 219–222.

Hunt, E. B., Frost, N., & Lunneborg, C. Individual differences in cognition: A new approach to intelligence. In G. Bower (Ed.), *The psychology of learning and motivation* (Vol. 7). New York: Academic Press, 1973.

Landauer, T. K., Galotti, K. M., & Hartwell, S. *A computer command by any other name: Study of text-editing terms.* Unpublished manuscript, Bell Laboratories, August, 1980.

Lewis, C., & Mack, R. Learning to use a text processing system: Evidence from "thinking aloud" protocols. *Proceedings of Human Factors in Computer Systems.* Gaithersburg, MD, March 15–17, 1982.

McLeod, C. M., Hunt, E. B., & Mathews, N. N. Individual differences in the verification of sentence–picture relationships. *Journal of Verbal Learning and Verbal Behavior,* 1978, *5,* 493–508.

Nelson–Denny Reading Test, Form D. Boston: Houghton Mifflin, 1973.

Parker, J. F., Jr., & Fleischman, E. A. Ability factors and component performance measures as predictors of complex tracking behavior. *Psychological Monographs,* 1960, No. 16 (Whole No. 503), 1–36.

Roberts, T. L. *Evaluation of computer text editors.* Unpublished doctoral dissertation, Stanford University, 1980.

Roberts, T. L., & Moran, T. P. The evaluation of text editors: Methodology and empirical results. *Communications of the ACM,* 1983, *26,* 265–283.

Sharma, D. K., & Gruchacz, A. M. The display text editor TED: A case study in the design and implementation of display-oriented interacting human interfaces. *IEEE Transactions on Communications,* 1982, Vol. COM–30, No. 1, 111–119.

Sternberg, R. J. *Intelligence, information processing and analogical reasoning: The componential analysis of human abilities.* Hillsdale, N.J.: Lawrence Erlbaum Associates, 1977.

Sternberg, R. J., & Weil, E. M. An aptitude-strategy interaction in linear syllogistic reasoning. *Journal of Educational Psychology,* 1980, *72,* 226–239.

Two-Dimensional Space Test. Richardson, Bellows, Henry, 1948.

8

The Role of Individual Differences in Learning Strategies Research*

Larry W. Brooks, Zita M. Simutis, and Harold F. O'Neil, Jr.

INTRODUCTION

Given a relatively complex learning environment, how can an individual make the most of the available resources, both internal and external, to acquire and use information and skills in an efficient manner? This is the central question underlying learning strategies research. Unlike instructional strategies, in which an authority, such as the teacher, manipulates the learning situation in some fashion, learning strategies are skills that allow individuals to manipulate the learning situation. This focus on learning strategies, as opposed to instructional strategies, has received increased attention during the last decade. A partial explanation for this shift may be the broader integration of cognitive and educational psychology. With the em-

*The authors thank Judith A. Englert for her comments and criticisms on earlier drafts of this paper. The authors also express their appreciation to Wayne Sampson, Doris Bitler, and David Shurtleff for their help in the preparation of this manuscript.

phasis in cognitive psychology on the mental processes that operate on information, it was only natural that educationally inclined researchers would become more concerned with the strategies students use to learn new material (see Calfee, 1981; Wittrock, 1978).

The purpose of this chapter is to examine the role of individual differences in learning strategies research. In the first section, we introduce the reader to learning strategies by discussing a number of dimensions by which learning strategies can be conceptualized. Following this section, we briefly discuss why so little attention has been paid to how differences among individuals influence the acquisition and use of learning strategies. In the next section, we overview a representative example of learning strategies related research concerning individual differences. We then offer a general framework for learning strategies research that incorporates individual differences and end with remarks about future directions in this area of research.

Because we are applied researchers at the Army Research Institute, the context of our research in learning strategies is the development of a research base on which to build a learning strategies curriculum for training soldiers. The tasks that soldiers are being trained to perform in the Army are becoming increasingly complex as modern technology plays a larger role in the development of new weapon systems. For example, the documentation required for learning and performing maintenance on an M1 tank consists of more than 40,000 pages; the tools required to perform maintenance on the M1 fill a large truck. Among many other required cognitive tasks, enlisted soldiers with a ninth grade average reading level must be able to comprehend, retain, and retrieve large amounts of technical information.

Our research in learning strategies is based on a recognized need in the Army to equip soldiers with the appropriate cognitive tools to acquire and use information in the performance of their duties. Because of time and funding constraints, soldiers are required to learn the skills necessary to perform their specific Army jobs in 6 to 10 weeks after 6 weeks of basic training; thus, soldiers are in the field operating and repairing sophisticated equipment such as tanks, radar systems, and computers in the performance of their Army jobs after only 12–16 weeks of Army training. Efficient as Army training is, soldiers must continually learn new skills while on the job. Our research, then, is directed largely toward integrating learning strategies with Army training to assist soldiers in meeting their training requirements and in upgrading their skills and knowledge while on the job.

Our concern with the need for research on individual differences in learning strategies is two-fold as it relates to developing learning strategies training for the Army. Foremost is the realization that soldiers have a wide variety of abilities and skills. We are concerned with selecting and developing the optimal learning strategies for soldiers based on these differences. Second, we are concerned with matching soldiers of varying abilities and skills with the most appropriate tasks. Therefore, we are interested in how task demands, along with learning strategies, interact with individual differences among soldiers.

DIMENSIONS OF LEARNING STRATEGIES

Learning strategies were, of course, used by people long before the current popular interest in them developed. One only has to think of the Socratic method or Galton's work on imagery techniques (Galton, 1883) to realize that techniques for improving a person's comprehension and memory abilities have been around for a considerable time. At present, however, there is no well-defined set of techniques that can be pointed to clearly as learning strategies. From a very general perspective, we can think of learning strategies as those techniques that an individual consciously controls and that are typically beneficial to the individual's acquisition, retention, and use of information. This definition could include prelearning activities such as mood modification via relaxation techniques, learning activities such as summarization, and postlearning activities such as rewarding oneself for studying for 2 hours. Somewhat in line with this broad view of learning strategies is Dansereau's (in press) definition of an effective learning strategy as a "set of processes or steps that can be used by an individual to facilitate the acquisition, storage, and/or utilization of information." A more strict definition of learning strategies would include only those strategies that are applicable to the direct manipulation of information such as, for example, Dansereau's (1978) networking method.

Regardless of the position one takes on the issue of definition, a number of general dimensions on which learning strategies vary can be enumerated. Because there are a variety of situations in which learning takes place, it is not surprising that different strategies have been developed to deal with these situations. What is offered here is one possible framework for representing cognitive learning strategies. Previous researchers (e.g., Dansereau, in press; Dansereau, Actkinson, Long, & McDonald, 1974; Rigney, 1980) have discussed dimensions on which learning strategies may vary. The present list should not be considered exhaustive but instead, is intended for use as a heuristic for categorizing different types of learning strategies. Figure 8.1 is a summary of the six dimensions presented below.

GENERALIZABILITY — DEGREE TO WHICH A LEARNING
STRATEGY IS APPLICABLE TO A WIDE VARIETY OF LEARNING
SITUATIONS.
SCOPE — DEGREE TO WHICH A LEARNING STRATEGY IS
APPROPRIATE FOR PROCESSING VARYING AMOUNTS OF
INFORMATION.
DIRECTNESS — EXTENT TO WHICH A LEARNING STRATEGY IS
USED TO DIRECTLY FACILITATE THE ACQUISITION OF NEW
INFORMATION.
LEVEL — EXTENT TO WHICH A LEARNER DIRECTS HIS OR HER
PROCESSING AT AN EXECUTIVE LEVEL.
MODIFIABILITY — DEGREE TO WHICH A LEARNING STRATEGY
CAN BE CHANGED TO MEET THE NEEDS OF A PARTICULAR
LEARNING SITUATION.
MODALITY — THE SENSORY OR PROCESSING SYSTEM
EMPHASIZED TO ACQUIRE AND UTILIZE INFORMATION.

FIGURE 8.1   Six dimensions for conceptualizing learning strategies.

GENERALIZABILITY

One way in which learning strategies can vary is in their generalizability. A generalized learning strategy (or coherent set of strategies) is applicable across a wide variety of situations. Robinson's (1946) SQ3R system is an example of this type of learning strategy since it is applicable to almost any text-learning situation. If a student follows the five steps comprising the SQ3R system in sequence while learning, for example, a chapter of text, he or she will first *S*urvey the chapter, paying particular attention to the headings, boldface print, and other author-provided cues for important ideas contained within the text. Next, the student will develop *Q*uestions about the chapter based on the preliminary survey. After this step is accomplished, Robinson suggests that the student *R*ead the chapter and attempt to answer the questions formulated in the preceding step. The final two steps require the student to *R*ecall and *R*eview the text material. This approach is easily adapted to any situation requiring text learning, and in fact, it is one of the building blocks on which much later research in learning strategies is based. Its primary drawback, a common one in this area, is that explicit instructions are not given on the actual use of these strategies.

An example of a less generalized learning strategy is one developed by Brooks and Dansereau (1983) specifically for learning scientific theories. This approach, which the authors call structural schema training, is based on the assumption that unfamiliar text, such as a scientific theory, is difficult to learn because students do not have previous experience (and consequently they have no framework) to guide them in knowing what information is important and what information is not as important to understanding the theory. Students using this technique are given the following list of categories of information important to the understanding of a scientific theory: (1) description of the theory, (2) inventor–history of the theory, (3) consequences of the theory, (4) evidence of the theory, (5) other theories, and (6) X-tra information regarding the theory. Each of these categories is further divided into subcategories of information. The student is instructed to use this framework of categories as a guide while taking notes on the theory being studied. At least two benefits may be gained by the student using this technique. One benefit is that even if the student cannot easily relate a given scientific theory to existing knowledge, she or he has a set system for deciding which information is most relevant to understanding the theory. The second benefit to the student is that the same structure can be used across a number of theories to represent similar information. Of course, this technique is not necessarily limited to scientific theories, and its developers plan to continue research on alternative applications.

SCOPE

Another manner in which learning strategies may differ is in the degree to which they are applicable in processing varying amounts of information. This dimension can be referred to as the scope of a learning strategy. Some strategies may be more useful in learning large amounts of material, while others may be more useful for learning small amounts of information. An example of a learning strategy (actually, a coherent set of strategies) that has a large scope is Dansereau's MURDER system (Dansereau, McDonald, Collins, Garland, Holley, Diekhoff, & Evans, 1979).

Because this particular system incorporates techniques common to many learning-strategy systems, it is described here in some detail. The system was developed by Dansereau and his colleagues as an omnibus studying system that could be used by college students. In many ways MURDER can be seen as an expansion of Robinson's (1946) SQ3R system. The main differences between the two systems are that the MURDER system specifies exact methods for using various study strategies and the MURDER technique includes affective–conative components.

The first component of MURDER is *M*ood. This step consists of a number of techniques for creating a positive and relaxed internal environment for the student. It was borrowed from the work of Meichenbaum (e.g., Meichenbaum & Goodman, 1971) on positive self-talk, Ellis (1963) on rational behavior therapy, and Wolpe (1969) on systematic desensitization. The second step is *U*nderstand, in which the student is encouraged to identify those portions of the text that are meaningful and those that require further processing by the student to be meaningful. While this aspect of the

MURDER strategy is not well defined, it appears similar to what others refer to as metacognitive strategies (see Flavell, 1979). In other words, students are to identify the information they understand, as well as the information they do not understand. The next step is *R*ecall, during which the student engages in the active use of specific text-processing strategies; for example, the student is instructed to network the text to make the relationships among the various topics clearer. The final three steps in the MURDER system are *D*igest, *E*xpand, and *R*eview. In these phases, the learner is asked to further expand her or his knowledge base by finding out what information is easy to remember and what information is hard to remember. Question asking and explicit feedback are two of the suggested techniques to use in expanding the student's understanding and memory for the text. Finally, the learner is asked to adjust his or her study techniques on the basis of test results in class.

Strategies that are less inclusive in scope include imagery, mnemonic, and keyword techniques. Weinstein and Mayer (1985) refer to these as basic elaboration strategies. Mnemonics and other similar techniques are frequently used as aids in remembering lists of items (such as the familiar *"every good boy does fine"* to aid in remembering the names of musical notes on the treble clef). Recently, considerable attention has been paid to the use of mnemonics in the acquisition of a second language (e.g., Paivio & Desroches, 1981). One of the more popular techniques in this area is the keyword method developed by Atkinson (e.g., Atkinson, 1975). This method consists of associating a mediator word with the word to be learned and then creating a mental image of the object referred to by the mediator interacting with the object referred to by the word to be learned. For instance, Pressley and Levin (1981) had subjects use the keyword *car* to remember the English word *carlin*. Since *carlin* means "old women," they instructed students to create an interactive image, such a that of an old woman driving a car, to help them remember the word to be learned. Obviously, this approach is very different from the SQ3R or MURDER approach to prose learning. The choice of an appropriate strategy depends on the amount and type of material to be learned.

DIRECTNESS

A third dimension on which learning strategies can be distinguished is their directness. Certain strategies, such as outlining, may be used directly to acquire new knowledge; other strategies, like relaxation training, may indirectly influence the acquisition of new information. Dansereau (1978) refers to these two kinds of learning strategies as primary strategies and support strategies, respectively. Examples of direct strategies are Holley, Dansereau, Collins, Brooks, & Larson's (1981) networking and Anderson's (1979) mapping strategies. Both of these techniques require the student to construct a spatial outline of a text that consists of a number of idea nodes representing the major and minor concepts, facts, and so on in the passage. The idea nodes are connected by means of relational links that represent a variety of different relationships among the nodes.

Indirect strategies may deal with the learner's affective–emotional and conative–motivational strategies for studying. Particularly popular in this area are methods for dealing with test anxiety. According to researchers such as Sarason (1960) and Spielberger (e.g., Spielberger, Golzalez, & Fletcher, 1979), test anxiety is a situation-specific trait that is characterized by feelings of tension and apprehension, self-centered worry, and activation of the autonomic nervous system. An example of one approach to dealing with test anxiety is Meichenbaum's (e.g., Meichenbaum & Butler, 1980) cognitive modification strategy system. Meichenbaum views test anxiety as a type of causal chain of components that interact with one another to produce a self-perpetuating cycle of anxious thoughts and behavior. According to his model, this chain consists of viewing physical arousal to testing situations as evidence of anxiety, which in turn causes the individual to further believe that he or she is anxious and therefore, to avoid these situations in the future. This avoidance increases the individual's anxiety toward testing situations, which may increase her or his physical response. Hence, the cycle reinforces itself. Meichenbaum suggests that a program consisting of the following three basic components be used to decrease test anxiety in individuals: (1) education, where the individual is made aware of how anxiety or stress operate both in his or her particular case and in general, (2) rehearsal, where the individual practices using specific strategies for coping with test anxiety, and (3) application, where the individual uses these strategies in an ecologically valid environment, such as the classroom.

LEVEL

A fourth way in which learning strategies can vary is in their level. That is, some strategies may require students to operate at a fairly high level of conscious awareness of their cognitive activities, while other strategies may require only minimal conscious awareness of cognitive functioning. A high level of awareness is required when a learner directs his or her studying at an executive level, that is, decides which learning strategies to use, as opposed to blindly applying a single strategy to any learning situation. In effect, this dimension distinguishes between metacognitive and cognitive strategies. Metacognitive strategies are involved in studying when a learner must select and implement specific cognitive and/or affective strategies to effectively process information (see Armbruster, Echolis, & Brown, 1982).

To date there has been little research on the combination of metacognitive strategies and cognitive strategies for learning text. Although a portion of both elements are involved in the Dansereau et al. (1979) MURDER system, only in a few studies have the interaction of these two kinds of strategies been the focus of attention (e.g., Brown & Day, 1983). Brooks, Bitler, and Shurtleff (1984) assessed the role of cognitive monitoring as one component of a three-component learning strategy system. This system involved training students to use the text's structure as a guide for creating outlines and summaries representing the content of written material. Furthermore, each student was trained to use the text's structure as a guide for formulating metacognitive questions about his or her understanding of the text. Preliminary results indicate that this training procedure significantly increases students' memory for main ideas from text material. This study, along with the Brown and Day (1983) study, are two examples of research concerned with the effects of both cognitive and metacognitive strategic processing in learning situations.

MODIFIABILITY

Another dimension on which learning strategies can be distinguished is their modifiability, or the degree to which they can be changed to meet the needs of a particular learning situation. Dansereau (in press) refers to the extremes of this dimension as algorithmic strategies, which are relatively inflexible, and heuristic strategies, which are easily modifiable. An example of an algorithmic strategy is Atkinson's (1975) keyword method or Brooks and Dansereau's (1983) structural schema training. Both of these strategies require the learner to perform similar or identical procedures across learning situations. In contrast, heuristic strategies, such as those outlined by Rigney, Munro, and Crook (1979), allow learners to adapt their studying procedures to the learning environment. Rigney et al. developed a generalized learning system called Aids. This system is computer-based and offers the student guidelines to break down complex learning tasks into simpler components. One reason that this system is heuristic in nature is that the learner helps to identify what subtasks must be performed in order to complete the overall task. This characteristic allows the learner to use the system in a relatively flexible manner.

The sixth learning-strategy category is modality. That is, strategies may vary according to what sensory or processing systems are emphasized in their acquisition and use. For example, Singer (e.g., Singer, 1978; Singer & Gerson, 1979; Singer & Pease, 1976) has conducted research on learning strategies and motor skills for a number of years. Singer argues that similar processes are involved in the learning of verbal and motor strategies and skills. If this is the case, it may be that the strategies that are currently being developed primarily as text-processing strategies will, at least in generic form, transfer across a wide variety of learning situations.

To summarize, we have specified six general dimensions on which learning strategies may differ: generalizability, scope, directness, level, modifiability, and modality. In conjunction with these categories, we have given some examples of the more relevant research that illustrates the differences among strategy systems along these dimensions.

LEARNING STRATEGIES
AND INDIVIDUAL DIFFERENCES

In this section we discuss research that relates individual differences to the acquisition and use of learning strategies. Although there has been substantial research examining the relationships among individual differences in other cognitive areas such as reading and instruction (see Carroll & Maxwell, 1979; Cronbach & Snow, 1977), there is little research on how differences among individuals are related to learning strategies. In *Individual Differences in Cognition,* Volume 1 (1983), Schmeck reviews research on study styles and learning strategies. This section complements Schmeck's earlier chapter by emphasizing other areas of research relating strategy systems to individual differences.

IMPEDIMENTS TO RESEARCH ON INDIVIDUAL DIFFERENCES
AND LEARNING STRATEGIES

Learning strategies can be considered a new area of research. Only since the 1970s have many researchers devoted their attention to this field of inquiry. In a majority of cases, it seems that one implicit assumption is that a strategy should be useful to a large number of individuals regardless of differences that may exist among individuals in knowledge, verbal abilities, and other cognitive characteristics. Although this is not a bad assumption when one is first developing a system, it does seem reasonable to expect that the effectiveness of different types of learning strategies will vary depending on the characteristics of individual learners.

One impediment to the integration of individual-differences and learning-strategies research is the lack of an appropriate model relating them. While there are a number of excellent models for representing individual differences (e.g., Carroll, 1983; Pellegrino & Glaser, 1982; Royce, 1973; Sternberg, 1977), to the authors' best knowledge these models have not been adapted in any consistent manner to the problems associated with learning-strategies research. However, a few researchers have suggested some interesting starting points for developing a model relating the two areas (e.g., Dansereau, Actkinson, Long, & McDonald, 1974; Lohman & Kyllonen, 1983).

Another impediment to the integration of learning-strategies and individual-differences research is that few tests have been developed to measure specific cognitive abilities or styles that the learning-strategy researcher may wish to assess and ultimately improve. There have been attempts to develop learning-strategy inventories (e.g., Schmeck, Ribich, & Ramanaiah, 1977; Schulte & Weinstein, 1981) and tests of affective measures such as test anxiety (e.g., Richardson, O'Neil, Whitmore, & Judd, 1977). Other cognitive or conative–affective measures, however, have received little attention by persons interested in learning strategies. It is reasonable to assume that with the changing perspectives in how we think about individual-differences research (e.g., Sternberg, 1977, 1981; Sternberg & Powell, 1983), more learning strategists will become interested in individual constructs related to the development and use of learning strategies.

Two related constraints to assessing individual differences within a learning-strategies framework are (1) the time to train learning strategies, and (2) the number of subjects required to perform individual differences research. Most learning strategy training requires an extensive period of time. For example, the Dansereau et al. (1979) MURDER system was offered as a semester course (e.g., 4 hours per week for approximately 3½ months). Even relatively simple strategies usually require a minimum of 2–4 hours to train. Given the pragmatic concerns with time constraints in most experimental situations and learning environments, it is understandable that many researchers have been reluctant to require subjects to spend the additional time needed to collect data on individual differences. Because of the time and cost involved in training large groups of individuals, many learning-strategy studies are conducted with a small number of subjects. As pointed out by researchers in individual differences (e.g., Cronbach & Snow, 1977), a fairly large number of individuals are needed when trying to determine the relationships among two or more different treatments and one or more attributes of learners. Often learning strategy researchers are not in a position to adequately measure many individual differences that they would otherwise be only too interested in assessing.

OVERVIEW OF PAST RESEARCH

A number of models have been proposed for how individual differences in abilities are related to one another and how these differences relate to other behavioral constructs. The development of models relating cognitive styles and affective components has not received as much attention but should be of interest to the learning strategist (see Royce, 1973). Those individual differences that may be most relevant to the acquisition and utilization of learning strategies can be subsumed under four general categories: (1) abilities, (2) cognitive style, (3) prior knowledge, and (4) affect and motivation (see Figure 8.2). In this section, we look briefly at some representative examples of learning-strategy studies from each of these categories.

ABILITIES

The influence of abilities on the acquisition and use of learning strategies has received the most attention from learning strategists. Specific areas that we cover in this section are verbal–reading ability, mathematical ability, learning rate, and visualization–spatial ability.

Previous research on the relationship between mental abilities and learning strategies has focused on verbal aptitude. In one study, Doctorow, Wittrock, and Marks (1978) assessed the difference between good and poor readers as measured by the Science Research Associates Reading Placement Test (Parker & Scannell, 1969) and the difference in their comprehension and recall of text material after receiving training on using generative pro-

ABILITIES — AN INDIVIDUAL'S CAPACITY TO PROCESS A SPECIFIC TYPE OF INFORMATION. EXAMPLES: VERBAL/READING ABILITY, MATHEMATICAL ABILITY, PROCESSING SPEED, VISUALIZATION/SPATAL ABILTIY.

COGNITIVE STYLE — THE PREFERRED MANNER IN WHICH AN INDIVIDUAL PROCESSES A SPECIFIC TYPE OF INFORMATION.

PRIOR KNOWLEDGE — THE PREVIOUSLY ACQUIRED KNOWLEDGE AN INDIVIDUAL PROCESSES ABOUT A SPECIFIC TOPIC.

AFFECT/MOTIVATION — AN INDIVIDUAL'S ATTITUDES, VALUES, INTERESTS, TEMPERAMENT, ESPECIALLY TOWARD A SPECIFIC LEARNING SITUATION.

FIGURE 8.2 Four general categories of individual differences related to learning strategies.

cesses in reading. Good and poor readers were assessed separately in two similar experiments. The major difference between the two experiments was in the reading level of the material to be learned. High-ability students (good readers) were given relatively longer and more difficult material to read than were low-ability students (poor readers). In both experiments, training consisted of having students (10–12-year-old children) create or generate a sentence describing each paragraph in a story. Students were to generate sentences for one of three different versions of the same text. In one version, each paragraph was preceded by a two-word heading describing that paragraph. In the second version, a one-word heading replaced the two-word heading; and in the final version, each paragraph was presented without any heading. One dependent measure used in the study was a multiple-choice (comprehension) test requiring students, in either a cued or noncued condition, to combine information across paragraphs to answer some items or to use only information contained within a single paragraph for other items. The second test was a cloze (recall) test with blanks inserted in place of certain key words in the stimulus passage.

The results of the two experiments were similar for good and poor readers with a few exceptions. For example, both good and poor readers scored higher on the multiple-choice and cloze tests if they were given the generative instructions in combination with the text containing the headings than if they were given the text without headings. Additionally, students given the generative instructions outperformed those students not given the generative instructions on the dependent measures. However, training students to write their own sentences summarizing each paragraph proved to be more beneficial for readers classified as low ability than for readers classified as high ability. The authors suggest that poor readers are less likely to use this kind of learning strategy spontaneously than are readers of higher ability. Also, it was found that high-ability readers were able to make more effective use of the text headings in combination with the generation strategy than were low-ability readers for the comprehension test. This result suggests that poor readers may be less able to make efficient use of multiple cues at a single sitting than high-ability readers. Such an hypothesis is supported by results of another study (Holley et al., 1981) in which college students were trained to use text headings as either acquisition aids, retrieval aids, or as both acquisition and retrieval aids. Results indicated that these learners were able to use the headings as either acquisition or retrieval aids but could not effectively use these strategies in combination. An alternative hypothesis is that readers who are classified as having low ability may have problems using text structural cues as processing aids. This reasoning would be generally congruent with past research in this area (e.g., Meyer, Brandt, & Bluth, 1980). If this is the case, then more explicit training in the use of text structural cues may be required for these types of students.

The implication of these findings for learning strategies research is that in comprehending fairly complex textual information, different strategies may need to be used by high- and low-ability readers. One hopes that as low-ability readers acquire more efficient strategies for comprehending prose material, their performance will more closely approximate that of high-ability readers. A second implication of the Doctorow et al. (1978) study is that the explicitness of training is a very important variable in the development of learning strategy systems. The effectiveness of any learning strategy will depend on the learner's awareness of what is expected of him or her.

Mayer (1980) investigated the relationship between mathematical ability as measured by the SAT-M (Scholastic Aptitude Test-Mathematics) and the use of advance organizers and elaboration strategies. This research is based partly on Mayer's (1975) assimilation theory, which suggests that at least three conditions must be met for meaningful learning to occur. One condition is that the information to be learned must be received by the learner. A second condition is that the learner must have previously acquired knowledge that can be used as an assimilative context in which to incorporate newly acquired information. Third, the learner must relate the new information to this assimilative context in an active manner. Elaboration strategies, in general, require the learner to relate what is being learned to what is already known. As such, these types of strategies should affect the third element in Mayer's assimilative theory.

In a series of experiments, Mayer (1980) tested whether elaboration techniques and an advance organizer (see Ausubel, 1963) would facilitate the learning of a computer programming language. Two types of elaboration were investigated. The first type was model elaboration, which required the student to relate new information (text descriptions of computer commands) to a familiar, concrete model of a computer. The second type, comparison elaboration, required the student to relate new commands to one another by stating how they were alike and how they were different. Learning was assessed by interpretation questions for which the student explained the function of a given program and by generation questions for which the student wrote a program that would accomplish a given task. Additionally, each type of question was asked at five different levels corresponding to the directness of transfer from the learning task to the question answering task. For example, Level 1 questions, which involved simple sorting, primarily involved near transfer, while Level 5 questions, which required putting new information together in novel ways, involved far transfer. The other three levels of questions represented different degrees of complexity and directness of transfer.

Results of two experiments comparing elaboration techniques with a control (read only) condition showed that the model-elaboration group surpassed the control group on both interpretation and generation questions and that the difference between the model-elaboration group and control group increased with questions involving more remote transfer. The comparison-elaboration group similarly outperformed the control group on far-transfer problems when the questions were interpretive in nature; for generation questions, the comparison-elaboration group performed better than the control group regardless of whether remote or more direct transfer was required.

A measure of learners' mathematical ability (SAT-M) was included as a factor in another experiment in this study (Mayer, 1980, Experiment 4). The results of this experiment reveal that learning techniques benefited students with low mathematical ability more than students with high mathematical ability and that the performance differences between these two ability groups were more pronounced on problems requiring the transfer of information to novel situations. Mayer suggests that his results support the notion that students classified as having high mathematical ability have already developed strategies for understanding mathematical concepts that students classified as having low mathematical ability do not have. Thus, students with low mathematical ability are more likely to benefit from explicit training in the use of effective learning strategies.

The results of Mayer's study are supportive of our contention that the explicitness of training in learning strategy programs is a factor of great importance. They also suggest that learning strategists should be interested in assessing the procedures that experts, both in content areas and in learning techniques, use in acquiring new information. If the strategies that high-ability experts use to process information can be taught to low-ability nonexperts, then, hopefully, the performance difference between these two groups can be minimized.

In one of the very few studies concerning learning rate and learning strategies, Wang (1983), compared fast and slow processors–learners on their use of elaborative strategies for learning paired-associative nouns. Wang hypothesized that fast learners generate more mediating elaborators and/or more appropriate elaborators than slow learners during acquisition. The types of elaborators that could be generated by subjects were classified as belonging to one of four categories: (1) related to both stimuli and response nouns, (2) related only to the stimulus, (3) related only to the response, and (4) idiosyncratic, not directly related to either the stimulus or the response. Wang reasoned that if fast learners merely generate more elaborators than do slow learners, no differences between the two groups would be expected on the proportion of elaborators belonging to each of the four categories. If, however, fast learners differ from slow learners in the quality of elaborators they generate, one would expect fast learners to construct more elaborators belonging to Categories 1 and 2, relative to slow learners.

In the first of three experiments, students were classified as fast learners if they reached a criterion of one perfect trial within four trials of a paired-associate task. Students classified as slow learners needed six or more trials to reach criterion. On experimental trials, each subject was presented with instructions to construct an elaborator (e.g., picture, rhyme, or sentence) to associate the two nouns in each pair and to give the elaborator a one-word label. All item pairs were presented at 4-second intervals. After the last pair had been presented, subjects were asked to use their generated words as cues to recall the elaborators they had just constructed.

Results from this experiment indicated that fast learners constructed more elaborators, especially during initial stages of learning, than did slow learners. Fast learners also produced better quality mediators than slow learners, reporting a greater percentage of elaborators related to either the stimulus noun or both the stimulus and response words.

In the second experiment, the elaborators identified in the first experiment were given to students to use in place of their generating their own mediators. These elaborators were divided into two groups: those used only by fast learners and those used only by slow learners. Results indicated that students given the fast-learner elaborators needed significantly fewer trials to reach criterion than did students given slow-learner elaborators. These results further support the notion that learning speed is related to strategy application.

In the third experiment, Wang again presented subjects with elaborators generated by either fast or slow learners. In this case, elaborators were also divided by quality for both sets of learners. In other words, there were eight different sets of elaborators: fast- and slow-learner–generated elaborators crossed with elaborators related to both stimulus and response, stimulus only, response only, or idiosyncratic. Other procedures were similar to Experiment 2.

Results from this experiment support the findings of the second experiment in that fast-learner elaborators were superior to slow-learner elaborators in their usefulness for learning paired-associate nouns. Also, results of these experiments support the notion that the different quality mediators affect acquisition rates more strongly as the criterion for learning becomes more stringent (i.e., from 1 out of 10 to 10 out of 10 items). This finding is also true of the acquisition rates for subjects using fast- and slow-learner–generated elaborators; that is, their acquisition rates became more disparate as learning progressed, with fast-learner mediators being more efficient learning aids.

This study supports the idea that the different strategies learners use to acquire paired-associate information greatly influence the rate of learning. Fast learners appear to be able not only to generate more elaborators but also to generate more effective elaborators that are related to either the stimulus or both the stimulus and response terms. The effectiveness of the products (elaborators) of fast-learner elaborative strategies was shown to transfer to other learners who were given these same elaborators. The next logical step in this line of research is to develop teaching methods that will help slow learners produce effective elaborators for paired-associate learning situations.

Thorndyke and Stasz (e.g., Stasz, 1980; Stasz & Thorndyke, 1980; Thorndyke & Stasz, 1980) investigated the relationship between learner strategies, visual abilities, and map reading. According to these authors, abilities may affect the use of learning strategies in at least two ways: (1) An individual's ability may help determine which strategy, if any, the learner will use in acquiring new information, and (2) the ability level of an individual may influence how effectively that person will be able to use a particular strategy.

In particular, Stasz (1980) was concerned with the global strategies individuals use in reading and learning maps and the relationship of these strategies to the learner's visual–spatial ability. In this study, 25 subjects were asked to study and reproduce two maps. One map depicted an imaginary town and the other depicted an imaginary continent. Each student was given 2 minutes to study a map and was then asked to reproduce the map from memory. Verbal protocols were collected concerning the study strategies each individual used during and immediately after map learning. Additionally, two individual-differences scales were given to all subjects. One test measured the students' degree of field independence and dependence, and the other measured visual-memory ability (i.e., the ability to remember the configuration, location, and orientation of visual information).

Five strategy categories were constructed based on the verbal protocols collected during map learning. The first category, the divide-and-conquer strategy, consists of dividing a map into smaller submaps for study. In other words, a map is divided into three to five smaller maps, and each of these sections is studied separately. The second category, is the global network strategy, in which learners select some of the more salient features on the map and use them as reference points for learning the rest of the map. The third strategy is the progressive expansion strategy, which involves selecting a starting point on the map (for instance, the right side) and learning the rest of the map by surveying it from that point. The final strategy is the narrative elaboration strategy, which differs from the first three in that it is verbally based and not directly related to focusing the learner's attention through specific visual procedures, as is the case in the other strategies. A learner using this strategy creates a narrative based on mnemonics and verbal elaboration to associate major spatial features on the map to one another. Finally, some students did not use any apparent strategy to learn the maps. Twenty of the 25 subjects were also divided into high- and low-ability groups on the basis of their visual-memory and field-dependence scores.

Results of this study revealed that high-ability subjects tend to use the global network strategy more often than any other strategy and that low-ability subjects tend not to use any strategy at all. It was also found that high-ability subjects and subjects who used one of the three visual and attention-directing strategies had higher recall scores for map features than did low-ability subjects and subjects who used either the verbal narrative strategy or no strategy.

Results of this research imply that low-ability subjects can be trained to use the more effective strategies of high-ability subjects. However, another study by Thorndyke and Stasz (1980) failed to provide support for this notion. The authors found that only medium- and high-ability subjects were able to profit from visual-strategy training. Additional research needs to be done in this area before more than tentative conclusions can be reached. A better approach may be to match strategy and instructional presentation with the abilities of each individual. Future research in this area should help delineate which parameters of this learning situation can be effectively manipulated.

COGNITIVE STYLE

Differences in cognitive style are potentially as important as differences in abilities to the formulation of a reasonable model of strategic information processing. Cognitive styles differ from abilities in a number of ways (see Messick, 1978). Whereas abilities are typically seen as unipolar and specific in nature, cognitive styles are often construed as bipolar and more general in nature. Abilities may also be conceptualized as being related to the amount of information processed, while cognitive styles may be related to the manner in which information is processed. A plethora of cognitive styles have been postulated by various researchers. Some that seem relevant to cognitive-strategies research include (1) educational set, (2) field dependence and independence, (3) top-down and bottom-up processing, (4) leveling and sharpening, and (5) preference for learning in different sensory modalities. We discuss two studies that looked at two different cognitive styles (educational set and field dependence) as variables in the acquisition and use of learning strategies.

Educational set is defined by Siegel and Siegel (1965, 1967) as a preference for learning new material in a factual-to-conceptual or a conceptual-to-factual sequence. These authors argue that students may be able to process information more effectively if it is presented to them in a sequence that is congruent with their cognitive style. In some respects this idea is similar to Pask's (1975) differentiation between holistic and serialistic problem solvers.

Holley, Dansereau, and Fenker (1981) investigated the utility of educational set in the context of learning-strategy research. These investigators modified the Educational Set Scale (ESS) developed by Siegel and Siegel (1965) on the basis of item analysis to create a more homogeneous set of items. Students in this study were classified as being either conceptually set or factually set by their scores on the ESS. Dependent variables included free-recall and multiple-choice (recognition) scores on a non-narrative passage as well as verbal-ability scores. The revised ESS scale was further divided into two subscales on the basis of a factor analysis. Factor I scores were highly correlated with total scores on the ESS (.99), while Factor II scores had a low correlation with total ESS score (.01). A series of discriminant analyses was computed to see if conceptual and factual subgroups could be differentiated reliably from one another. It was found that the two ESS groups could be distinguished from each other, especially on the basis of their free-recall and verbal-ability scores. Furthermore, it was found that not only was Factor I significantly related to verbal ability, but also that verbal ability was not related to Factor II. These results indicate that learners who are conceptually set do better on a text-comprehension task than do learners who are factually set. Holley et al. also found that conceptually set learners do better on free-recall (conceptual) performance measures, while factually set learners do better on recognition (factual) performance measures. Finally, it was shown that conceptually set learners score consistently higher on both measures than do factually set learners.

The implications of this research for learning strategies include the possibility of trying to change a student's preference for conceptually versus factually set sequencing and the possibility of teaching students to use the strategies that are most appropriate for the sequencing of materials. We know of no studies that have been conducted in which the different processing procedures of conceptually set students have been evaluated. Such work would seem to be a logical step for further research on cognitive style.

In another study investigating the relationship between cognitive style and learning strategies, Brooks, Dansereau, Spurlin, and Holley (1983) investigated the role of field independence and dependence in the training of a text-processing strategy emphasizing the use of text headings as comprehension aids. This notion was based in part on the assumption that field-independent students may be able to relate the superordinate information contained in headings to the relevant subordinate information (details) contained in the text more effectively than field-dependent students. This assumption is supported by Spiro and Tirre (1980), who found that field-independent readers were more successful at using high-level structured knowledge (schemata) in the processing of text material than were field-dependent individuals. Because headings and strategies employing headings as learning aids emphasize the top-level structure, or schema, of a text, Brooks et al. (1983) predicted that field-independent readers could use headings more effectively than field-dependent readers.

The second experiment of the study required students to use text headings to (1) develop expectations about the material in the passage, (2) understand why each heading was appropriate for its section of text, (3) memorize the headings, and (4) practice using the headings as recall aids. Three treatment groups were used. One group received a text with headings plus instructions in the use of strategies for using the headings, a second group received the passage with headings but not training, and a third group received the passage without headings or training on strategies.

Field dependence in this study was assessed using the Group Embedded Figures Test (GEFT; Oltman, Raskin, & Witkin, 1971). The Delta Vocabulary Test was used as a measure of verbal ability (Deignan, 1973). Dependent variables in this study consisted of a free-recall test, a multiple-choice test, and an outline test in which readers were asked to produce an organized outline of the text from memory.

Results indicated that the learning strategy involving the use of text headings proved effective in helping students free-recall the materials. Similar but nonsignificant results were also found for the outline measure. On the other hand, the multiple choice–recognition measure did not discriminate between groups. In assessing the relationship of field dependence to strategy use, these authors used a hierarchical regression approach whereby variables were entered into a regression equation in a specified order. Two sets of equations were computed for each of the three dependent variables. One set of equations used the verbal-ability measure (Delta) as a covariate before entering the field-dependent measure (GEFT) into the equation. A second set of equations was computed using only dummy coded variables to represent the treatment groups, the GEFT, and the appropriate interaction terms. Results of these equations showed that when verbal ability is covaried, field dependence does not account for a significant amount of variance in any of the dependent variables. However, when verbal ability was not included in the equations, a significant amount of the variance accounted for in the dependent variables could be attributed to the field-dependence variable. In none of the equations was a significant interaction found between field dependence and the use of learning strategies.

These findings have implications for researchers interested in considering individual differences in their learning-strategies research. When investigating the role of individual differences, the investigator should be careful in defining the appropriate equations expressing relationships between these variables and strategy training. As Brooks et al. (1983) indicate, conclusions that the researcher reaches can be different depending on the variables and/or statistical strategies used in assessing the relevance of individual differences to the use of learning strategies. A second implication concerns the relationship between field dependence and text processing. It appears that only when highly organized prior knowledge is relevant to the learning of new material, as was the case in the Spiro and Tirre (1980) study, does field dependence account for a significant proportion of the variability in students' recall.

Learning style, as defined by Schmeck (1983) is another cognitive style with implications concerning learning strategies and individual differences. According to Schmeck, learning style is an individual's habitual strategy for processing information regardless of the demands and characteristics of the learning environment. Heuristically, at least, we can differentiate learning styles from learning strategies by ascribing to learning style the connotation of a stable processing strategy and to learning strategy the idea of a flexible, conscious change in processing style to meet the demands of a particular learning situation (see Battig, 1979).

Since Schmeck in *Individual Differences in Cognition,* Volume 1 (1983) reviewed the work on learning styles and learning strategies, we do not go into detail here on the relationship between these constructs. The reader is also referred to Schulte and Weinstein (1981) for information concerning the development of learning strategy inventories.

PRIOR KNOWLEDGE

The relevance of prior knowledge to the acquisition of new knowledge has been emphasized repeatedly in the cognitive literature. It is curious that relatively little attention has been paid to the role of domain-specific knowledge within the context of learning strategies. The relationship between learning strategies and content-specific prior knowledge should certainly prove to be a fruitful line of research.

A study by Walker (1982) was a preliminary attempt to establish the relationship between high and low domain knowledge and individual verbal recall. This study was based on earlier work by Voss and his colleagues (e.g., Chiesi, Spilich, & Voss, 1979; Spilich, Vesander, Chiesi, & Voss, 1979) on the influence of prior knowledge on text processing. According to Voss, prior knowledge consists of the concepts, goals, rules, and other information already stored in memory about a particular topic. A common assumption underlying learning-strategies research is that strategies are content-independent and, therefore, generalizable across a variety of domain-related learning situations (see Brooks & Dansereau, 1983). However, transferability of strategies across domains has yet to be demonstrated to any great extent. Walker argues that domain-specific knowledge is a prerequisite to the effective use of strategies in a given area of knowledge. Although this particular study does not address this issue directly, the results offer some insights into the relationship between strategic thinking and domain-specific knowledge in acquiring new information. In this experiment, Walker tested low verbal-ability Army recruits on their knowledge of the game of baseball. A soldier's knowledge of baseball was assessed by a 45-item test covering the concepts, goals, and rules of baseball. Then verbal ability was measured by the Test of Adult Basic English typically given to new Army recruits. Finally, soldiers were given a short, narrative account of a half-inning of a fictional baseball game and were asked to complete a free-recall and a multiple-choice test concerning the game.

Results of this experiment are relevant to learning strategies research in two respects. First, individuals obtaining relatively high scores on the baseball knowledge test were able to infer more goal-related states implicitly mentioned in the passage (e.g., score of the game) than were individuals with low baseball knowledge. This result indicates that high-knowledge persons were employing a more effective monitoring strategy than were the low-knowledge persons. Second, it appears from the results of this experiment that high-knowledge individuals are using a more effective retrieval strategy than are low-knowledge individuals given that the difference between these two groups of individuals was greater on the free-recall task than on the recognition–multiple-choice task (see Holley, Dansereau, Collins, Brooks, & Larson, 1981; Yekovich & Thorndyke, 1981).

If the use of more-effective strategies is actually due to the greater amount of prior knowledge on the part of high-knowledge, low-ability individuals, future studies need to be conducted to determine whether or not these strategies are indeed content-dependent. Also, it would be interesting to see if the strategies of high-knowledge individuals can be incorporated by low-knowledge individuals into their repertoire of study skills.

In a study concerned with the effects of prior knowledge, Miyake and Norman (1979) investigated how high- and low-knowledge persons differ in the number and kinds of questions they ask about instructional material. Although not a learning-strategy study per se, this study does have implications for learning-strategy research. The major hypothesis of Miyake and Norman was that in order to ask questions about a specific knowledge domain, one must first know something about the domain. That is, high-knowledge individuals could ask more questions about newly presented information than could low-knowledge individuals. It could also be expected that high-knowledge individuals would ask more questions when presented with relatively difficult material than when presented with relatively easy material. This would be expected because high-knowledge individuals would not experience any gaps or inconsistencies between their knowledge and the new, relatively easy incoming information. In contrast, low-knowledge individuals may not ask very many questions when presented with relatively difficult material because they do not have the appropriate knowledge needed to generate questions about the material. However, with relatively easy material, low-knowledge individuals are more likely to have enough previously acquired knowledge concerning the topic to generate more questions than they would with more-difficult material.

Subjects in this experiment were instructed in the use of a computer text editor. Two versions (easy and difficult) of the instructional material were developed. The difficult version was more technical in nature than the easy version. Subjects were placed into high- and low-knowledge groups on the basis of whether or not they received experimentally provided training on a different computer text editor (high knowledge) or not (low knowledge). Thus, four experimental groups were created: (1) high knowledge–difficult material, (2) high knowledge–easy material, (3) low knowledge–difficult material and, (4) low knowledge–easy material. Verbal protocols of each student's freely occurring thoughts and questions were collected under all four conditions.

Questions generated by students while learning the text editor were classified by Miyake and Norman (1979) into one of five categories: (1) overall questions—the total number of questions, (2) number of concepts—the total number of questions minus repetitions and paraphrases, (3) the hypotheses—the number of speculations generated by the student about the material, (4) confirmations—comments that were not questions generated by the students about their interpretations of the material, and (5) look-backs—the total number of times the student turned back to previous pages of the material.

Results of this study support Miyake and Norman's hypotheses. Overall-category questions and concept-category questions were more often generated by high-knowledge students given hard material and by low-knowledge students given easy material. Similar, but not significant, results were found for the confirmation-category statements. Look-backs, however, were more often performed by students given the hard material regardless of the knowledge condition.

From a learning-strategy standpoint, it would be interesting to know if low-knowledge individuals can be taught strategies that would allow them to ask appropriate questions even when they do not have a sufficient knowledge base to generate questions without an algorithm. Brooks and Dansereau (1983) addressed this issue to some extent by creating a structural schema that learners can use to guide their studying of new material even if they are not familiar with a particular topic. This area of research has been largely ignored by learning strategists but should receive more attention in the future.

AFFECT AND MOTIVATION

Affective and conative variables have been of continuing interest to learning strategists. The need to fully integrate these variables into any full-scale learning-strategy program has been pointed out by O'Neil and Richardson (1980), Dansereau et al. (1979), and Spielberger, Gonzalez, and Fletcher (1979) among others.

Test anxiety has long been a subject for research by instructional psychologists (see Sarason, 1980); its relationship to learning-strategies research is noted by Spielberger et al. (1979). From a learning-strategy viewpoint, test anxiety is troublesome because it may cause a decrease in performance when it is present in a learner. Weinstein, Cubberly, and Richardson (1982) investigated the relationship between test anxiety and the two different learning strategies. Weinstein and her colleagues argue that the learner has a limited capacity to process information during a specified period of time and that the occurrence of anxious thoughts make demands on the individual learner's information-processing capacity. Therefore, highly test-anxious persons should have less capacity to process incoming information than persons not highly test anxious. This difference between high and low test-anxious persons should be more apparent when complex cognitive tasks are performed than when simple cognitive tasks are performed. The two learning strategies that students were trained to use during this experiment were (1) a shallow processing task in which individuals were told to compare and contrast paired-associate words by similarities between their physical representations (i.e., the same group of letters appear in both words), and (2) a deep processing task in which students were told to use a semantic-processing strategy to compare each word pair (i.e., both words may have similar meanings in different contexts). It was assumed by these authors that shallow processing tasks would place less processing demand on the learners than would the deep processing task.

Test anxiety in this experiment was measured by the Test Anxiety Scale (TAS; Richardson, O'Neil, Whitmore, & Judd, 1977). High test-anxious individuals were defined as those scoring above the median for this sample on the TAS, and low test-anxious individuals were defined as students scoring in the lower half of the range for the sample. Results for this study confirmed the hypothesis of Weinstein and her colleagues. The deep processing strategy led to better performance on the dependent measure for all individuals regardless of test-anxiety score. Low test-anxious individuals, however, outperformed high test-anxious individuals when both groups used the deep processing strategy. There was no difference between the groups when the shallow processing strategy was employed. The authors suggest that these results support a cognitive-attentional theory of test anxiety (i.e., the learner as a limited-capacity processor can only attend to a small number of processes at once).

Weinstein et al. (1982) note that this study can form the basis for a series of studies investigating whether high test-anxiety persons use different cognitive strategies than do low test-anxiety persons. Results of this latter type of studies also may help in developing appropriate learning strategies for highly test-anxious individuals.

In an extensive literature review and data analysis project, McCombs and Dobrovolny (1980, 1982) investigated the relevance of conative, affective, and cognitive skill variables to a computer-managed instructional system for the Air Force. Based on analysis of a number of individual-difference variables and on instructor and student interviews, they found that the following characteristics discriminated poor learners from effective learners:

1. *Conative variables.* Poor learners exhibited low motivation to learn, few professional and personal goals, little self discipline and responsibility, and low vocational maturity.
2. *Affective variables.* Poor learners exhibited high test anxiety and lack of skills for dealing with stress and anxiety.
3. *Cognitive variables.* Poor learners exhibited a lack of reading, comprehension and problem solving skills.

McCombs and Dobrovolny constructed a battery of individual difference measures based on these variables to discriminate between effective and noneffective learners. They constructed eight scales consisting of 140 items covering both conative and affective domains plus reasoning. These items were administered to two groups of military trainees (sample sizes were 195 and 117). The items and scales were revised on the basis of item and factor analysis and were then used in a series of discriminant analyses to predict which students would perform satisfactorily and unsatisfactorily in their military courses. It was found that approximately 80% of students could be correctly classified on the basis of the revised items and scales.

Finally, McCombs and Dobrovolny developed seven training modules covering the strategies that previous research has indicated are effective. Six of the training modules cover the following areas: (1) career development,

(2) values clarification, (3) goal setting, (4) assertiveness, (5) stress, and (6) management and problem solving. An introductory module was also developed to act as an advance organizer (see Mayer, 1978). Preliminary results concerning an evaluation of these modules indicated the modules were highly effective in reducing drop-out rates from Air Force training.

A FRAMEWORK FOR LEARNING STRATEGIES

Learning strategists increasingly emphasize that the understanding and training of effective information-processing skills involves the complex interaction of a variety of variables. The growing interest shown by cognitive-skill researchers in individual differences is ample demonstration that an integrative approach to learning strategies can be developed. We have discussed two domains that we propose as requirements for a general framework: learning strategies and individual differences. However, at least two other areas of concern should be included in a general framework for learning-strategies research. In creating and applying learning-strategies programs, researchers should consider the effects of task demands on the learner. Additionally, the nature of the information that the learner is expected to process should be anticipated by the learning strategist. In this section we briefly outline some of the prominent characteristics of these two domains—task demands and the nature of incoming information—as they relate to learning strategies.

TASK DEMANDS

Task demands are related to the skills and/or knowledge an individual must have to adequately meet the requirements of a learning situation. At present, very little research in the area of learning strategies has focused on the interaction between particular learning strategies and learning task demands.

1. *Similarity.* Similarity refers to how closely the situation in which the information learned resembles the situation in which the information is used. This dimension is related to near and far transfer as discussed by Dansereau and Brooks (1980) among others. According to these authors, near transfer occurs when the learning and performing situations are similar, and far transfer occurs when the two situations are not similar. The most appropriate learning strategy depends to some extent on the similarity between the acquisition and performance tasks.

2. *Level.* Depending on the task demands of a given situation, the learner may have to remember only higher-level or global information. In contrast, the learner may only need to know detailed information to perform a task. More realistically, the learner will probably need to know some combination of global and detailed information to adequately accomplish a given task. The learning strategy the individual uses will depend on the emphasis given to different levels of information.

3. *Modality.* The learner may be expected to output information in a number of different ways. For example, the learner may be required to perform a verbal task, or alternately, a motor task. The type of learning strategy the learner uses should be determined to some extent by the modality the learner uses in completing a task.

4. *Construction.* Construction refers to the amount of integration and inference in which an individual must engage to perform a task adequately. In one prose comprehension and recall task, for instance, the learner may be asked to recall verbatum the information in a text. In another, the learner may be asked to construct answers to questions that require the use of inferences based on information provided in the text.

NATURE OF INCOMING INFORMATION

The information that is presented to the learner and how it is presented varies across learning situations. In general, learning strategies have been developed for a wide variety of information sources. The following is a list of dimensions along which the presentation of information may vary:

1. *Amount.* The amount of information the learner must process is an obvious distinction. The learner may be required to process either large or small amounts of information, and selection of a strategy may depend upon the amount of information to be processed.

2. *Modality.* As mentioned previously, the information may be presented to the learner in different modalities. For example, the information one receives in learning a motor skill, such as driving a car, is likely to be different than the information that one receives when processing written text.

3. *Complexity.* The information presented to the learner can vary in terms of its complexity. One would likely use a different learning strategy to learn graduate-level scientific text than to memorize a shopping list.

4. *Structure.* The presentation of information may be structured differently to represent or emphasize certain characteristics of the information. Two text authors may present the same set of concepts in

different sequences depending upon their own idiosyncratic representation of that information. The same could be true of pictorial
material describing how to perform a physical task.

5. *Rate:* The learning strategy a person uses may depend upon the rate at
which the information is presented. A fast presentation rate may
preclude the use of certain strategies that require a minimum process-
ing-time interval that exceeds the constraints set by the task.

THE FRAMEWORK

We propose that four domains—learning strategies, individual differences, task demands, and the nature of the incoming information—form
the basis of a coherent framework for learning strategies. For heuristic purposes, we can classify the repertoire of learning strategies and the abilities,
cognitive styles, prior knowledge, and affective and motivational dispositions of a person as individual variables and classify task demands and the
nature of the incoming information can be viewed as interindividual or environmental variables. The combination of these two broad domains in a
learning situation determine the outcome of that learning situation. For our
purposes, the outcome of a learning situation consists of at least three
categories: (1) performance, or the actual change in the effectiveness with
which an individual completes a task; (2) knowledge base, or the measurable
changes in knowledge, both in content (what a person knows) and in structure (how a person's knowledge is organized) that occur as a result of learning; and (3) attitudes and styles, or the demonstrable changes that occur in an
individual's affective, conative, and cognitive dispositions and strategies. A
schematic representation of this framework is presented in Figure 8.3.

Of course, other variables such as social background, age, and gender
should be mentioned when speaking of representing the learning situation.
These and other relevant individual differences (Messick, 1978) can easily be
incorporated into our framework. The major purposes in presenting this
simple model of learning strategies research is to highlight the need for more

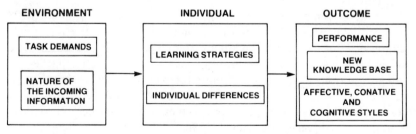

FIGURE 8.3   A schematic representation of a learning-strategies framework.

research that emphasizes the combination of a variety of variables in the learning situation in order to create optimal learning-strategy systems.

FUTURE DIRECTIONS

One of the foremost issues that should concern learning strategists is the development of a heuristically valuable model for conceptualizing the relationships between individual differences and learning strategies. A reasonable approach would be to investigate which metacomponents (see Sternberg, 1977) of intellectual and affective processing are directly involved in the acquisition and utilization of learning strategies. The emphasis on the use of higher-level constructs is due to the relatively weak findings that are typically reported between strategic behavior and basic, simple processing variables (e.g., Brooks et al. 1983; Campione & Brown, 1979). From a transfer-of-learning perspective (e.g., Dansereau & Brooks, 1980; Voss, 1982), a greater degree of predictability would be expected when the individual differences that a researcher measures are similar in processing level to the learning strategies being investigated. Exactly which processing components will prove to be reliable and predictive is a subject for future research.

In the process of developing a heuristic model for individual-differences and learning strategies research, it is probable that new individual variables will be identified or receive more attention than has been the case in the past. To date, with few exceptions, the majority of individual-differences measures used by learning strategists have been previously developed for use in other fields of psychology (for example, field-dependence tests). It may be that measures (and possibly constructs) developed specifically for identifying relevant individual differences within the domain of learning strategies will be especially sensitive to the types of changes that learning strategists expect in students' thinking and behavior. The addition of such variables to preexisting and traditional individual-difference measures should prove valuable to constructing a comprehensive framework for representing learning situations.

The development of learning strategy scales (e.g., Schmeck, 1983; Schulte & Weinstein, 1981) is one promising effort in the direction of creating new measures of individual differences directly related to the acquisition and use of learning strategies. This is one area in that learning strategists may have unique insights into the type of processes that should be measured to represent accurately the internal world of the learner. An interesting development would be scales to measure the learner's flexibility in the utilization of learning strategies in his or her repertoire. The executive strategies that learners use to select appropriate procedures for acquiring information should be a subject for research in this area. The information gained from the use of such scales would be valuable to the formulation and application of learning strategy systems.

Not only should individual differences be considered when developing a learning strategy system, but the possible interactions among individual differences, task demands, and the nature of incoming information should receive attention. In order to create an optimal learning environment for each learner, the characteristics of a particular learner as they relate to task demands and the type of information being processed have to be considered. Within the domain of learning strategies, the representation of the learning situation as an integration of the four basic domains mentioned in our framework has yet received very little research attention. Research such as that being conducted by McCombs (McCombs & Dobrovolny, 1980) does, however, represent a step toward this approach to designing learning-strategy studies.

Also, in line with this view of representing the learning situation as a combination of various interacting domains is research by Dansereau (e.g., Larson & Dansereau, 1981; Spurlin, Dansereau, Larson, & Brooks, 1981) on the possible interactions between individuals with either similar or dissimilar cognitive styles. This research suggests that the similarities and differences in cognitive and affective styles of students who study together may influence the effectiveness with which they acquire new information. One interesting variation on this notion is to program a computer to have a specific cognitive style that would either be similar or dissimilar to a student in a computer-aided learning situation. This type of research may be one way to develop flexible computer-directed instructional systems.

Finally, a longitudinal approach to individual differences and learning strategies would be of benefit in supplementing our knowledge of the interactions among learning strategies and the abilities, styles, and affect of each learner. For example, How do various individual differences affect the continued use of learning strategies over long periods of time? Alternately, as students become more expert in the use of learning strategies, are there noticeable and consistent changes in affective and cognitive styles? Also of interest would be the changes in the strategies that students use as they become more effective learners. It is possible that the abilities, prior knowledge, affective and conative predispositions, and styles of the learners will influence both the changes they make in their learning strategies and the choice of which learning strategies they will use. The manner in which various individuals utilize learning strategies over long periods of time should influence the design of a learning-strategy system.

Learning-strategy systems are intended to enable learners to make the most efficient use of their available resources to acquire, retain, and utilize information. Since each learner has his or her own unique set of abilities, styles, knowledge, and affective and motivational predispositions, the role of individual differences in learning-strategies research is of the utmost importance. Additionally, the influence of task demands and the nature of the incoming information should be considered in the development and implementation of learning-strategy systems. Future research combining these various variables in the learning situation in a consistent and coherent manner will greatly improve our understanding of how learners use strategies and will allow us to create efficient strategies for learners to use across a variety of learning situations.

REFERENCES

Anderson, T. H. Study skills and learning strategies. In H. F. O'Neil, Jr. (Ed.), *Learning Strategies.* New York: Academic Press, 1979.

Armbruster, B. B., Echolis, C. H., & Brown, A. C. The role of metacognition in reading to learn: A developmental perspective. *Volta Review, 1982, 84,* 45–56.

Atkinson, R. C. Mnemotechniques in second-language learning. *American Psychologist, 1975, 30,* 821–828.

Ausubel, D. P. *The psychology of meaningful verbal learning.* New York: Grune & Stratton, 1963.

Battig, W. G. Are the important individual differences between or within individuals? *Journal of Research in Personality, 1979, 13,* 546–558.

Brooks, L. W., Bitler, D., & Shurtleff, D. *Text processing and metacognitive strategies.* Paper presented at the Ninth Annual Department of Defense Psychology Symposium, Colorado Springs, CO, April, 1984.

Brooks, L. W., & Dansereau, D. F. Effects of structural schema training and text organization on expository prose processing. *Journal of Educational Psychology, 1983, 75,* 811–820.

Brooks, L. W., Dansereau, D. F., Spurlin, J. E., & Holley, C. D. Effects of headings on text processing. *Journal of Educational Psychology, 1983, 75,* 292–302.

Brown, A. L., & Day, J. D. Macrorules for summarizing texts: The development of expertise. *Journal of Verbal Learning and Verbal Behavior, 1983, 22,* 1–14.

Calfee, R. Cognitive psychology and educational practice. *Review of Research in Education, 1981, 9,* 3–73.

Campione, J. C., & Brown, A. L. Toward a theory of intelligence: Contributions from research with retarded children. In R. J. Sternberg & D. K. Detterman (Eds.). *Human intelligence: Perspectives on its theory and measurement.* Norwood, NJ: Ablex, 1979.

Carroll, J. B. Studying individual differences in cognitive abilities: Through and beyond factor analysis. In R. F. Dillon & R. R. Schmeck (Eds.), *Individual differences in cognition* (Vol. 1). New York: Academic Press, 1983.

Carroll, J. B., & Maxwell, S. E. Individual differences in cognitive abilities. *Annual Review of Psychology, 1979, 30,* 603–640.

Chiesi, H. L., Spilich, G. J., & Voss, J. F. Acquisition of domain-related information in relation to high and low domain knowledge. *Journal of Verbal Learning and Verbal Behavior, 1979, 18,* 257–273.

Cronbach, L. J., & Snow, R. E. *Aptitudes and instructional methods: A handbook for research on interactions.* New York: Irvington, 1977.

Dansereau, D. F. The development of a learning strategies curriculum. In H. F. O'Neil, Jr. (Ed.), *Learning Strategies.* New York: Academic Press, 1978.

Dansereau, D. F. Learning strategy research. In J. Segal, S. Chipman & R. Glaser (Eds.), *Thinking and learning skills: Relating instruction to basic research.* Hillsdale, NJ: Erlbaum, in press.

Dansereau, D. F., Actkinson, T. R., Long, G. L., & McDonald, B. *Learning strategies: A review and synthesis of the current literature* (AFHRL-TR-74-70, Contract F41609-74-C-0013). Lowry Air Force Base, CO: Air Force Human Resources Laboratory. (AD-07722), 1974.

Dansereau, D. F., & Brooks, L. W. *Transfer of learning from one setting to another.* Paper presented at the National Technical Institute for the Deaf, Rochester, New York, October 1980.

Dansereau, D. F., McDonald, B. A., Collins, K. W., Garland, J., Holley, C. D., Diekhoff, G. M., & Evans, S. H. Evaluation of a learning strategy system. In H. F. O'Neil, Jr. (Ed.), *Learning strategies.* New York: Academic Press, 1979.

Deignan, G. M. *The Delta reading vocabulary test.* Lowry Air Force Base, CO: Air Force Human Resources Laboratory, 1973.

Doctorow, M., Wittrock, M. C., & Marks, C. Generative processes in reading comprehension. *Journal of Educational Psychology,* 1978, *70,* 109–118.

Ellis, A. *Reason and emotion in psychotherapy.* New York: Lyle Stuart, 1963.

Flavell, J. H. Metacognition and cognitive monitoring: A new area of cognitive-developmental inquiry. *American Psychologist,* 1979, *34,* 906–911.

Galton, F. *Inquiries into human faculty and its development* (1st ed.). London: Macmillan, 1883.

Holley, C. D., Dansereau, D. F., Collins, K. W., Brooks, L. W., & Larson, D. Utilizing intact and embedded headings as processing aids with non-narrative text. *Contemporary Educational Psychology,* 1981, *6,* 227–236.

Holley, C. D., Dansereau, D. F., & Fenker, R. M. Some data and comments regarding educational set theory. *Journal of Educational Psychology,* 1981, *73,* 494–504.

Larson, C. O., & Dansereau, D. F. *Field dependence-independence and text processing.* Paper presented at the annual meeting of the Southwestern American Educational Research Association, Austin, Texas, February, 1981.

Lohman, D. F., & Kyllonen, P. C. Individual differences in solution strategy on spatial tasks. In R. F. Dillon & R. R. Schmeck (Eds.), *Individual differences in cognition:* (Vol. 1). New York: Academic Press, 1983.

Mayer, R. E. Information processing variables in learning to solve problems. *Review of Educational Research,* 1975, *45,* 525–541.

Mayer, R. E. Can advanced organizers influence meaningful learning? *Review of Educational Research,* 1978, *49,* 371–383.

Mayer, R. E. Elaboration techniques that increase the meaningfulness of technical text: An experimental test of the learning strategy hypothesis. *Journal of Educational Psychology,* 1980, *6,* 770–784.

McCombs, B. L., & Dobrovolny, J. L. *Rationale for the design of specific types of student skill training in the conative, affective, and cognitive skill domains* (Contract No. MDA 903-79-C-0193, ARPA order No. 3690). Lowry Air Force Base, CO, 1980.

McCombs, B. L., & Dobrovolny, J. L. *Student motivational skill training package: Evaluation for Air Force technical training* (Contract No. MDA 903-74-C-0193, Report No. AFHRL-TP-82-31). Lowry Air Force Base, CO: Logistics and Technical Training Division, 1982.

Meichenbaum, D. H., & Butler, L. Toward a conceptual model for the treatment of test anxiety:

Implications for research and treatment. In I. G. Sarason (Ed.), *Text anxiety, theory, research and applications.* Hillsdale, N.J., Erlbaum, 1980.

Meichenbaum, D. H., & Goodman, J. Training impulsive children to talk to themselves: A means of self-control. *Journal of Abnormal Psychology,* 1971, *77,* 115–126.

Messick, S. Personality consistency in cognition and creativity. In S. Messick & Associates (Eds.), *Individuality in learning.* San Francisco: Jossey-Bass, 1978.

Meyer, B. J. F., Brandt, D. H., & Bluth, G. J. Use of author's textual schema: Key for ninth-graders' comprehension. *Reading Research Quarterly,* 1980, *16,* 72–103.

Miyake, N., & Norman, D. A. To ask a question, one must know enough to know what is not known. *Journal of Verbal Learning and Verbal Behavior,* 1979, *18,* 357–364.

Oltman, P. K., Raskin, E., & Witkin, H. A. *Group embedded figures test.* Palo Alto, CA: Consulting Psychologists Press, 1971.

O'Neil, H. F., Jr., & Richardson, F. C. Test anxiety reduction and computer-based learning environments. In I. G. Sarason (Ed.), *Test anxiety: Theory, research, and applications.* Hillsdale: NJ: Erlbaum, 1980.

Paivio, A., & Desroches, A. Mnemonic techniques in second-language learning. *Journal of Educational Psychology, 73,* 780–795, 1981.

Parker, D. H., & Scannell, G. *Primary reading laboratory (Series IIB and IIC).* Chicago: Science Research Associates, 1969.

Pask, G. *Conversation, cognition and learning.* Amsterdam: Elsevier, 1975.

Pellegrino, J. W., & Glaser, R. Analyzing aptitudes for learning: Inductive reasoning. In R. Glaser (Ed.), *Advances in instructional psychology* (Vol. 2). Hillsdale, NJ: Erlbaum, 1982.

Pressley, M., & Levin, J. R. The keyword method and recall of vocabulary words from definition. *Journal of Experimental Psychology: Human Learning and Memory,* 1981, *7,* 72–76.

Richardson, F. C., O'Neil, H., Whitmore, S., & Judd, W. A. Factor analysis of the test anxiety scale. *Journal of Consulting and Clinical Psychology,* 1977, *45,* 704–705.

Rigney, J. W. Cognitive learning strategies and dualities in information processing. In R. E. Snow, P. Frederico, & W. E. Montague (Eds.), *Aptitude, learning and instruction* (Vol. 1). Hillsdale, NJ: Erlbaum, 1980.

Rigney, J. W., Munro, A., & Crook, D. E. Teaching task-oriented selective reading: A learning strategy. In H. F. O'Neil, Jr., & C. D. Spielberger (Eds.), *Cognitive and affective learning strategies.* New York: Academic Press, 1979.

Robinson, F. P. *Effective study.* New York: Harper, 1946.

Royce, J. R. The conceptual framework for a multi-factor theory of individuality. In J. R. Royce (Ed.), *Multivariate analysis and psychological theory.* New York: Academic Press, 1973.

Sarason, I. G. Empirical findings and theoretical problems in the use of anxiety scales. *Psychological Bulletin,* 1960, *57,* 403–415.

Sarason, I. G. (Ed.). *Test anxiety: Theory, research, and applications.* Hillsdale, NJ: Erlbaum, 1980.

Schmeck, R. R. Learning styles of college students. In R. F. Dillon & R. R. Schmeck (Eds.), *Individual differences in cognition* (Vol. 1). New York: Academic Press, 1983.

Schmeck, R. R., Ribich, F., & Ramanaich, N. Development of a self-report inventory for assessing individual differences in learning processes. *Applied Psychological Measurement,* 1977, *1,* 413–431.

Schulte, A. C., & Weinstein, C. E. *Inventories to assess cognitive learning strategies.* Paper presented at the Meeting of the American Educational Research Association, Los Angeles, CA, April 1981.

Siegel, L., & Siegel, L. C. Educational set: A determinant of acquisition. *Journal of Educational Psychology,* 1965, *56,* 1–12.

Siegel, L., & Siegel, L. C. A multivariate paradigm for educational research. *Psychological Bulletin*, 1967, *68*, 306–326.

Singer, R. N. Motor skills and learning strategies. In H. F. O'Neil, Jr., (Ed.), *Learning strategies*. New York: Academic Press, 1978.

Singer, R. N., & Gerson, R. F. Learning strategies, cognitive processes, and motor learning. In H. F. O'Neil, Jr., & C. D. Spielberger (Eds.), *Cognitive and affective learning strategies*. New York: Academic Press, 1979.

Singer, R. N., & Pease, D. The effect of different instructional strategies on learning, retention and transfer of a serial motor task. *Research Quarterly*, 1976, *47*, 788–796.

Spielberger, C. D., Gonzalez, H. P., & Fletcher, T. Text anxiety reduction, learning strategies, and academic performance. In H. F. O'Neil, Jr., & C. D. Spielberger (Eds.), *Cognitive and affective learning strategies*. New York: Academic Press, 1979.

Spilich, G. J., Vesonder, G. T., Chiesi, H. L., & Voss, J. F. Text processing of domain-related information for individuals with high and low domain knowledge. *Journal of Verbal Learning and Verbal Behavior*, 1979, *18*, 275–292.

Spiro, R. J., & Tirre, W. C. Individual differences in schema utilization during discourse processing. *Journal of Educational Psychology*, 1980, *72*, 204–208.

Spurlin, J. E., Dansereau, D. F., Larson, C. O., & Brooks, L. W. *Cooperative learning as an active and passive process*. Paper presented at the Annual Meeting of the Southwestern Educational Research Association, Austin, Texas, February 1981.

Stasz, C. *Planning during map learning: The global strategies of high and low visual-spatial individuals* (N-1594-ONR). The Rand Corporation, 1980.

Stasz, C., & Thorndyke, P. W. *The influence of visual-spatial ability and study procedures on map-learning skill* (N-1501-ONR). The Rand Corporation, 1980.

Sternberg, R. J. *Intelligence, information, processing, and analogical reasoning: The componential analysis of human abilities*. Hillsdale, NJ: Erlbaum, 1977.

Sternberg, R. J. Testing and cognitive psychology. *American Psychologist*, 1981, *36*, 1181–1189.

Sternberg, R. J., & Powell, J. S. Comprehending verbal comprehension. *American Psychologist*, 1983, *38*, 878–893.

Thorndyke, P. W., & Stasz, C. Individual differences in procedures for knowledge acquisition from maps. *Cognitive Psychology*, 1980, *12*, 137–175.

Voss, J. F. Organization, structure and memory: Three perspectives. In C. R. Puff (Ed.), *Memory organization and structure*. New York: Academic Press, 1982.

Walker, C. H. *Effects of ability and prior knowledge on the spontaneous development of learning strategies*. Paper presented at the meeting of the American Educational Research Association, New York, March 1982.

Wang, A. Y. Individual differences in learning speed. *Journal of Experimental Psychology: Learning, Memory, and Cognition*, 1983, *9*, 300–311.

Weinstein, C. E., Cubberly, W. E., & Richardson, F. C. The effects of test anxiety on learning at superficial and deep levels of processing. *Contemporary Educational Psychology*, 1982, *7*, 107–112.

Weinstein, C. E., & Mayer, R. E. The teaching of learning strategies. In M. C. Wittrock (Ed.), *Handbook of research on teaching* (3rd ed.) New York: MacMillan, 1985.

Wittrock, M. C. The cognitive movement in instruction. *Educational Psychologist*, 1978, *13*, 15–29.

Wolpe, J. *The practice of behavioral therapy*. New York: Pergamon, 1969.

Yekovich, F. R., & Thorndyke, P. W. An evaluation of alternative functional models of narrative schemata. *Journal of Verbal Learning and Verbal Behavior*, 1981, *20*, 454–469.

Author Index

Numbers in italics refer to the pages on which the complete references are cited.

A

Ackerman, P. L., 48, 52, 55, *64*
Actkinson, T. R., 162, *169*
Adams, J. A., 39, *64*
Addy, M. L., 167, *169*
Ahlfors, G., 167, *169*
Albert, M. L., 120, *141*
Allison, R. B., 61, *64*
Als, H., 109, *115*
Anastasi, A., 40, *64*
Anders, T., 101, 103, *117*
Anderson, J. R., 42, 56, 58, *64*
Anglin, J. M., 146, *169*
Apgar, V., 96, *115*
Arndt, S., 129, *139*
Ashcraft, M. H., 19, 30, *31*
Asher, J. J., 149, 154, *169*
Atkinson, R. C., 150, 158, 165, 166, *169*
Aurentz, J., 157, 159, *169*

B

Bakan, P., 128, *139*
Bamman, H. A., 167, *169*
Banich, M., 126, 127, *142*
Barnard, K., 98, 99, 101, 102, 105, 114, *115*
Baron, J., 82, *92*
Bartholomeus, B., 135, *139*
Bayley, N., 96, *115*
Bee, H., 98, 99, 101, 102, 105, 114, *115*
Behar, L. 98, *115*
Beilin, H., 10, *31*
Bellezza, F. S., 150, *169*
Bellugi, U., 122, 125, *139, 142*
Belmont, J. M., 6, *31*
Benedict, H., 146, *171*
Bennett, G. K., *64*

Berger, D. E., 129, *139*
Berlin, C. I., 123, *139*
Berry, J. K., 146, 154, 155, 158, 166, *169, 170*
Bever, T. G., 135, *139*
Bisanz, J., 8, 9, 10, 21, 22, *31, 32*
Bishop, S. L., 158, 166, *172*
Bispo, J. G., 162, 163, *172*
Blade, M. F., 81, *92*
Blake, J., 10, *31*
Blumstein, S., 121, 130, *139, 143*
Bobbitt, B. L., 8, 24, *32*
Bobrow, D. G., 45, *65*, 131, *142*
Bogen, J. E., 121, *140*
Bond, N. A., 56, *64*
Borkowski, J. G., 164, *169, 170, 171*
Bradley, R., 97, *115*
Bradshaw, J. L., 123, 130, 131, 136, 137, *139, 140*
Bransford, J. D., 158, *171*
Brazelton, T. B., 96, 109, *115*
Brickner, M., 131, *140*
Broca, P., 120, *139*
Broussard, E., 98, *115*
Brown, A. L., 147, *169*
Brown, R., 146, *169*
Bruder, G. E., 126, *139*
Bruner, J. S., 7, *31*
Bryant, S. L., 154, 158, 159, 163, *171, 172*
Bryden, M. P., 78, *94*, 125, 130, 137, *139, 142*
Burt, C., 43, *64*
Burton, L., 126, 127, *142*
Butler, D., 136, *142*
Butterfield, E. C., 6, *31*

C

Calaway, E., 106, *115*
Calderon, M., 130, *140*

253

S

Saltz, E., 7, *33*
Sameroff, A., 114, *117*
Samuel, J., 158, 166, *172*
Scarr, S., 101, 103, *117*
Schmid, J., 52, *66*
Schmidt, A., 107, *116*
Schneider, W., 3, *33*, 38, 39, 41, 42, 43, 45, 46, 56, 57, 62, 63, *66*, 131, *143*
Schvaneveldt, R. W., 3, 4, 5, *32, 33, 34*
Schwartz, J., 134, *142*
Schwartz, S., 25, *32*
Scruggs, T. E., 161, 163, 164, *170*
Searleman, A., 124, *142*
Seashore, H. G., *64*
Segalowitz, S. J., 106, *117*, 125, 137, *142*
Shannon, B., 135, *142*
Shatz, M., 147, *172*
Shaughnessy, J. J., *172*
Shepard, R. N., 73, *92, 93*
Shevron, I., 128, *143*
Shiffrin, R. M., 3, *33*, 41, 42, 45, *66*, 131, *143*
Shoben, E. J., 3, *33*
Shriberg, L. K., 147, 148, 149, 151, 154, 155, 158, 159, 160, 166, *170, 172*
Shuman, H., 96, *115*
Siegel, L., 97, 98, 99, 100, 101, 102, 104, 105, 114, *117*
Sigel, I. E., 7, *33*
Sigman, M., 99, 114, *116, 117*
Simpson, G. B., 16, 17, 22, *33*
Simrall, D. V., 36, *66*
Smith, C. B., 167, *169*
Smith, E. E., 3, *33*
Smith, I. M., 70, *93*
Smokler, I. A., 128, *143*
Snow, R. E., 89, *93*, 161, *169*
Snyder, C. R., 3, 4, 17, *33*, 41, *66*, 98, 99, 101, 102, 105, 114, *115*, 131, *142*
Soller, E., 7, *33*
Sostek, A., 101, 103, *117*
Spache, E. B., 167, *172*
Spache, G. D., 167, *172*
Spearman, C., 44, *66*
Spellacy, F., 130, *143*
Sperber, R. D., 12, 13, 16, 28, 29, *32, 33, 34*
Sperry, R. W., 121, *140*
Spietz, A., 98, 99, 101, 102, 105, 114, *115*

Stake, R. E., 61, *66*
Stasz, C., 92, *94*
Stazyk, E. H., 30, *31*
Sternberg, R. J., 74, 82, *93*, 148, 152, 154, 167, *172*
Stewart, M., 25, *32*
Stoll, E., 167, *171*
Stringfield, S., 98, *115*
Stroop, J. R., 42, *66*
Surwillo, W. W., 6, *34*

T

Tallal, P., 134, *142*
Tapley, S. M., 78, *94*
Taraldson, B., 101, 103, 105, *117*
Tartter, V., 121, *139*
Teng, E. L., 125, 137, *143*
Terbeek, D., 135, *142*
Terman, L., 96, *117*
Thorndyke, P. W., 92, *94*
Thurstone, L. L., 68, 69, 90, *94*
Tobin, A., 98, *115*
Toms-Bronowski, S. A., 147, 148, 149, 151, 154, 155, 158, 159, 160, *170*
Torgesen, J. K., 147, *172*
Toye, A. R., 162, 163, *172*
Trevarthen, C., 126, *143*
Tronick, E., 109, *115*
Tucker, L. R., 61, *66*
Tueting, P., 106, *115*
Tulving, E., 2, *34*
Tversky, A., 138, *143*
Tweedy, J. R., 5, *34*
Tzeng, O. J. L., 122, 123, 125, 133, 134, 135, 136, 137, 138, *141, 143*

U

Uzgiris, I., 100, *117*

V

Vaid, J., 125, *143*
van Daalen-Kapteijns, M. M., 152, *172*
Varro, L., 78, *93*
Vaughn, B., 101, 103, 105, *117*
Vernon, P. E., 43, 44, 45, *66*
Vidulich, M., 62, 63, *66*

Subject Index